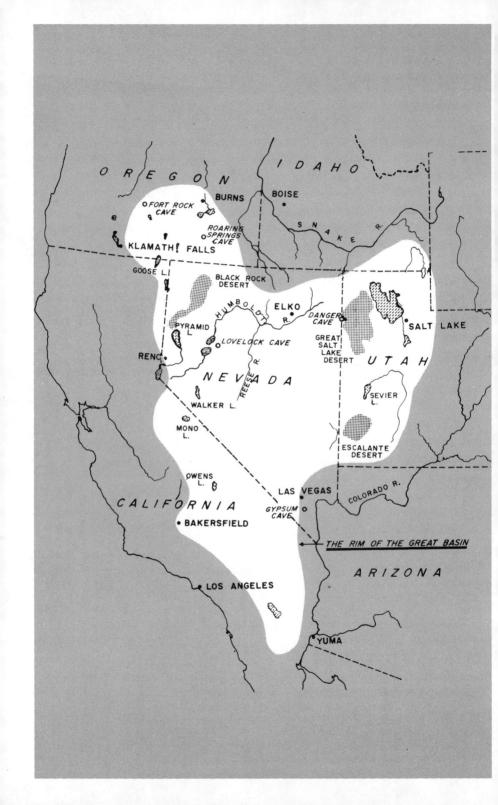

STONE AGE

in the

GREAT BASIN

by

Emory Strong

Binford & Mort Publishing

Portland, Oregon

Stone Age in the Great Basin

Printed in the United States of America

First Edition 1969
Second Printing 1976
Third Printing 1989

FOREWORD

By Dr. L. S. Cressman

This book was written for the non-professional, the relic hunter, the collector, for anyone who has an interest in ways of life of the past in that vast area known as the Great Basin. I am sure the professional archaeologist too, as I have, will find this book of value.

Private collections often harbor valuable specimens that are unknown to the professional, yet these products of the aboriginal craftsman are frequently of critical importance for his work. These artifacts are generally widely scattered, in possession of the ranchers, cowboys, trappers, collectors and skillful amateur archaeologists; only rarely do they find their way to museums. We professionals think that to preserve these objects for future generations they should be placed in museums and not be subjected to the risks of fire, sudden death of the owner, or other disaster which might cause their loss. Such disposal, however, is not likely to take place on a wide scale.

The specimens are prized possessions cherished for their aesthetic value, the sense of achievement derived from their discovery, and the memories they recall of pleasant trips on the hunt, often with good companions, always stimulating, sometimes even dangerous. Every professional knows very well how he recalls the enjoyment of successful field trips and, not infrequently, the excitement of the experience develops with the recounting, especially at social gatherings. We do not condemn a wealthy patron of the arts who purchases expensive works to expand his private collection. Much as I prefer to see objects of aboriginal handicraft preserved in a museum, as a person I know perfectly well that the owners who derive pleasure from their possessions have as much right to keep and enjoy them as the art collector.

It is important, however, for the enrichment of our understanding of our fellow men, past and present, that we have knowledge of the existence of the material under individual ownership and the opportunity to study it.

Mr. Strong in this book, as he did in his earlier *Stone Age on the Columbia River,* has performed a distinct service to archaeology by providing a photographic record of many artifacts widely scattered in private collections. Some of these will be enlightening to those who have a tendency to look with disdain on the Indians of the Great Basin and their past. Exquisite pieces of stone work represented by weapons and tools, figurines fashioned in stone perhaps with religious significance, and basketry, together with an amazing skill and flexibility in adaptation to the harsh environment of the Great Basin testify to the skills, to the hopes and fears of those ancient men and women and their efforts to attain some fulfillment of life and avoidance of disaster. Only a person with the author's feeling of sympathy with the people, a knowledge of their life conditions, a wide acquaintance with the owners of collections, and a solid reputation for integrity, could do the kind of valuable work represented by both this and his earlier book.

Professional archaeologists are deeply in debt to amateurs, to local residents in an area, and others who provide them with information essential to their work. Mr. Strong makes available his knowledge to help us, reversing the relationship in which we seek out the amateur and other informed individuals one by one.

Finally, I am sure the author will find that there will be those who will disagree with some of his interpretations and explanations. If everyone agreed with an author he would not have written a good book. Mr. Strong has written a good book.

PREFACE

Throughout the Americas and the world there are numerous geographical divisions each of which has fostered a culture adapted to its particular ecological advantage or disadvantage. The Northwest Coast with its vast natural resources nourished a people with a complex social structure, rich in the arts. The Bushmen of South Africa still endure an environment so bleak that no existence seems possible, their way of life is the very simplest. In the Great Basin, once called the Great American Desert, there evolved a culture that survived and expanded in an unfriendly territory, a desert culture that must be considered low in the standards that men have established to judge each other, yet one that is of great interest to students and laymen, for it exemplifies the ability of a people to survive in a region where nature is most frugal with her gifts.

In their exploitation of the meager resources of the desert, inventive and ingenious traits resulted in a wealth and variety of artifacts, the weapons with which the battle for survival was made victorious. The long vanished owners of these tokens—relics now eagerly sought by the weekend archaeologist—left in their refuse fragmentary records of their passing, fragments that scientists have sifted from the dust of centuries, meticulously analyzed, and fitted to a pattern.

Many learned scientists have excavated and postulated and published, but the mass of information is so scattered that the layman does not care to search for it, carrying the thread of unity to weave a continuous pattern. This is the sole contribution of this book—to extract from the literature and abridge the story of the Desert Culture, its origin, adaptation and demise. Not a single thing new has been contributed by the author.

In a treatise like this, covering over 200,000 square miles, some sort of parameters must be set to avoid a confusing mass of data that overwhelms the reader with a flood of statistics. I have chosen to picture the industrious inhabitants of the desert as human beings battling for life in an unfriendly land; there are no ethnic divisions, linguistic groupings or cultural subdivisions herein; all people are classified as people with everyday problems of survival that differed mainly with geologic changes that affected the biota, only in minor details with geography. Included are areas adjacent to but not strictly within the Great Basin for the culture spilled over the rim of it. The cultural boundary is not precise nor is that of the Basin itself.

Ruth and I have traveled thousands of miles in the Great Basin and in every mile there was something of interest. Traces of Early Man were everywhere, the caves that housed him, the lake beds and swamps in which he hunted, the trails he followed, his camp-fires and workshops and artifacts. The plants and shrubs that fed and clothed and housed him were present in a wondrous array, and overall was always the fresh clean invigorating smell of the desert.

The gratifying acceptance of the author's "Stone Age on the Columbia River" is convincing evidence that people have a wide interest in the prehistory of their particular area. A surprising number of enthusiasts range the desert in search of mementoes of its vanished people; weekenders and vacationers can find no better place to escape the vicissitudes of civilization. They can go as far back as they wish, to where only the coyote and jackrabbit or horned lizard peer at them from beneath the sagebrush clump, or relax in luxury in a motel before wandering over the nearby hill into adventure. The searcher never lacks for reward, if not materially at least spiritually in the peace and tranquility of this rugged land, and the proximity—even injection into—the past. To these people we hope this book will give some guidance and pleasure.

Without the help of the following individuals and their families, who so willingly permitted their collections to be photographed and answered so many questions, this book could never have been written: Horace Arment, Richard Cowans, John and Georgia Crow, Richard DePaoli, Eugene Favell, Tom Gerity, LeRoy Gienger, Howard and Stephen Hughes, Earl Jarrett, Louis Johnson, Brent Kenyon, C. D. Lair, Reub Long, George and Alfred Luke, Bill McClure, Elizabeth Miller, Rees Mortensen, Wallace Munk, Jack Nicolarsen, Johnny O'Shea, Vic Overman, Ben Pruitt, Lt. Col. Robert Rae, Norman Reimers, George Sanford, Vernon Schiele, Delmar Smith, Norman Sweeney, Jimmie Thomas, Stephen Tieber, Peter Ting, Peter Ting Jr., George Warner, Ann Webb, John Wendler, Harry Winnemucca, Ronald and Garry Zumwalt. A very special thanks goes to Dr. L. S. Cressman for checking the manuscript and for many, many other favors, and also to Dr. Robert Stephenson and Peter Ting for reading the manuscript and offering helpful criticism and suggestions, to Campbell Grant, Don Martin, Glen Ainsworth, Dr. Dale Ritter, Dr. Robert Heizer, Jim Anderson and Donald Tuohy for their information on interesting sites and for furnishing pictures, to George Phebus of the Smithsonian Institution for selecting and furnishing photographs, to Dewey and Harry Samson for allowing us to partake of their extensive knowledge of plants used by their people, and to Mrs. Ella Swarner for her assistance in typing and correcting the manuscript. My gratitude to Ruth I shall acknowledge in person.

All sketches and photographs are by the author unless otherwise credited in the text.   E. S.

Contents

STONE AGE IN THE GREAT BASIN

Part One

The Setting

1. The Great American Desert

Confined within the rims of the Great Basin lies one of the great deserts of the world. It is a broken and inhospitable region, but one where for more than 10,000 years Ancient Man hunted and gathered for a precarious existence. And it is a land where one may yet find readable traces of his way of life and manner of death. So unknown to the white invaders was this vast area of internal drainage—equal to all the original 13 states together except Pennsylvania—that it was only 125 years ago that the search was abandoned for the famed San Buenaventura.

This mythical Great River of the West, rivaling the Columbia in reach and flow, was thought to empty somewhere south of San Francisco. Colonel John Charles Fremont, after circling the Great Basin, was able finally to dispel that legend forever. In 1849, he wrote: "The Columbia is the only river which traverses the whole breadth of the country, breaking through all the ranges, and entering the sea" (Fremont 1849).* He was also convinced that the huge region was without a drainage outlet to the sea: "The existence of the Basin is . . . an established fact in my mind: its extent and contents are yet to be ascertained."

*References to the bibliography in the back of this book are made by enclosing the author's name and date of publication in brackets, or the date only if the name is used in the text.

1

The extent and content of the prehistoric population needed to be ascertained too, but the references in the early journals were far more emotional than intellectual. The writers were intent upon impressing their readers with the hardships and annoyances and strange adventures experienced on the trail, not with recording factual descriptions of the natives. Almost without exception the explorers considered the inhabitants of the desert to be repulsive, decadent, miserable creatures scarcely deserving to be classed as human beings.

Listen to Thomas Farnham: "They wore no clothing of any description—build no shelters. They eat roots, lizards, and snails, they provide nothing for future wants. And when the lizard and snail and wild roots are buried in the snows of winter, they are said to retire to the vicinity of timber, dig holes in the form of ovens in the steep sides of the sand hills, and having heated them to a certain degree, deposit themselves in them, and sleep and fast till the weather permits them to go abroad again for food. Persons who have visited their haunts after a severe winter have found the ground around these family ovens strewn with the unburied bodies of the dead, and others crawling around them, who have various degrees of strength, from a bare sufficience to gasp in death, to those that crawl upon their hands and feet, eating grass like cattle. It is said that they have no weapons of defense except the club, and that in the use of that they are very unskilled. Those poor creatures are hunted in the spring, when weak and helpless, and when taken, are fattened, carried to Santa Fe and sold as slaves." (Quoted in Steward 1938). Fortunately, few others were as imaginative as Farnham, although his last sentence is not imaginary. There are enough descriptions of the Desert Culture by early travelers to permit the selection of reasonable accounts.

Strictly speaking, the name Great Basin is improper. It is not a single basin but a series of disconnected, flat-floored desert valleys, each with its own interior drainage system separated by a series of north-south oriented ridges. Theoretically, each basin could have its own outlet to the sea without disturbing the others.

The Klamath River, for instance, has been able to cut a channel to the sea so that the Klamath Basin is now partially drained. The Malheur Lake area formerly discharged into the Pacific by way of the Snake and Columbia rivers, but was cut off by a lava block (Jaeger 1957a). Now it is a basin receiving the Silvies River and the Donner und Blitzen River, forming lakes and marshes that have been set aside as the Malheur National Wildlife Refuge. The refuge harbors a magnificent array of water and marsh birds and animals.

Some 90 desert valleys comprise the Great Basin and cover an area of 210,000 square miles. The Basin's western boundary is the Sierra Nevada, and its eastern the Wasatch Range, 570 miles distant. Its total length is about 880 miles, including most of Nevada and large parts of Oregon, California, and Utah. Some of its lakes are very large; Pyramid Lake covers 120,000 acres, Great Salt Lake over 1,000,000.

All precipitation that falls evaporates either from the ground surface or after it flows into the lowest areas of the basin. At present the rainfall averages between five and ten inches per year but evaporation is so rapid that little of this meager portion can be utilized by plants. Because of the dry air, hot sun, and frequent winds, the evaporation rate is enormous, reaching 120 inches a year at Boulder City, Nevada (Jaeger 1957a). The average evaporation rate in the Great Basin is about ten inches a month during the summer. At the rate of 120 inches, a permanent lake would lose to the atmosphere ten acre-feet of water annually for every acre of surface. It is enough to dispel the waters of rivers like the Bear, Carson, Truckee, and Walker. When the precipitation is more than average, the water simply spreads wider over the playas or drainage basins that the sediments have built up over the centuries—presenting more area to the thirsty air until balance is again achieved.

But it was not always so. There were times when the water gradually rose in the basins until it spilled over the margins, creating lakes hundreds of feet deep and thousands of square miles in extent. It was then that the climate and ecology were entirely different from that of the present. Early Man could peer from the portal of his cave and overlook a land of lush vegetation, and perhaps see a band of primitive horses or camels, or a giant ground sloth. And then there were times like the present when the lakes again dried up, as Great Salt Lake must do if it continues to shrink. Here, in this vast area, one with an eventful and colorful history, lived the people of the Desert Culture.

The very existence of the Desert Culture—where every economic resource must be fully exploited to sustain a bare existence—was not envisioned until quite recently. Excavations in Lovelock and other caves, especially Danger, revealed an ancient, food-gathering economy, and Dr. Jesse Jennings (1957) was one of the first to substantiate it with well-documented evidence.

The plant and animal life of the Great Basin is as varied and rhythmic as the landscape. In measured cadence the valleys and ranges march from the Sierra Nevada to the Wasatch, and the life zones lie in uniform layers. Even on foot one can pass through a series of zones, from the Lower Sonoran with its desert bush to the Canadian with aspen and fir, in only a few hours. With their variation of resources, they were of immense importance to the inhabitants of the Great Basin. The seeds in the lower elevations ripened first, followed in succession by those in zones of increasing elevation. So tedious was the gathering of desert seeds that existence would not have been possible had the harvests all been ready at once.

The Desert Culture might be defined as gastronomic; the orientation toward food gathering was specific, and starvation was an ever-present menace. Upon the desert, Man was a total parasite; he reaped but he did not sow. Fremont (1849) observed that these ancient people had adapted themselves almost like plants and seemed to be growing on what the locality afforded. Mobility was essential to existence; every resource of seeds or nuts or roots had to be vigorously attacked in the proper season lest it be lost. To linger was to miss the harvest, for the season might last but a few days. Adaptation had to be complete.

Mobility meant but few possessions and those of the most essential nature. Little time or effort could be expended on elaborate ceremonial functions or the embellishments of such rites. It is true that at one time, during the Pluvial, the desert bloomed with richer flora and fauna, but the culture failed to respond to the additional nourishment. The traces, therefore, of the ancient peoples of the desert do not reveal the elaborate and artistic utilitarian and ceremonial objects that were possessed by those in the more culturally favorable areas surrounding the Great Basin. What they do reveal is a way of life in harmony with a stringent environment imposing rigorous limitations over the social and material organization of the group.

The normal organization was the family unit, including perhaps some in-laws and friends, numbering as few as two or three or as many as 20 or 30. The wanderings of the group followed a pattern consistent with the seasonal resources, broken only by weather conditions or by the threat of slave raiders from the north or east. Generations of experience in their own territory guided their route; they knew the location of every seed patch and root field and when to descend for the harvest.

Late summer and fall were the most important seasons, for then seeds and nuts must be gathered, and roots dug and dried in sufficient quantity to last throughout the long winter. Before cattle and sheep destroyed the range, the ancient people gathered sand grass, rye grass, sunflower, blazing star, wild celery, sweet sage, and many, many other plants. They knew the delicious sweetness of the root of the wild caraway; they harvested the wild parsley and dug the bulbs of the sego lily and camas. They knew what grew in the sandy and in the moist places; they gathered fungi in the woods and even the lichen from the trees.

In the fall, family groups might assemble for the pine harvest, or for a rabbit drive. With this type of social organization there could be no great chiefs such as existed in the Plains, nor any skill in the civilized art of war. The annual gathering for the pine-nut harvest did, however, give the scattered bands a chance to congregate for a feast or a dance, for gambling, trading, and visiting, and for the selection of mates.

On the approach of winter the family groups established themselves in a winter village in some sheltered valley, usually one that had been used for generations. Sometimes, if the pine-nut crop had been good, they spent the winter in the vicinity of their stored harvest. The Reese and Owens river valleys were two favorite wintering sites. There nearly every stream, every sheltered draw, had a village at its outlet. The word village is perhaps not correct, for the group might have consisted of only one family, yet another year might have brought a gathering of more than enough to the same site to justify its being called a village.

Spring was a time of starvation. The stores of seeds and roots usually were consumed before the end of winter, before the fresh spring greens had burst through the snow. Hunting was poor; the fish had not started their annual spawning runs. For the young, the old, and the weak it was a time for death. As the warm days approached, the misery was relieved; edible leaves and shoots could be gathered, and the hibernating rodents emerging from their dens could be captured. Hordes of fish, leaving the deep lakes to spawn, could be netted, speared, or trapped by those fortunate enough to have a stream in their territory. There would be no more leisure until winter again closed in.

The sexual division of labor existed but the line was not sharply drawn. The women gathered the seeds and roots, prepared the food, and did the cooking; the men exploited the animal kingdom. Both assisted in the nut harvest and the rabbit drive, perhaps also in the quest for fuel for the campfire. Women were the textile experts; they gathered the fibers and wove that hallmark of the Desert Culture, the basket. The men chipped the stone and manufactured their weapons, made the digging sticks, built the houses, and wove the rabbit-skin robes (Steward 1938). In general, each sex made its own implements while those things used by both were made by both. Usually, when men and women together assist in the food harvest as in the Desert Culture, the women enjoy a more equal status than do those where, as in the buffalo country, the men are the providers.

The population of the immense area of the Great Basin was meager in the extreme. The normal method of depicting population density is by the number of persons per square mile—for the Basin it was by square miles per person. In the more favorable regions, such as the Owens Valley or along the Humboldt River, there might be as few as two square miles per person, in Death Valley as many as 40. For the State of Nevada the average was about 14 square miles per person, a total population of 7,000 or 8,000, according to estimates made in the 1860's (Steward 1938).

There were in the Basin comparatively rich, well-watered valleys and lake basins where, when first they were seen, Stone Age men must have said, "This is the place." Here the culture rose to higher levels; there might even have been permanent villages such as were occupied by the later Klamath. The cultures advanced not only because of the more advantageous environment but because the people were naturally more vigorous and aggressive or they would not have won out over the competition, nor have been able to retain possession. Still, considering the vast area and the immense time span since the first man slipped over the rim of the Basin, the culture was not too highly diversified. To better understand and appreciate it, though, one should know something of the history of the Great Basin and of the geologic disturbances and convulsions that brought it into being. First, however, it would be interesting to know how the earliest of the white invaders viewed the desert and its inhabitants.

2. The White Invaders

The Spaniards were the first white men known to enter the confines of the Great Basin. The Spanish missions had already been established along the coast of California—San Diego in 1769, Monterey in 1770, and San Antonio and San Gabriel in 1771. Others followed in rapid succession, spaced one day's journey by horseback apart, approximately 60 miles. Supplying the missions became quite a problem to the Spanish. The aborigines had no agriculture; they could not support the invaders. Conscripting the entire native population into slavery to labor on the mission buildings and grounds, to the total disruption of their culture, only aggravated the need for supplies from the homeland. It was clear that an annual ship was not the answer; an overland route must be blazed between California and the Spanish settlements in the Southwest, over which both colonists and essential goods could be taken.

The Franciscan Father Francisco Hermenegildo Garces was the earliest and one of the most aggressive of the explorers of the Great Basin. In 1774, with a party commanded by Juan Bautista de Anza, he left Tucson and journeyed westward in search of a route, crossing the Colorado River near Yuma. From there the expedition struck through the Colorado Desert and the southern extension of the Basin to San Gabriel. The route was not considered feasible "because of the extreme scarcity of water and pasturage and of the vast sand dunes." Anyone who has been into the southeastern part of California will agree with Garces and marvel that a crossing could be made by an explorer who knew neither the way nor the distance.

A second expedition including Garces left Tucson for Cali-

8

fornia in October, 1775, with colonists and supplies. Garces
parted from the main group at Yuma and followed the Colorado
to a crossing near Needles. He was probably the first white
man to see the Mojave Indians. From there he followed approximately parallel and between the present routes of U.S. 40
and 15 past Soda Lake, Barstow, and San Bernardino to Los
Angeles and Bakersfield. Some conception of the remarkable
geographical sense of these early explorers of an unknown land
can be conceived by following Garces' return route: he was able
to strike out east and slightly southward from Bakersfield through
Tehachapi Pass and pick up his old trail somewhere near Vic-
torville. He left the Great Basin on May 25, 1776, near the
point where he had entered in March. He had passed twice
through the most difficult and hazardous part of the Great Basin
in three months, a total distance of something like 700 miles.

Garces was partly responsible for the legend of the San
Buenaventura River. Had such a river existed, it, like the Columbia, would have been of immense value as a trade route.
Not understanding the nature of the Great Basin, all the early
explorers thought there had to be a great river somewhere to
drain the immense land. Maps drawn as late as 1840 showed
the Buenaventura, and men like Lewis and Clark, von Humboldt, and Zebulon Pike—who enjoyed great stature in scientific
circles—drew the undiscovered river on their maps. Many fruitless years of effort were expended in a vain search for this
legendary river and the fame that would go with its discovery.
It was finally the Humboldt and the Carson that usurped the
trade route—a poor but important substitute for a water-level
road by the San Buenaventura had it existed. Man, both primitive and modern, has ever followed the nourishing rivers and
the passes they sculpture through the hills. Where none exist
the path is indeed a weary one.

Father Garces, still tramping the sands of the Great Basin,
was killed by Yuma Indians in 1780 in the massacre of a small
settlement and mission near the junction of the Yuma and Colo-

rado rivers, a mission founded as a way point on the trail that Garces had traced.

Perhaps the most famous of all the explorers of the Great Basin was Fray Silvestre Velez de Escalante, renowned not only because he was so tenacious but because he was a most excellent chronicler. A facile pen accentuates his exploits, one of the great adventures of all time. Unlike those of Lewis and Clark, his documents are colored by emotion, but his observations were keen and his recording meticulous. He sweetened his journal with sentimental elaborations of the desires of the natives for the blessings of the Cross, but that was usual for recorders fired with missionary zeal. Their words were eagerly devoured by the citizenry at home where, even as today, the appeal of emotion opened wide the purse that reason alone would transfix.

Escalante, with Fray Atanasio Dominguez, left Santa Fe on July 29, 1776. With them were nine Spanish gentlemen, numerous servants, horses and mules, and a herd of cattle for food along the way. Traveling generally northwest, they approached the Great Basin on September 14, when, "We arrived at a large river which we called San Buenaventura"—the Green River near Jensen, Utah. Traveling now westward, they passed near Duchesne, Myton, and Fruitland close to present Highway 40. On September 21, "We continued through the grove which became more dense the further we went, and having traveled half a league west, we emerged from it, arriving at a high ridge from which our guide pointed out to us the direction to the Lake (Utah Lake), and, to the southwest of it, another part of the sierra in which he said there lived a great many people of the same language and character as the Lagunas" (Bolton 1950). The expedition had passed over the Wasatch Range near Twin Peaks and were now in the Great Basin.

Descending the western slope of the Wasatch, "We saw in front of us and not very far away many large columns of smoke arising in the same Sierra." Smoke signals arose all around as they descended the mountains. On reaching the valley near the present Spanish Fork they found the meadows burnt or burning. Escalante replied with signals of his own and "They replied with larger signals . . . this is the most prompt and common signal used in any extraordinary occurrence by all the people of this part of America." This was the genuine Indian smoke signal, setting the grass afire to warn of the approach of strangers or an enemy.

The stories of communication by puffs of smoke or any manipulation of the column are pure fiction, romantic nonsense. All the early travelers of the Great Plains and Basin tell of the prairies being fired to announce the arrival of visitors; Lewis and Clark often mention the practice. Stansbury (1852) says, "Just before descending this valley, we observed from the high ground, the smokes of numerous Indian Signal fires, rising in several directions—an intimation that strangers have been discovered in the country." Fremont (1849) says, "Columns of smoke rose over the country at scattered intervals—signals by which the Indians, as elsewhere, communicate to each other that enemies are in the country. It is a signal of ancient and very universal application among barbarians."

Camp was made on the Provo River. The Indians, at first ready to fight in defense of their families, were pacified and "took them very joyfully to their poor little houses, and after the father had embraced each one separately and made known to them that we came in peace and that we loved them as our best friends he gave them time to talk at length with our guide." Soon the natives were clamoring (according to the journals) for the fathers to return and "rule and teach them," promising the Spaniards all their land and protection from the Comanches— but, "We told them that although our people would believe what we might say about them, they must give us a token showing they wished to become Christians . . . we then presented the chief, who was a man of good presence, with a hunting knife and strings of beads, and Don Bernardo Miera gave him a hatchet."

The token was brought next day, a painting on buckskin "saying that the figure which on each side had the most red ochre or, as they called it, the most blood, represented the head chief, because in the battles with the Comanches he had received the most wounds. The two other figures, which were not so bloody, represented the two chiefs subordinate to the first, and the one which had no blood represented one who was not a war chief." The irony of the situation seems to have escaped Escalante; at least he does not mention it. They tried to teach the natives a prayer to ward off sickness and the enemy but they were unable to handle the words and were told to say merely "Jesus Maria!"

Escalante was very much impressed with the Utah Lake country and the natives there—"Round about it are these Indians, who live on the abundant fish of the lake, for which reason the Yutas Sabuanganas call them Fish Eaters. Besides this, they gather in the plain grass seeds from which they make atole, which they supplement by hunting hares, rabbits and fowl of which there is a great abundance here. They speak the Yuta language but with notable differences in the accent and in some of the words. They have good features and most of them have heavy beards. In all parts of this sierra to the southeast, southwest and east live a large number of people of the same tribe." Traveling near the present route of Highway 91, the party progressed southward. Near Mills they "met an old Indian of venerable appearance. He was alone in a little hut, and his beard was so thick and long that he looked like one of the hermits of Europe."

The next morning at their camp on the Sevier River, "Very early twenty Indians arrived together with those who were here yesterday afternoon, wrapped in blankets made of the skins of rabbits and hares. These people here have much heavier beards than the Lagunas. They have holes through the cartilage of their noses and wear as an ornament a little polished bone of deer, fowl, or other animal thrust through the hole. In features

they look more like Spaniards than like the other Indians hither-
to known in America, from whom they are different in the fore-
going respects."

Following roughly the present route of the Santa Fe Railroad
south of Delta, Utah, the party suffered greatly from rough and
rocky trails, lack of pasture, and scarcity of water. Near Sevier
Lake, "the men who had gone seeking water arrived, accom-
panied by some Indians whose ranchos they accidentally reached
on the bank of the Rio de Santa Ysabel (Sevier). These were
some of the people with long beards and pierced noses who, in
their language, are called Tirangapui. The five who first came
with their chief had such long beards that they looked like Ca-
puchin or Bethlemite fathers. The chief was an attractive man
of mature years but not aged. We preached the Gospel to them
as well as the interpreter could explain it. . . . We said goodby
to them and all, especially the chief, took our hands with great
fondness and affection. But the time when they most emphatical-
ly expressed themselves was when we were leaving this place.
They scarcely saw us depart when all of them, imitating their
chief, who set the example, broke out weeping copious tears, so
that even after we were a long distance away we still heard the
tender laments of these miserable little lambs of Christ who had
strayed only for lack of The Light." They were before many
years to see "The Light" but to them it brought only misery,
sickness, and the final Long Darkness.

The party was now in desperate straits; it was October and
the weather was wet and cold; mud and stony ground impeded
their progress; they were out of food, and their guides left without warning. After a bitter conference it was decided to return
to Santa Fe, although some members thought that Monterey was
but a short distance away to the west.

They proceeded with many hardships almost due south
through Cedar City, where they left the Great Basin, and on to
Hurricane Cliffs, a little less than half way between the Arizona
line and the Colorado River. Here they turned eastward, again

crossing the Arizona line near the Paria River. Twelve days they spent in search of a crossing of the Colorado, finally finding one near the outlet of Last Chance Creek, thereafter known as the Crossing of the Fathers. The transit was made on November 7, 1776, and Escalante says, "In order to lead the animals down the side of the canyon mentioned it was necessary to cut steps in a rock with axes for the distance of three veras or a little less. The rest of the way the animals were able to get down, although without pack or rider."

Before the waters of Glen Canyon Dam buried this historical site forever, we descended the canyon down which the party passed and saw the steps laboriously cut into the slickrock two hundred years ago. Standing on the very ground brings to stark reality the hardships and sufferings of early explorers, in winter with no food, far from home and not knowing whether the land ahead was even passable.

The first Americans, as far as known, to enter the Great Basin were John Hoback, Jacob Reznor, Joseph Miller, Edward Robinson, and Martin Gass, all members of John Jacob Astor's Overland Expedition led by Wilson Price Hunt. They left the party, which was on its way to the mouth of the Columbia River, near Idaho Falls in October 1811 to trap the surrounding mountains. Apparently they discovered and traveled down the Bear River, a sizable stream flowing into Great Salt Lake. They were robbed of everything they owned by the Indians. Nearly a year later all except Gass were found by Robert Stuart in a destitute state. They kept no journal and contributed little to the knowledge of the Great Basin, but they were the first and should be accredited that honor.

Jedediah Strong Smith, a staunch, colorful, non-swearing, Bible-carrying frontiersman, was perhaps the most persistent and unlucky of all the rangers of the Great Basin. He was a partner in the firm of Smith, Jackson and Sublette and his business was furs, but his insatiable curiosity and energy sent him on many a perilous journey where "I of course expected to find Beaver which with us hunters is a primary object but I was also led on by the love of novelty common to all which is much increased by the pursuit of its gratification" (Morgan 1953). Once he was attacked by a grizzly bear that crushed his ribs and "had taken nearly all of his head in his capacious mouth and laid the skull bare to near the crown leaving a white streak where the teeth passed one of his ears was torn from his head after stiching all the other wounds I put my needle stiching the ear through and through and over and over and laying the lacerated parts together as neat as I could . . ." Jedediah ever after wore his hair long to cover the scars.

In August of 1826 Smith left Bear Lake with 18 men, traveling southward past Utah Lake to cross the Colorado near the mouth of the Virgin. He then crossed the Mojave Desert by an old trail along the Mojave River, a route that had been used since ancient times by the Mojave on trips to the coast to trade for sea shells. After visiting the Spanish settlements he returned eastward past Walker Lake to Utah Lake, arriving in June 1827. In July he again started on his old track with a party of 18 men and two women. At his former crossing of the Colorado, where the Mojave had been very friendly, they suddenly fell upon and massacred ten of his men and captured the two women, all of his horses, most of his goods and all of his guns except five. "After weighing all the circumstances of my position as calmly as possible," he struck across the desert with what few possessions the party could carry on their backs, only to be imprisoned by the Spanish when he arrived on the coast. Talking himself out of this predicament, he started for Fort Vancouver with a band of horses. Following along the coast of Oregon, all of the party except himself and two others were killed by the Rogue River Indians, and all of his property taken. The trio managed to reach Fort Vancouver, and Smith eventually returned east only to be killed in 1831 by the Comanches on the Santa Fe Trail. He was 32 years old.

From the few portions of Smith's journal that have survived

it appears that he had more compassion for the Indians than most of the travelers of that day. At one place in the desert, "We galloped after them and overtook one who appeared very much frightened and pacified her in the usual manner by making her some presents. I then went to the place where I had seen one fall down. She was laying there and apparently lifeless. I got down from my horse and found that she was indeed dead. Could it be possible, thought I, that we who called ourselves Christians were such frightful objects as to scare poor savages to death?" Smith was merely trying to overtake them to find out the trail. He was also quite incensed at the treatment of the Indians at the California missions, where they were hanged or beaten almost to death for trying to escape.

Traveling across the Utah deserts, almost completely devoid of water, Smith says, "when we found some water in some of the rocky hills, we most generally found some Indians who appeared the most miserable of the human race having nothing to subsist on, (nor any clothing) except grass seeds, Grasshoppers, &c." At Utah Lake "passed through a large swamp of bullrushes, when suddenly the lake presented itself to our view. On its banks were a number of buildings constructed of bullrushes, and resembling muskrat houses. These we soon discovered to be wigwams, in which the Indians remained during the stay of the ice. As there is not a tree within three miles, their principal fuel is bullrushes" (Daniel Potts, from Morgan 1952). It is a pity that all of Smith's journals were not left to us, but the fact that he did keep one while beset with every invidious hazard and hardship that the desert could conjure attests to his force of character.

The most far-reaching and wide-ranging of all the early travelers in the Basin were the Snake Country brigades of the North West and Hudson's Bay companies. The first one was in 1818, their purpose to trap the streams in the vast and unknown areas west of the Rockies, most seriously the Snake River and its tributaries. Eventually they explored and trapped nearly every river of the West. These brigades must have presented a colorful scene on the grey hills of the Great Basin; fifty or a hundred men on horseback, twice as many women and children and pack animals, noise and confusion and dust. They would be out a year or more, with no contact with civilization. Towards the end they must have exhibited an appalling appearance, after the hard winter and hot summer, the rocky trails and thorny branches, the hunger and thirst had taken their toll. Each leader was supposed to keep a journal but except for that of Peter Skene Ogden (Rich 1950, Davies 1961) they are not much value ethnographically. Ogden had a little compassion for the Indians —he realized they were human beings and at times treated them as such.

Ogden left the Flathead Post near Missoula, Montana, on December 20, leading the 1824-26 expedition at the head of 58 men and 268 horses. He trapped the tributaries of Clark's Fork and Snake rivers until late in April when he crossed the divide south of Blackfoot, Idaho, into the Great Basin. Following down Bear River he passed the foot of the Wasatch Range near present Ogden, Utah, a city named after him. Troubled with deserters and plagued by American competitors, he had little time or inclination for recording ethnological material. His only reference of interest was written on Bear River near the Utah border, "Last evening about Sun Set 7 Indians came in Sight on the opposite Side of the River they were hailed in the Snake Language but made no answer they appear very doubtful of us & we so equally their Camp at a Short distance from this only 4 leagues they inform us Pe-i-em with all the Snakes are now absent on a trading excursion for Shells with another nation Some distance from this & are expected back this month . . ."

On his next expedition Ogden left Fort Vancouver on September 11, 1826, with about 36 men and an uncounted number of women and children, picking up 100 horses at The Dalles. Heading south and southeast, he entered the Great Basin in October, traveled to Malheur Lake, then west past Newberry Crater and southward to Klamath and Tule lakes. Here he again turned westward, crossed the Klamath and followed the Applegate to the Rogue River, then retraced his steps to Tule Lake. Following closely the present route of State Highway 139, Ogden discovered and named Pit River early in May, 1827, near present Canby, California. He then followed the route of 395 past Goose Lake to Lakeview. Turning east, he passed through Warner Valley back to Malheur Lake, leaving the Great Basin late in June, 1827.

The first experience the party had with the Indians was shortly after entering the Basin north of Burns, Oregon, where three Indians stole seven horses. Horse stealing was considered a game and not a crime by the Indians but not so by the two trappers who pursued and overtook them. The Indians handed back the horses "at the same time smiling"—they had lost the game but were good losers. Not yet satisfied (for to the trappers the loss of their horses was serious and could well be fatal) one man started beating them "with his Whip handle. The Indians for some time endured the blows but at length becoming vexed one seased Baptiste and the two others Payette, now a long scuffle ensued one of the Indians was killed both the men were severely wounded and saved themselves by flight abandoning their arms and horses, the two remaining Indians finding they had gained so desided an advantage . . . made off." Payette soon recovered, but Baptiste the Iroquois suffered greatly and was a burden for weeks.

In the vicinity of Malheur Lake they were alarmed many times by attempts to steal horses. The Indians had gathered in this valley to winter—"it is almost incredible the number of Indians in this quarter . . ." In the hundred-mile trek over the barren plains between Harney Lake and Newberry Crater no Indians were seen. In the valley of the Little Deschutes River, Ogden says, "In this part of the country I really had no idea of finding Snakes but it is almost incredible the extent of country this nation are to be found in but the poverty of it is the cause for a more baren one since leaving the Columbia cannot be found . . ."

On the Williamson River, they "found the Village composed of 20 Tents and strange as it may appear built on the water and surrounded on all sides by the water and from its depth impossable to approach them on foot or on Horseback but with Canoes with which they are well provided." Near here, too, "A Number of Indians collected round the Camp and traded Roots and 1 dog they appear well versed in trade but comported themselves peacibly and I am of opinion are good Indians but will not long remain so, two years intimacy with the Whites will make them like all other Indian villians, this was the case with the Snakes when first discovered by the Traders and in fact with any tribe I am acquainted with."

Ogden describes a Klamath Indian village: "a few Huts but of a very large size square made and flat at the top composed of earth and roots the dore at the top they are well constructed for defence against arrows but are not proof against Balls, in course of the day about 200 of them collected about our Camp, they appear to live in dread of enemies constantly waring their Arms, their dress appears rather strange—their Leggins being made of reeds also their shoes of the same well adapted for snow but would not answer in the Summer season—there is scarcely a difference in the dress of the men & women the latter are very ordinary while the former are generally fine stout looking men." They traded for 40 dogs, a favorite food of the trappers, and "some small Fish not more than two inches in length and far from being good."

On Lower Klamath Lake, "The natives traded some Camass of an inferior quality, this Country in many parts appears to abound with this Root and appears to be the principal support of the natives in this quarter they have also no doubt at times Fish to assist them but do not appear either from want of ingenuity or laziness to be expert Fisherman." Here Ogden was wrong on both accounts—the wokas was heavily harvested by the Klamath, and they were good fishermen.

While in the vicinity of the present Lava Beds National Monument, Ogden early in January, 1827, expressed his views of the country. "Here a number of Indians collected round our Camp complaining of starvation but we could afford them no relief in regard to food for the last four days we have been without and for some time previous one Half of the party have been in a similar state and consequently many curses are bestoed on this Country and justly so for certainly it is poverty itself it cannot even support its own inhabitants still less a few solitary strangers amongst the number first rate hunters and marksmen." The brigade, of course, had to subsist off the country at all times.

When they reached Pit River the trappers were "warn'd to avoid the Indian paths along the banks of the River from the number of deep Pits that they have made for entrapping Wolves and Deer still three fell in with their horses two escaped fortunately without injury but the third was kill'd a serious loss to his master, at the bottom of the Pits a number of stakes are driven, the Natives inform us at times they kill a number of Animals, some of them are nearly thirty feet deep." And later, "It is almost incredible the number of Pits the Indians have made along the River on both sides of the track as well as in it they are certainly deserving of praise for their industry but from our not seeing the track of an Animal I am not of opinion their labour is rewarded from the number of Pits so as to warn others who may chance to travel in this quarter I have nam'd this River Pit River, it is true we have lost a Horse and a most valuable one and it is now almost surprising to me we have not lost more."

One of the longest and most expensive expeditions to pass through the Great Basin was that of John Charles Fremont in 1844. His is also one of the best known because of the numerous editions of his journal and his colorful career. Crossing the Rockies at South Pass, Fremont followed the Bear River to Great Salt Lake, thence to Fort Hall, across the Blue Mountains to The

Dalles and then southward, leaving the Great Basin at Carson Pass over the Sierra Nevadas. In April, 1844, he started homeward by Tehachapi Pass, traveling northeast to Utah Lake. Most of the country traversed by Fremont, who had the famous Kit Carson as a guide, had been explored before. He added little new information concerning the Great Basin but was the first to recognize the nature of this great land: ". . . the Pacific side differs from it (the Atlantic) in another and most rare and singular feature—that of the Great Interior Basin, of which I have so often spoken, and the whole form and character of which I was so anxious to ascertain."

Fremont does make a few references to Indians, most of whom were already acquainted with the white men but still living much as they had for thousands of years. It is a pity that Fremont did not have the ability or the desire of Lewis and Clark to observe and record, because he could have left as vivid a picture of the Desert Culture as did Lewis and Clark of the Plateau Indians. Like most writers of that day, Fremont described either the misery and debasement or the brutality and ferocity of the natives as was best suited to flavor a particular portion of the narrative to please the literary appetites of his Eastern readers.

In the vicinity of Great Salt Lake, Fremont met a ". . . tribe of root-diggers. We now had entered a country inhabited by these people; and as in the course of the voyage we shall frequently meet with them in various stages of existence, it will be well to inform you that, scattered over the great region west of the Rocky Mountains, and south of the Great Snake river, are numerous Indians whose subsistence is almost solely derived from roots and seeds, and such small animals as chance and great good fortune sometimes bring within their reach. They are miserably poor, armed only with bows and arrows, or clubs; and, as the country they inhabit is almost destitute of game, they have no means of obtaining better arms. In the northern part of the region just mentioned, they live generally in solitary families; and farther to the south they are gathered together in villages. Those who live together in villages, strengthened by association, are in exclusive possession of the more genial and richer parts of the country; while the others are driven to the ruder mountains, and to the more inhospitable parts of the country.

"Roots, seeds, and grass, every vegetable that affords any nourishment, and every living thing, insect or worm, they eat. Nearly approaching to the lower animal creation, their sole employment is to obtain food; and they are constantly occupied in struggling to support existence."

Floating down the Bear River in a rubber boat that he had in his equipment, Fremont ". . . came unexpectedly upon several families of Root-Diggers, who were encamped among the rushes on the shore, and appeared very busy about several weirs or nets which had been rudely made of canes and rushes for the purpose of catching fish. They were very much startled at our appearance, but we soon established an acquaintance; and finding that they had some roots, I promised to send some men with goods to trade with them. They had the usual large heads, remarkable among the Digger tribe, with matted hair, and were almost entirely naked; looking very poor and miserable, as if their lives had been spent in the rushes where they were, beyond which they seemed to have very little knowledge of any thing." The men sent to trade brought back both roots and bear meat, showing that the natives could not have been so miserably poor after all.

After procuring supplies and equipment at Fort Vancouver and The Dalles, Fremont headed south where at Klamath Lakes he visited a Klamath village—"The chief was a very prepossessing Indian, with handsome features and a singularly soft and agreeable voice—so remarkable as to attract general notice.

"The huts were grouped together on the bank of the river, which, from being spread out in a shallow marsh at the upper end of the lake, was collected here into a single stream. They were large round huts, perhaps 20 feet in diameter, with rounded tops, on which was the door by which they descended into the interior. Within, they were supported by posts and beams.

"Almost like plants, these people seem to have adapted themselves to the soil, and to be growing on what the immediate locality afforded. Heaps of straw were lying around; and their residence in the midst of grass and rushes had taught them a peculiar skill in converting this material to useful purposes. The women wore on their heads a closely-woven basket, which made a very good cap. Among other things, were parti-colored mats about four feet square, which we purchased to lay on the snow under our blankets, and to use for table cloths. Unlike any Indians we had previously seen, these wore shells in their noses." The shell was the *Dentalium,* see Figure 93.

Passing Summer Lake they "Decided to follow a plainly-beaten Indian trail," which carried them into Chewaucan Marsh where "large patches of ground had been turned up by the squaws digging for roots, as if a farmer had been preparing the land for grain. I could not succeed in finding the plant for which they had been digging. There were frequent trails, and fresh tracks of Indians." They soon came to Abert Lake, bordered by one of the highest fault scarps in the world, Abert Rim. On Christmas Day they named a lake on which they had been camping Christmas Lake; it was in Warner Valley and far from the present lake of that name. The "plainly beaten trail still continued, and occasionally we passed camping-grounds of the Indians, which indicated to me that we were on one of the great thoroughfares of the country." Still traveling southward, Fremont discovered and named Pyramid Lake after crossing a barren desert that severely taxed both men and animals—although Fremont still dragged along his howitzer. Crossing the Sierra Nevada Range and again returning to cross the Mojave Desert, he had many adventures with the Mojave Indians but his journals carry little more of ethnographic interest.

3. In the Beginning

Geologists have spent months and years tracing the vagaries of fossil weather and geological disturbances in the Basin. A wave-cut terrace, a stream-eroded glacial moraine, microscopic marine shells, or plant pollen, all are clues on which scientists can reconstruct the past. Far back in geologic time, millions of years, were the structural changes, the rumbling and spasms and violent convulsions that eventually produced the Great Basin landscape of today and the environment that engendered the Desert Culture.

The Great Basin is called by geologists a physiographic province because that phrase describes the area concisely: an area where the geological features are more or less uniform and related. The province is not unique—the interior turmoil and turbulence that caused the earth's surface to warp and rumble is not limited to the West. The Sahara, the Libyan and the Kalahari in Africa, the deserts of Western Australia, and large areas in South America are basins.

But the Great Basin has one feature possessed by no other— it is here, within our reach, where we can visit, explore, and enjoy it. Stone Age Man ranged the Basin from rim to rim and beyond, and shifting sands and flash floods uncover his traces on every ridge and plain. You today can tread the same paths and seek out the same sunlit valleys and pinon-covered slopes as did Stone Age Man himself. You can stand on the rimrock from which he saw horses and camels and elephants grazing or browsing and where now grow only the hardiest of plants. Here he camped on pluvial lake shores and tracked mud on sagebrush bark sandals into sheltering caves. He fashioned hunting darts and throwing-sticks long before the bow and arrow were invented, while Stone Age Woman wove matting and baskets and gathered seeds and roots and berries and bore his children and milled his grain. He stalked giant bison that had a spread of horns nearing a fathom, and saw the ground sloth, a great lumbering stupid creature, claw down tree limbs for their leaves. All this you too can see, if you let the desert stimulate your imagination.

The Great Basin lies in a plane of weakness in the earth's crust called the Cordilleric Geosyncline, stretching nearly from pole to pole. If one could have taken a time-lapse moving picture of the Cordilleric, compressing 180 million years into an hour, the earth would be shown as a relatively quiet land ocean, with sudden disturbances when the surface would burst and heave and subside like a storm at sea. These great "storms" have been traced and dated and are called "revolutions," periods of great mountain building. They are the basis for the geological divisions on Chart No. 4 in the Appendix.

The story of Stone Age man is concerned with only one of these divisions, the Pleistocene, a word derived from the Greek meaning "most recent." But it is interesting to know a little of the history of the Great Basin far back in geologic time, to better understand and appreciate the landscape and its forms that engendered the Desert Culture.

Mountains are not the everlasting hills of the poets. Many times they have risen only to be eroded into a plain, to arise again and repeat the cycle. In the Jurassic Period, mountains rivaling the Alps or the Andes were thrust up—oriented north and south—extending from the central Great Basin of the present to beyond the Pacific Coast. These high mountains caused the clouds to cast down their loads, forming rivers and glaciers that eventually reduced the ranges to a broad belt of low hills. Then the land subsided, in the Cretaceous, and a great inland sea reached from the Arctic Ocean to the Gulf of Mexico in the Cordilleric Geosyncline.

The remaining hills along the present Pacific region were then separated from the inland sea by a wide plain across which rivers flowed to the eastward, much as the Missouri and the Platte now flow across the Great Plains. The silts eroded from the hills settled in the inland sea, forming the colorful banded sandstones and mudstones lying beneath the Pleistocene deposits in Arizona and Utah. The Cretaceous, which lasted about 70 million years, is known as the Age of the Dinosaurs. Vast forests and fetid swamps covered much of the present Great Basin; the climate was humid and tropical.

The Tertiary and Quaternary geological periods were as different as peace and war. Large areas of the world were covered with lush tropical vegetation in the Tertiary, palm trees approached the Arctic Circle, and redwood and fig and magnolia trees grew in Alaska. This was the age of mammals, some of them reaching prodigious size both physically and numerically. The later stages of the Tertiary were to know an animal kingdom never equaled even in the time of the dinosaurs. With such numerous animals and widespread vegetation the mathematics of chance dictated a profusion of fossils, which have been studied by paleontologists until the history of this most interesting period is well known. There were no great apes nor any trace of primates that could have been an ancestor to man.

The Miocene Epoch was a time of extensive crustal unrest in the West. One of its most cataclysmic outbursts was the ejection of the vast Columbian lava fields, covering an area of 250,000 square miles with lava up to a mile thick. It extends far into the northern Great Basin, where it dominates the present spectacular desert scenery. During the Pliocene the mountains that had been formed during the later stages of the Miocene were effective barriers to the moisture-laden winds from the ocean. Lacking rain, the rich-forested plains that were to become part of the Great Basin evolved into grasslands that supported a profusion of horses, camels, antelopes, and their parasites. Those browsers were unable to make the change from lush tropical vegetation to harsh grazing, which required much stronger and harder teeth. The grasslands then must have looked much like the mid-West once did, with its great herds of bison, elk, and antelope.

In the late Pliocene and early Pleistocene strong compressive forces were generated that caused warping along the Pacific Coast and inland—forces that built or revived the Coast, Sierra Nevada, Wasatch, and other ranges. The bending and faulting was on a grand scale. Sections of land many miles long and wide were tilted, one edge rising sharply. Whole blocks were sometimes pushed high above their former positions. Abert Rim, not far north of Lakeview, Oregon, is one of the greatest fault scarps in the world. The eastern side of the Steens fault block abruptly rises a mile above the plain at its base, while the western side is a gentle slope. The Wasatch Mountains are a fault block, as are the Sierra Nevadas. The upheavals and deformations and faulting, after erosion had rounded the edges, became the measured succession of plains and ridges of the present Great Basin landscape.

Some faults are clean-cut faces, ground and polished where they have been sliding in contact with each other for ages; such a smooth face is called a slickenside. A remarkable exposure of a slickenside is on the eastern side of Klamath Lake six miles north of Klamath Falls on U.S. 97; see Figure 9. It is being exposed by the removal of the talus for road construction. Sometimes a fault is a mass of shattered and ground rock many feet or perhaps hundreds of feet wide. Figure 9 also shows a fault of this type in central Nevada. In one place along this fault is a tree split in half, each half lying on opposite sides several feet apart. Fissures of this type sometimes bear rich veins of valuable ore, formed when the hot broth from the nether regions rises to the surface bearing a burden of dissolved minerals. The Comstock Lode, which is perhaps the most famous example, produced millions for the promoters but only misery and death for the local Indians.

All these changes were slow, covering hundreds of thousands or even millions of years and were imperceptible except for earthquakes that at times reached calamitous proportions, and occasional volcanic eruptions of violence beyond comprehension. The faulting and slipping are still in progress, still in the process of being formed. In the United States, nine of every ten earthquakes is in the Nevada-California region (Byerly 1952). In the past, earthquakes greater than any that have been recorded must have occurred as the huge fault blocks were born. Some of them were tragic, as stones from the roofs of caves crushed to death the Stone Age occupants clustered around the fire on the floor below. On March 26, 1872, the Owens Valley fault, along the base of the Sierra Nevada, slipped with a terrific shock; in the village of Lone Pine 52 of the 59 houses were thrown down and 23 people killed. The San Francisco and Yellowstone earthquakes are well known and there have been others as severe but less destructive in recent times.

Along the fault lines, reaching far into the bowels of the earth, lava has sometimes risen to the surface and spread over the land, and hot springs may be seen steaming on the hillsides. Ejection of hot ashes built beautiful, symmetrical cinder cones. Between Little Lake and Independence on Highway 395 all these results of internal fires may be seen in a fine display.

As stated before, the geologic events that occurred up to the end of the Pliocene are of small interest to the archaeologist, except that the land forms had been created to receive the Basin and Range culture. It is the Pleistocene in which he is interested, the geological epoch that started perhaps one million years ago. During this time, vast areas of the earth were covered with ice. The Pleistocene may still be with us; perhaps we are in one of the interglacial stages, a period when the ice retreated only to advance again. One reads sensational newspaper articles now and then, asserting that the ice is returning or retiring. The truth is that no one knows for sure. Measurements would have to be taken over a span of many centuries to be significant.

4. The Ice Age

The Pleistocene Epoch, more familiarly known as the Ice Age, is generally considered to cover the last one million years. Geology is not an exact science like mathematics, and the time is not definite. It was during the Pleistocene that the destiny of man was determined (as far as man is concerned the Ice Age has always been here) and it is perhaps well to discuss the series of events in some detail. The reader will have a clearer picture of man and his environment if he is familiar with the geological history, and while combing the sands of the Great Basin for mementos of its ancient inhabitants, be able to vicariously associate with them through the visible traces of the Time of the Great Cold.

The Ice Age theory was proposed quite recently, and with considerable controversy. It began when it was noticed that, in many places in the world, stone boulders were found resting on entirely different rocks: igneous granite on sedimentary sandstone or perhaps basalt upon limestone. They were called erratics and the strange combination was a wondrous puzzle to early scientists. Some thought that a great flood brought the stones from distant mountains while others believed they might have been rafted in on floating ice and become stranded when the ice melted. Arguments were sometimes conducted with more sound than logic, for many were deaf to all evidence except that supporting their own views.

As early as 1847 it was realized that glaciers might be the transporting agent for the strange deposits, as mountaineers recognized the similarity to those of existing glaciers. But a glacier in the desert? It was apparent that it could not be. Still, more and more clues were uncovered—unmistakable glacial moraines far from mountains were identified, and stones scratched and faceted and polished as only moving ice can do it were found on barren hillsides and in the valleys. Largely through the efforts of Louis Agassiz, a Swiss scientist who came to America to study the evidence, the glacial hypothesis that vast areas of the earth's surface were once covered with ice was accepted. Subsequent work has resulted in maps that show the extent of the ice and approximate dates of the advances and retreats, dates about which few authorities agree and like national boundaries are constantly changing.

No one knows what causes an ice age. One theory states that the radiation given off by the sun may fluctuate, and sometimes be less than normal. Another maintains that the sun becomes obscured by clouds of cosmic dust that the planetary system encounters in its great swing about the center of the universe. Yet another claims that an increase of the sun's heat will cause more evaporation and precipitation. Whatever the reason, ice ages do occur and some very ancient ones have been partially traced from long-buried deposits. So delicate is the balance in nature that a difference of but a few degrees in the average temperature—some scientists say only three or four— is enough to cause the glaciers to start forming, or rather those already in existence to grow. An ice age is not a time of extreme cold, although colder than the present, but merely a period when more snow falls in the northern latitudes than can melt in the summer. After the glaciers are formed, however, there are alterations in the climate and weather pattern, and these are the important changes as far as Early Man was concerned.

Like a government bureau, an ice age is self-perpetuating. Ice crystals are the best natural reflector and they cast the sun's heat back into space so it cannot be utilized to melt the snow, and the more area covered with the coruscating crystals, the more of the sun's energy is wasted. As the snow piles up, the delicate flakes are subject to sublimation, melting and refreezing, and eventually become granular crystals called "firn" or "neve." The layers of firn pack closely together from the weight of new snow above and as the weight increases, combine into hard, blue, glacial ice. When the ice gets thick enough, gravity causes it to flow outward like a spoonful of batter on a griddle. It is in the latitudes around 50 and 60 degrees that the ice was formed because there is not enough precipitation in the more northern latitudes to make sufficient glacial ice to cover the land. Cold air cannot hold as much vapor as warm air, and in the polar regions there is not much moisture being transported by the wind. Large areas in Alaska were free of ice in the Pleistocene.

The glaciers fluctuated widely, sometimes melting only to again reform. The interglacial or retreat periods were much longer than the glacial or advance stages. Sometimes the ice disappeared for thousands of years, long enough for forests to grow and meadows to become populated with strange animals— only to be overwhelmed by another advance of the creeping, white mantle. It is interesting to note that there are millions of cubic miles of water still locked up in Ice Age glaciers. If they all melted, the level of the ocean would rise over 100 feet, drowning many of the world's major cities. Civilization will be fortunate if we remain in the Ice Age.

The only one of the several ice stages during the Pleistocene with which man is concerned is the Wisconsin. It too fluctuated and authorities differ by wide margins on all dates except that of the final retreat. Any ages given here should be considered approximate and are stated only to give a sense of time. The last advance of the Wisconsin was a minor one called the Cochrane, which ended about 7,000 years ago. The greatest advance was the Iowan, perhaps 35,000 years ago, and this is the time many scientists believe man first entered the New World. It should be made clear that the ice sheet did not reach into the Great Basin; the area was free from ice except for glaciers on some of the mountains. It was not the ice itself but its effects on the weather that concerned the first inhabitants—except for one very important feature.

Early Man was a hunter, a roamer following the game herds as the Laplanders follow their flocks of domesticated reindeer. As the ice crept southward the game animals and the carnivores, including man, were gradually pushed forward or sideways. As more and more water became locked up in the glaciers, the sea level fell until there was dry land hundreds of miles wide between Asia and America. It is believed that over this land passage Early Man followed the game herds into the Americas— the one important direct result of the glaciers. It is certain that there was such a passage for there were Pleistocene animals of the same species in both Asia and America, an impossible condition without it. Animals that originated in America and migrated to Asia include the camel and horse, both of which became extinct in America rather recently. Animals that originated in Asia and crossed the passage to America include the bear, caribou, bison, musk ox, and elephant.

The vast ice sheets that started in Canada and flowed many hundreds of miles by the energy of their weight extended about one third of the way across Montana. In the Mississippi Valley one lobe reached some distance beyond St. Louis. Scientists have estimated that the apex of the ice sheet must have been three miles thick, to spread so rich a batter over so large a griddle. The evidence of the Ice Age so clearly seen on every hand in the Great Basin—wave-cut terraces, wide lake beds, lacustrine gravel deposits, dry river channels—is not that of the ice but the climate.

5. Fossil Weather

In the deserts of Africa and Asia are hills and hummocks resulting from the dust and rubble of once-great cities. Even in the shifting sands of the Sahara are the remains of ancient cities. Of much greater antiquity, but in the same area, drifting dunes reveal fist axes and flaked blades of Mousterian Man, over 50,000 years old. How could such a barren desert support a flourishing civilization or foster an ancient culture? The answer is simple—it was not a desert then. What is now a wasteland, like the Sahara and the Great Basin, was once a fertile, well-watered, temperate, productive region. Climates change, sometimes drastically, for many reasons, most of which are unknown. Local changes might be due to eustatic movements of the earth uplifting mountains which cut off moisture-laden winds, or lowering lands enough to permit invasion of a sea with its tempering effects.

The study of fossil weather is a most interesting but exacting study. Clues are scarce and difficult to interpret. One of the most helpful tools is the study of ancient pollen. Bogs which have been filled by the accumuation of centuries will have in the deposits various kinds of pollen. Knowledge of the age of the pollen-bearing layer (which can be established by geologic or other means) can establish the climate at the time of its formation. This expanding science is called palynology, and it is fortunate that pollen is such a durable substance. An entirely new science is the study of cores brought up from the bottom of the ocean. The different species of marine invertebrates in the varying levels of the cores are an indication of the water temperature at the time the material was deposited. The work done so far indicates that most of the time the weather has been much warmer than it is now.

Clues to the weather are found in the physical appearance of the landscape, such as an ancient lake terrace which could have been formed only in a wet period, or an isolated stand of trees— a remnant of a once extensive forest. Animals and fish, too, show weather changes by their distribution.

The effect of the Ice Age on the local weather was drastic but still caused by the same well established but little understood meteorological laws that control our present climate. In the winter there is a difference in the temperature and pressure of the air over the snow and ice of the North, the open oceans and the snow-free lands, and the tropics. The farther north, the colder and heavier is the air; the farther south the warmer and lighter. The cold air tends to flow beneath and displace the warmer air like water under oil. The warmer air as it rises expands and cools. Since cool air cannot hold as much moisture as warm air, some condenses and falls as rain or snow.

Such masses of cold air sweeping southward are called storm fronts and in winter bring rain or snow to whatever section of the country they pass over. In the summer the temperature difference between the north and south latitudes is not so great. The cold fronts do not form in the same way and there is less precipitation. During the Ice Age the summer meteorological conditions were more like those of the present winter; there were storm fronts throughout the year, resulting in a cool, wet climate in the Great Basin.

The shifting of the storm fronts had some interesting effects. There was not only more precipitation but less evaporation. Water accumulated in the basins until it spilled over the lips to cut deep channels which are now dry and barren. These were the times of the great pluvials, and there were two in the Great Basin, the Bonneville and the Provo. Their traces are strikingly evident as the highest terraces on the shores of the old lakes, especially in the vicinity of Salt Lake City. There were some fluctuations of water levels; the terraces were formed during still-stands when climatic conditions were in balance. There is evidence that early man overlooked these ancient lakes; artifacts are found on the old strand lines including cobble choppers, stone blades, and atlatl points. Geological evidence dates them at from 9,000 to 11,000 years ago. One such site is Hathaway Beach on Carson Sink, Nevada, and another is in the Mojave Desert at Soda Lake.

It is a paradox that there is less erosion during a pluvial than during a dry period. Plentiful moisture engenders lush vegetation even if the climate is relatively cool. Forests blanket the hills. Grass for grazing and shrubs for browsing support herbivorous animals which in turn support the carnivores. The vegetation covers and its roots bind the soil, resisting washing and runoff so that the precipitation soaks in, later to emerge as springs feeding permanent streams and rivers. During a dry or thermal period there is little or no vegetation to protect the soil, and rains generally come in scarce but violent storms. The copious runoff cuts deep gullies through which the soil is carried to form alluvial fans or lacustrine deposits on the basin floors. It is this rapid washing that exposes the old camp signs and relics of ancient man.

During the Bonneville Pluvial, about 35,000 years ago, Lake Bonneville stood about 1,000 feet higher than its present remnant, Great Salt Lake. At that point it overflowed into the Columbia River drainage system through Red Rock Pass. Lake Lahontan was over 500 feet deep, and Lake Chewaucan filled Abert and Summer Lake basins. Between the Bonneville and Provo pluvials the lakes Lahontan and Bonneville fell to about 325 and 110 feet, only to rise again to 625 and 320 during the Provo Pluvial.

Following the latter pluvial there was a time of gradually increasing temperatures called the Anathermal. The weather, although growing warmer, was for a long time about like that which now makes the West such a pleasant place to live. The lakes remained at high levels, and waves cut caves in the old shore lines—caves that were to offer shelter to Early Man. The great Ice Age animals still roamed the plains. The Anathermal lasted until about 5,000 B.C.; the climate was then growing definitely warmer and drier.

The long dry period that followed the Anathermal is called the Altithermal. It lasted from about 7,000 to about 3,000 years B.P. The change from wet to dry was very gradual and completely unnoticed by any any individual. It took centuries to metamorphose, nor was the transformation without fluctuations. Nevertheless, the final stage was catastrophic to both men and animals. The vast lakes that once lapped at shores well watered with gentle rain gradually disappeared, leaving great marshes that must have been heavily populated with both human beings and wildlife. Finally, the marshes too dried, leaving only desert.

How is it known that there was the Time of the Great Heat? One indication is the nature of sedimentary deposits; geologists can determine the difference between those laid down under dry and wet conditions, and their approximate age. Another is the salt content of the puny remnants of the immense pluvial lakes. Antevs (1948) made studies of Summer, Abert, and Owens lakes and believes that their saline content would have taken approximately 4,000 years to accumulate. He thinks that at the close of the Anathermal the lakes evaporated, leaving their salt-encrusted beds looking something like the present Death Valley—to be denuded by the wind, or buried beneath later sediments. Then, about 4,000 years ago, the basins again filled but the salt was no longer available to be re-dissolved. There were some exceptions; Great Salt Lake either did not dry or the salt was reclaimed. Pyramid, Klamath, and some others probably survived the shriveling heat.

There are other clues to the Altithermal, but not all authorities are convinced, and many believe that the weather has not changed significantly in the Great Basin for the past 10,000 years. But like the presence of the pre-projectile point culture, there seems to be too much evidence of the great desiccation to ignore it.

The Althithermal was followed by the Medithermal, when there were a few times of increased precipitation and severe droughts such as the one at the end of the 13th Century, and the lesser one of the 16th Century. But the weather on the average was not much different from that which we now enjoy.

6. The Antiquity of Man in the New World.

Belief in the antiquity of Man in the New World receives some support from evidence of the Ice Age transgressions. To emigrate from Asia it was necessary to have a dry-land crossing; as shown earlier such a passage did exist while so much water was locked up in the solid state. This dry-land route is frequently called a land bridge but the word bridge suggests a span over water and there was none. The sea level was so low the bottom was exposed as dry land, a passage several hundred miles wide which lasted probably for thousands of years. The warm Japanese Current tempered the southern shores of the isthmus. It must have been a pleasant land of forests and meadows, an attractive place for animals and the carnivores that hunted them, including man.

There are three schools of thought on the origin of the ancestors of the American Indians. All agree that they came by means of the land passage, although admitting the possibility that an insignificant number may have arrived by a very lucky and unplanned Pacific crossing. And all agree that there are no primates either existing or fossilized in the Americas from which man descended—he could have come only from the Old World. One group surmises that the first arrivals antedated the Mongoloids, another that there was a succession of invasions by Mongoloids and others, with the first entrants being pre-Mongoloid. A third theorizes that there were other strains arriving, including Amurians and Negritos. These differences in opinion are occasioned by the different physical types in the existing Indian nations. The problems are too academic for this book. Here we will

38

simply consider that they were men following the food supply and their natural propensity to see what was over the next hill.

After following the passage to America, an ice-free corridor southward was necessary to reach the Plains and the Great Basin, and there were three possible routes. One was by boat along the shores, the least likely approach because the culture was probably not sufficiently advanced to have adequate boats for braving the stormy coastal waters. The beach route is also unlikely, because it would have required an ocean-oriented culture and there is no evidence of its existence. The probable route was up the Yukon and down a corridor east of the Rocky Mountains, or through the lowlands of the McKenzie River, then southward. There is some evidence that both routes were used, even that men worked their way northward from where they had established themselves in the Great Plains, as they followed the game behind the retreating ice sheets. Remains of Pleistocene animals in the North are prolific but men were counted by tens and animals by thousands; it is not easy to find and untangle the faint traces of men. There is yet much work to do before the southward migration route is conclusively traced, but no other is generally considered feasible.

Glacial studies indicate that there was enough water locked up in terrestrial ice to uncover a land passage about 35,000 or 40,000 years ago, followed by another great freeze 20,000 or 25,000 years later. Scientists believe that between these periods there was a time lasting about 15,000 years when it would have been impossible for Early Man to have reached America or to have migrated southward from Alaska, because of ice and sea-level conditions. Man thus had to arrive either about 35,000 or about 15,000 years ago. Because tentative dates greater than 15,000 years have been obtained, many archaeologists will say that they believe Early Man crossed the passage soon after it was uncovered, about 35,000 years ago, but concede that absolute proof is lacking. Practically every one of them would be willing to rack up his trowel if he could find the evidence—for to him would go honors accorded Dr. J. D. Figgins when he first proved the association of Early Man with extinct Pleistocene animals—and Figgins was not an archaeologist but paleontologist. It is known from ample proof that the Americas were rather well populated by 12,000 years ago; some scienists say about 15,000, a date secured by Ruth Gruhn (1961) from Wilson Butte Cave in Idaho. The belief that the human animal first set foot on American soil about 35,000 years ago is based on reasoning backed up by some shovel and trowel work.

In very old sites in America are found some of the most refined projectile points in existence: beautifully chipped lanceolate points that were used to tip the spears or darts of the Big Game Hunters, sometimes called the Llano Culture. This migration came from Siberia where there are no such complex flaked projectile points definitely antecedent to the Llano. However, rough stone tools, principally choppers and scrapers, of a pre-projectile point culture are found in Siberia. If these people were the original immigrants and came over only 15,000 or 20,000 years ago, there was probably insufficient time for the sophisticated Llano Culture to develop. The pre-point culture, a flake and chopper tradition like that then existing in Europe, may have been the first to arrive and people the Americas many thousands of years prior to the Llano. Such a culture, with few artifacts and a meager population, would be difficult to trace, but some startling finds have been made.

Another—and very powerful—argument for the early population is the diversity of languages. There are more language groups in the Americas than in all the rest of the world combined (Bryan 1965). It has been argued that an arrival date much earlier than those yet obtained from cultural remains is necessary to explain the complexity of linguistic differentiation, especially since the relation of languages to those in the Old World are tenuous or non-existent except for the later arrivals such as the Eskimo. This lack of language relation could be explained by the early arrival of a culture with an extremely limited vocabulary, one that expanded during the thousands of years after arrival.

An interesting facet in regard to Early Man is that, for thousands of years, Europe and America were in about the same stage of development. We are so used to thinking that the Old World was much further advanced that it is startling to realize that a chopper from a Great Basin cave would have suited equally well either the American or his European counterpart. In fact, the textile and flaking techniques indicate that America was somewhat ahead of Europe in cultural advancement. When the two primary cultural revolutions—agricultural and writing—did come, the Europeans already had, or soon acquired, the horse. That animal provided a means of communication to spread the culture and, later, was a beast of burden to relieve the work load.

There are several places where impressive evidence of this pre-point culture has been uncovered. Dr. Alex D. Kreiger has summarized them in "Prehistoric Man in the New World" (Jennings and Norbeck 1964), listing over 200 references. One site is in Alaska; from it have been taken rather crude adtifacts showing chemical change and corrosion that must have taken many thousands of years to accomplish.

It is difficult to fit chemical change into the time scale. Generally the stone artifacts from old camp sites—even those of the ancient Big Game Hunters—are in good, even excellent condition, but then sometimes they are not. Ruth and I have found atlatl weights made of galena, a lead ore, that have been altered over the centuries into white lead; they were just a blob of paint. And in the same site were some that had only a thin white skin; the insides were solid galena. Indian village sites on the lower Columbia River are so full of deer, elk, and other game animal bones they can be hauled away in trucks, yet there are others where not the slightest trace of bone exists except that calcined by fire. Most chemical change is due to acid, and the amount and strength in nature varies widely. To alter such a resistant substance as silicon dioxide takes a great deal of time or a very powerful corrosive or both.

One of the earliest dates yet obtained from a suspected pre-projectile point site in the New World is 30,000 years ago, obtained by the C14 method from burned bones of pygmy mammoths on Santa Rosa Island off the coast of California. These little fellows were only about six feet high. The bones were taken from a clay that had been burned red, bones that strongly suggested that the animals had been butchered and eaten. A chipped artifact was found in one of the areas. The Santa Rosa dates have not been accepted, yet the evidence is strong enough to justify further research. There is no question of the antiquity of the sites; they are in a deep layer cut back by the sea into steep cliffs 50 to 75 feet high, cut into an alluvial fan that could have been deposited only when the sea was much lower than at present. The depth of the cultural remains in the face of the cliffs is so great that excavation presents a serious problem. It may be a long time before the debris is sifted and the residuum analyzed.

Lewisville, Texas, has yielded the oldest C14 date yet obtained —38,000 years—from a possible Early Man site. Perhaps it was 8,000 years older than Santa Rosa, but that will never be proved because the cultural remains are now deep beneath the water behind one of the numerous power dams. It is also suspected that in Lewisville a modern practical joker reached one of his greatest triumphs. In the deposit was a Clovis point, completely out of context but enveloping in a fog of doubt the entire operation, a serious work by capable and dedicated scientists.

The site was uncovered on the Trinity River at a depth of about 20 feet in a borrow pit for earth fill for the dam which eventually flooded the area. There were several hearths, some flakes, and numerous bones, some of which had been split, some charred. Pleistocene animals identified from the fossil remains were mammoth, horse, camel, bison, peccary, glyptodon, turtle, and tortoise. The glyptodon and tortoise could not survive in the existing climate at Lewisville; their presence shows that the weather was warmer then.

The dating specimen was obtained from two hearths which also contained three pre-projectile point artifacts—a scraper, hammerstone, and cobble chopper. Like the initial findings at the Folsom site, the association was challenged; the artifacts may have been injected into the hearths from above by earth-moving equipment. In view of the weight of the evidence—split bone, hearths, variety of animal remains, and number of artifacts— there should be no "reasonable" doubt.

Not long ago a C14 date of about 28,000 years was obtained from the very promising Tule Springs site in Nevada. It too contained split and burned bones of extinct fauna, flaked artifacts, worked bone, and possible campfire remains. But more recent and extensive excavations and studies have shown that the complicated geological structure had been misinterpreted. The tested samples were from mixed layers, and no date earlier than about 13,500 years could be assigned to the cultural remains.

Another Texas site where no C14 date was obtained but which bears evidence of extreme antiquity is Friesenhahn Cavern. Pleistocene animals identified from bones in this limestone cave were mammoth, mastodon, bison, horse, camel, peccary, dire wolf, bear, and two species of smylodon the saber-tooth cat. Artifacts found were worked bone (which could have been cut by carnivores), polished bone tubes (which could have been tumbled in the stomach of a prehistoric cat), chipped end scrapers (which could have been formed by weathering), and a freshwater clam shell for which no reasonable explanation could be given except transportation by man. Also uncovered were 40 or more scraper-like artifacts that have such a definite pattern that accidental formation must be excluded. Excavation of this cave is far from complete and may yet produce some conclusive evidence of the antiquity of man in America.

Some of the most interesting and abundant traces of Early Man—scrapers, choppers and blades—have been surface finds from the upper terraces of ancient pluvial lakes and the deserts of Southern California. Untold numbers of these historical heritages have been carted home by relic hunters to be later cast aside as unworthy of display. Many have been collected and studied by archaeologists. In some places a series of terraces marks different stillstands of Pleistocene lakes that might have been thousands of years apart. The abundance of the old-terrace material offers some of the strongest evidence of a pre-projectile point culture.

Southwest of Mexico City, along the Atoyac River in a stratified river deposit, have been found a number of flaked cobbles showing retouching; also stone scrapers and gravers, a number of triangular bone pieces with one edge beveled, some with perforations, and a large bone with incised design. Many bones, some split and charred, were found and from them were identified mammoth, mastodon, horse, camel, bison, deer, glyptodon, and rodent.

One interesting feature of this site is the way it was geologically dated. The bed below the deposit bearing the cultural debris is gravel. Since there were no andesite boulders in it—although Popocatepetl and other volcanoes in the vicinity are andesitic and also glacially eroded—it was postulated that the site predates the formation of the volcanoes; otherwise there would have been andesitic gravel in the stream bed associated with the cultural remains. This feature has not yet been clearly demonstrated, but it is a good example of the many clues for the geological dating of a project. The fossil record proves that this is an ancient site and the cultural remains suggest a pre-projectile point culture.

South America has produced some sites with interesting artifacts indicating an ancient flaking tradition. Near Maoca in Venezuela, in a thick bed of mud, paleontologists have found flake and pebble tools associated with such extinct Pleistoncene creatures as mastodon, horse, camel, sloth, glyptodon, and wolf. From the surfaces of high terraces of Rio Pedregal at El Jobo have been taken a series of scrapers and choppers. From lower terraces similar tools plus percussion-flaked lanceolate points have been removed, indicating a transition stage in the tool-making art. Another assembly of pre-point tools has been collected from the surface and the upper few inches of the clay shores of Lake Maracaibo and includes several forms of scrapers, hand axes, and knives.

On Tierra Del Fuego, at the southernmost tip of South America, there is a shell midden that has yielded points similar to those taken from a cave in the same land that were about 8,500 years old. Beneath the midden there is a 1.5-foot layer of sterile beach sand covering a stratum yielding bolo stones, percussion chipped cores and flakes, and a hand axe. The sea is now about 600 feet from the site, and the sterile beach sand over the remains indicates that there was a time after the cultural stratum was laid down that the sea rose and covered the spot, later to retreat and permit establishment of another village that accumulated the shell midden. It is thought that the advance and retreat of the sea would have taken considerable time.

These are only a few of the 15 or so possible Early Man sites in South America that have been investigated. If Siberia was the sources of the population, it must have taken a long, long time for a primitive people to traverse both continents, especially with their vastly different terrain requiring new techniques for mastery.

The ecology of the pre-projectile point culture—if it did exist—can only be surmised. Certainly they were hunters, for bones of the big-game animals are found in suspected early sites—but how they captured them is a mystery; they had no weapons except possibly wooden spears with fire-hardened points, weapons that have disappeared without a trace. Game could have been driven into bogs where they would mire down and could be slain with rocks and spears; the *National Geographic Magazine* for June, 1962, has a story of a mammoth in Wyoming that appears to have been captured that way. Or, the hunters could have driven herds over cliffs as did the Plains Indians with the buffalo. Small animals could have been trapped or dug from their burrows; birds' eggs, seeds, roots, berries, all could have been used. There were no milling stones and no tools or food preparation equipment except choppers that may have been used to butcher the animals captured.

The vast number of dated sites in the 9,000-14,000-year range is intriguing. During this period a remarkable culture was established, one that expanded and spread rapidly over North America. It must have arisen from within as it seems to have spread from the Great Plains area outward in all directions. This stage has been called Fluted Point, Early American Hunter, Upper Lithic, Paleo American and Llano. Characteristic of the stage was the production of thin, beautifully worked blades or projectile points showing an unsurpassed control of technique as demonstrated in the Clovis, Folsom, Cascade, Eden, and similar points. The workmanship of these efficient points indicates that the people had a well-disciplined character, a culture that would have been diligent in the chase and politically well organized.

The wide dispersion of diagnostic projectile points indicates an expansion of the big-game hunting tradition in the Great Plains and Intermontaine Plateau but not in the Great Basin. A number of fluted projectile points have been found in the Basin, yet no evidence exists that the Llano culture ever reached any substantial development there.

The big-game-hunting people roamed the plains of America for many centuries but the end was near. By about 7,000 years ago some of the larger animals were extinct and others were thinning fast. Some more reliable food source had to be searched for and exploited. The result was the Desert Culture, dating from the first appearance of the milling stone. This marks the beginning of the theme of this book, the story of a culture that lasted practically unchanged for about 10,000 years before the white invaders destroyed it.

7. Caves—Windows of the Past

Caves have always attracted men, both primitive and modern. In ancient times they were at once refuges and shelters, and no cave ever was long unoccupied if Homo sapiens was in the vicinity. Like islands, they were symbols of security, a concentrated area upon which to lavish the luxury of possession, an anchor about which to swing in the daily search for food. Here was a ready-made habitation, fashioned by nature and always, in the Great Basin, overlooking the lake whose wind-driven waves carved it from the rocks. From the entrance the inhabitants, probably a small family group, could watch for both human invaders and wandering game. Camels, horses, elephants, giant ground sloth, and bison came to drink from the lake, and there must have been many hurried conferences at their appearance, as hunters planned an assault with their puny weapons against the giant beasts.

Conditions in caves are ideal for the preservation of artifacts. The deposit on the floor continually builds up from human or animal debris and settling dust. Rarely do invading waters enter to wash away the evidence. Compressed beneath layers of fine silt, in perfect dryness, wood and fiber and sometimes even leather will remain preserved for hundreds or even thousands of years. Packrats befoul the deposit and rockfalls from the roof disturb the pattern, but in general a cave contains a chronological sequence, layer upon layer, of the occupation, inviting the skilled hand of the archaeologist to strip away the matrix and leave the cultural remains suspended in space with his classification charts. Thousands of years of history and generations of human beings

47

can be viewed in three dimensions and the past reconstructed with precision.

Unfortunately, caves also have a fascination for the amateur collector and they are being searched out and plundered of their contents at an alarming rate. Looting a cave can be considered in no other category than vandalism, for the contents, like all cultural heritages, belong to the public and not to the individual alone. With rare exceptions, the cave plunderer works only for the artifact, like the hunter for a trophy, with no thought of any contribution to knowledge. He has for his reward only a collection of trinkets, mere curious baubles without the historical record.

While it is unfortunate that there are so many cave looters in the Great Basin, it is fortunate that there are so many caves. The waves of vast Pleistocene lakes beat against exposed edges of rock layers in fault scarps, layers with varying degrees of hardness. The softer material eroded faster, leaving extensive rock shelters and caverns. Sometimes the waves enlarged existing openings in sedimentary formations, or removed the softer material around gas vents in lava flows. Limestone caves, too, are found and are usually the largest and deepest. These caverns are formed by the action of rain water, made slightly acid by carbon dioxide from the atmosphere, dissolving away the stone, some of which may be re-deposited in the form of stalagmites or stalactites. They do not necessarily have any relation to Pleistocene lakes or their terraces, as do eroded caves.

Although caves offered shelter and even a degree of comfort to their Stone Age inhabitants, they are not pleasant places in which to dig. Dust, heat and guano stench plague the searcher for history. The very qualifications that make a cave ideal for the preservation of archaeological evidence are those that make the extraction of the data so frustrating. Caves are dry—the good ones—and the fill is atmospheric dust, fine as smoke, saturating the debris of men and animals, a biologic deposit that forms by fits and starts, depending on the region's flora or fauna. During a pluvial, ruminants may deposit thick layers of dung and rodents may harvest and store hay in deep straw beds. Packrats will forage far and near for sticks, stones, and bones with which to build a miniature fort to protect their nests. During an altithermal, atmospheric dust floats in or is dropped from the windstream in an eddy. Always there are rocks falling from the roof to add their bulk to the deposit, and seemingly one stone can never be removed without picking out its neighbor first.

In this deposit every step, every thrust of the shovel, flushes a cloud of choking, permeating, foul-smelling dust that obscures the vision, ruins the camera, and penetrates the clothing. And over everything the dust pall settles continuously, obscuring stratification and artifact alike beneath a dull gray veil. The most efficient face mask fails to exclude it, and without a filter, work is impossible. To top everything off, it is pitch dark.

Twenty miles southward from Lovelock, Nevada, a limestone peak projects from the Humboldt basin like a nomad's tent. To the east lie the fault-scarp Humboldt Mountains, and to the west the broad Humboldt Sink—the sponge that absorbs the Humboldt River. (There is also a Humboldt Current off the coast of Chile, and a Humboldt County, Humboldt Salt Marsh, Humboldt Bay, and Humboldt Range in the West, all named in honor of Baron Alexander von Humboldt, one of the earliest and greatest of the naturalists, but one who never saw the Great Basin.)

At the apex of the limestone peak, overlooking the Sink, is Lovelock Cave, a limestone cavern that held one of the richest archaeological treasures ever found in the West, most of which was cast over the lip of the cave to be ground to dust or inundated beneath the rubble of guano miners. The cave, known but seldom visited, could be entered only by a small opening, the entrance being blocked by rockfalls. Two men from Lovelock, finding the cave contained a deep layer of bat guano, staked a mining claim in 1911 and removed perhaps fifty tons of guano from a layer three to six feet deep. Baskets, sandals, fur and feather blankets, bows and arrows, mummies, nets, skeletons, everything that would not go through the miners' grizzly, was thrown out—except a few of the more outstanding curios. One ancient warrior was spared the indignity of sepulcher beneath the guano rubble when a civic-minded local booster organization rescued his desiccated remains from the dump and boiled them down to a skeleton for use in their initiation rites.

After the miners finished their work, local collectors dug over the deposits for what treasures they might contain, most of which eventually were lost, including a perfect, carved atlatl. A beautifully worked feather plume and a large woven net for snaring rabbits were eventually purchased by the Museum of the American Indian; these so intrigued the museum officials that they sent Dr. Mark Harrington to investigate the cave. This would be normal procedure now, but at that time so much material was being acquired by museums as gifts and purchases that field work was ordinarily not considered. Mr. L. L. Loud from the University of California, who had made some collections from the cave in 1912, joined with Harrington to conduct further excavations and they collaborated on a report (Loud and Harrington 1929) that ends thus:

"In its original state Lovelock was a real source-book of pre-history, probably unique in its richness and scope. It is most unfortunate that some institution could not have made a complete study of it, and transcribed the information it had to offer before irresponsible hands destroyed so many of its pages."

Lovelock Cave is situated on a terrace of Pleistocene Dendritic Lake, one of the stillstands of the pluvial Lake Lahontan (see Fig. 18). One of the higher stages of the waters had covered the cave to a depth of 200 feet, partly filling it with debris, to which was added the erosion detritus from the cliff after the waters receded. From the entrance the ancient inhabitants could overlook the dying lake, bordered by extensive marshes teeming with wild life. The cave offered shelter during the cold, wet winters, perhaps protection from enemies. For nomads it would have been a refuge as they passed this way on the endless quest for subsistence. The Cave deposits showed occupation over a long period, but no permanent residency. There were extended intervals when only wild beasts sought its shelter.

The most feared section of the old immigrant road to California passes close to this cave, and is still followed by anyone wishing to visit it. The road is only a faint trace, rough and rocky, with an occasional washout, but passable with care. Old wagon-wheel rims or perhaps an ox shoe are occasionally found, wasted to a streak of rust in the sand by the chemical-laden waters. The road can be found by turning east off 1A on an unmarked road about ten miles south of 95—or, with difficulty, from Lovelock. It is not a trip to be taken casually, but with preparation and guidance.

The cave is about 40 feet wide and 160 deep. Like most caves, the floor slopes steeply downward to the rear. Huge rocks that fell from the roof project like outbuildings from the deposits, and a dank, musky smell beclouds and befouls the atmosphere. Deep holes penetrate the refuse abandoned by collectors. Time had covered the lacustrine gravels with a succession of layers of rubbish that exceeded ten feet, and was then topped with guano layers.

Mr. Loud first worked here in 1912, upon completion of the mining operation, selecting as best he could the undisturbed areas. Mr. Harrington arrived in 1924, secured the services of Mr. Loud, and together they conducted extensive excavations with the help of Indian labor. They found a number of graves in the cave, many of which had been previously destroyed. About 55 dead were represented, including several mummies. But burials appeared to be only incidental in the cave; it had been used primarily as a dwelling. The burials probably took place during times the cave was unoccupied and subsequent residents were unaware of their presence. In the several thousand years during which the cave was sporadically inhabited, the presence of 50 or 60 burials does not establish a trait nor signify a burial ground.

Some of the graves were rather elaborately furnished. One,

dating back to the Transitional Age, was found beneath a very large decorated basket which covered three other baskets. The body was wrapped in an animal skin and covered with woven nets. An elkhorn tool with a handle painted white and a lump of white paint completed the offerings. Another grave, at a depth of five feet, was covered with six fine baskets, inverted. Removing the baskets revealed the remains of a child wrapped in a woven fur blanket, encircled in a net. Some of the baskets had been decorated with feathers, and this feature, coupled with the depth which penetrated into the lacustrine deposits, indicated an early burial, for feather-decorated baskets appeared only in the lower levels.

One remaining undisturbed plot in the cave was chosen for stratigraphic study; the deposits were separated into six levels. The first (excluding the removed guano layer) was about 18 inches deep, partially disturbed. It produced a large number of basket and matting fragments, two arrow foreshafts with points in place, a stick bent into a loop similar to those used for stirring mush by recent Indians, and parts of a digging stick and fire drill. The second level was about 30 inches thick and contained large amounts of roof fall, possibly the results of a violent earthquake. Artifacts included arrow shaft fragments—some with pointed greasewood foreshafts—many basket, matting, and fiber fragments, and a bone awl. Two of the more unusual finds were foreshafts for flaming arrows, one wrapped with tule, the other with punky wood that had been burning when shot into the cave, perhaps a relic of an ancient siege. These two levels were designated as the Late Period because only arrows were found, no dart or atlatl fragments. Subsequent C14 tests, plus a little interpolation, dated this period about one thousand years ago.

The third to the sixth levels were each approximately two feet thick. The third consisted of grass and dust with few stones and was comparatively rich in artifacts. Found were many basket fragments, parts of fur and feather blankets, a feathered, painted cane arrow with a foreshaft slotted for insertion of a point, and two atlatl dart shafts. In Level 4 no arrow parts were found, but there were two atlatl dart fragments. Twined, flexible-weave basketry appeared for the first time, as well as feathers from large birds, that were tied to cord. Because of evidence of transition from atlatls to the bow and arrow, these two layers were designated as the Transitional Period. Again by C14 tests and interpolation, Level 3 was dated about 2,500 years and Level 4 about 3,000 years ago. (The C14 tests were made many years after the excavation.)

No arrow or atlatl shafts were found in Level 5, but there were fragments of flexible, twined basketry; a flexible, twined bag; and a coiled basket or hat decorated with feathers. In Level 6 there was an atlatl dart foreshaft and more flexible basketry, two wooden decorative pendants, a rabbit-skin blanket, and a headband made from hair.

A study of the stratigraphic section, supported by evidence elsewhere in the cave, shows that certain cultural objects were found throughout, such as matting and cordage, coarse coiled basketry, fur blankets, netting, pointed digging sticks, and Olivella shell beads. Other material, however, showed a cultural change, notably that of transition from the atlatl to the bow about 2,500 years ago.

The atlatl and the bow were contemporaneous for a considerable period, as more recent investigations also show. Soft, twined bags and baskets were phased out and the stiff wicker and twined baskets became fashionable. Duck decoys came late, about 1,500 years ago, and lasted until the present day, as did sandals and moccasins. The name Lovelock Culture has been assigned to this complex. Similar cultural components have been found as far away as Danger Cave, 250 miles east, and Massacre Lake Cave, 140 miles northeast. In Ocala Cave, ten miles south of Lovelock Cave, articles similar to those from Lovelock were found by Harrington in 1924.

Gypsum Cave was one of the most interesting and informative ever analyzed, and fortunately was excavated under the direction of a man with the feeling of an artist, the skill of a perfectionist, and a flair for prose, Dr. Mark Harrington (1933). Gypsum Cave is 15 miles east of Las Vegas, Nevada, in Paleozoic limestone forming the Frenchman Mountains. Gypsum or selenite crystals, formed in the folded, faulted limestone, gave the cave its name and twice tempted prospectors in search of a fortune to stake the cave as a mineral claim, but hopes were later abandoned. Local Indians had considered it sacred and placed offerings within. Local residents of Las Vegas considered it an interesting place to picnic.

Dr. Harrington worked in the Moapa Valley and Gypsum Cave in the late 1920's, completing the excavation of Gypsum Cave in 1932 when the blindfold of prejudice that had hindered the acceptance by the profession of late Pleistocene man was gradually being removed by the weight of evidence. Investigators had braved the fire of so well-armed and formidable a man as Ales Hrdlicka, whose withering blasts could be withstood only by one well fortified with facts. One needed to be sure of his ground before jousting with Hrdlicka, and his iconoclastic attitude undoubtedly advanced the profession by subduing the proponents of dubious evidence. The search for Ancient Man was being avidly pressed, and fame would be the reward for the discovery. Hrdlicka challenged one and all who assigned an age of over three or four thousand years to early man in the Americas. He was an able scientist, a leading physical anthropologist, but violently unreceptive to the Early-Man theory.

Dr. Harrington, then, as he admits in this report, was cautious: "So when the time came for the exploration of Gypsum Cave in Nevada I still approached the subject with some suspicion. I was not entirely convinced that Pleistocene man had existed in America, in spite of the extraordinary Folsom find of stone points among the bones of extinct bison and other discoveries which had been reported. To that extent I did not approach the Gypsum Cave problem with an unprejudiced mind; certainly in this case I can not be accused of the old practice of first forming my theories and then searching for evidence to support them."

Gypsum Cave lies at an altitude of about 2,000 feet. The entrance overlooks an eroded fossil-lake bed to the east, a couple of hundred feet below, sloping gradually toward the distant Colorado River. It is not in the Great Basin proper, but near the periphery thereof, and is here considered for reasons explained in the introduction to this book. In the Las Vegas Valley to the northwest once ran the Spanish Trail from California to Santa Fe, followed by the Mormon Road, then later by Highway 93 and the Union Pacific Railroad. And nearby is Tule Springs, a promising site that failed.

The entrance, 70 feet wide, is gained only after scrambling over a slope of broken rock, as is usual with most caves. Inside, the floor slopes sharply downward at an angle exceeding 30 degrees; the total depth of the cave is about 300 feet with a maximum width of 120 feet. Branching from the main cavern are four alcoves or rooms, designated Rooms 1, 3, 4, and 5. Room 2 encompasses the main entrance.

During preliminary investigations a few years earlier, Dr. Harrington was intrigued by a deposit of dung similar to that of a horse, but of some unknown creature. He surmised that it might be from some extinct animal, and if so, the association of Early Man with Pleistocene animals might be proved, a discovery that would be of immense value to science.

Shortly after excavation started on January 20, 1930, Mrs. Bertha Pallan, secretary of the expedition, while exploring the crevices within the cavern, discovered a skull unlike that of any known animal. While it was being identified, a visitor discovered some massive bones, dark hair, and claws that could have come from no other animal than a ground sloth. Then came the report on the skull—it was indeed a ground sloth, species *Nothrotherium shastense*, long extinct! Now indeed were excitement and interest aroused, and hopes for future discoveries. On the basis of the find, the California Institute of Technology, the Carnegie Institution, and the Southwest Museum offered financial and scientific support. The claws of the sloth and many of the artifacts secured from Gypsum Cave are now on display in the Southwest Museum in Los Angeles.

Room 1 (see Chart #1) measures about 65 by 35 feet and slopes downward sharply. The roof was blackened with smoke and there was a cultural deposit up to four feet deep. The area near the room entrance is fairly level and appeared to be the favorite haunt of the prehistoric occupants. At some distant time an earthquake had brought down from the roof a massive fall, including one rock 30 by 15 by 8 feet. This rockfall extended throughout the cave and was one of six distinct layers discovered in Room 1. Eventually, excavations reached a depth of 13 feet.

Layer 1 was a midden, the upper part containing numerous artifacts traceable to Basketmaker and Pueblo cultures. Since the area is unsuitable for agriculture, the cave was probably headquarters for hunters of mountain sheep. It also served as a source of selenite crystals for ornaments, specimens of which were found in all stages of manufacture. Two complete ones still containing the suspension cord threaded through the holes were uncovered.

Layer 2 was a nearly sterile composition of earth sprinkled with mountain sheep dung, the quantity of which indicated human occupants were rare. Layer 3 was a roof fall three feet thick, the result of the earthquake. Layer 4 was similar to Layer 2.

Layer 5 was up to seven feet deep, consisting of general debris mixed with sloth and mountain-sheep dung. It was in this deposit that the most important find was made: eight feet below the original surface and beneath a solid, unbroken layer of sloth dung was uncovered a fireplace, proving human occupancy contemporaneous with this Pleistocene animal. In this layer also were found two worked sticks and an oval knife made from chert.

The area about the cave entrance was designated as Room 2. Measuring 83 by 56 feet, it slopes downward so steeply that the far end is 34 feet lower than the entrance. Because the area selected for investigation was near the bottom of the slope, an elaborate cribbing was necessary to hold back the rockslide above. At a depth of eight feet, and beneath layers containing sloth dung and hair, were uncovered two painted atlatl dart fragments. This important find called for deeper digging, which in turn required extensive cribbing, performed by experienced miners previously hired for that purpose. Efforts were rewarded by another painted dart-shaft fragment at a depth of ten feet. These dart fragments served as type specimens for identification of all the ancient darts found throughout the cave. Another interesting find was the jaw and vertebrae of a small horse.

Entrance to Room 3 was gained through narrow passages polished by the traffic of animals. The area measures 75 by 50 feet, not including long alcoves and tunnels extending northward. The floor of this room also slopes sharply and, as in Room 2, the lower portion was selected for exploration. It was in this room that Mrs. Pallan found the sloth skull; and a few feet away, beneath a layer containing sloth dung, was discovered a perfect specimen of a dart point of an early style, named the Gypsum Cave type (see Figure 30). In this room also were discovered the skull of a prehistoric horse, basketry, and a hafted stone knife. (Dr. Harrington calls it a knife, but it looks like the hafted atlatl foreshaft shown in Figure 28.) More painted dart fragments, a complete flute fashioned from a reed, and the skeleton from a small horse were found. Most discoveries were made in the talus rock; extensive excavations in the midden uncovered little of interest.

Room 4, 125 by 175 feet, proved to be rich in paleontology but poor in archaeology. Men are not creatures of the dark, and Room 4 is far from the welcome light of the sun at the entrance. The outstanding discovery here was a dart point in a layer beneath one containing the bones of a small camel. Some dart fragments were found, as well as leather, feathers, and other indications of human occupancy. In one packrat's nest fortification there were bones of the extinct camel, horse, and sloth; also numerous bones of other desert animals who shared the habitat.

Room 5 proved to be practically barren. The most significant find here was a dart foreshaft discovered in the entrance to the room beneath an undisturbed layer of sloth dung.

At the time the report was written, the site was dated geologically at between 7,500 and 9,500 years. Subsequent radio carbon dates from samples collected six feet deep averaged 10,500 years.

The ground sloth was one of the curious beasts that failed to survive the Pleistocene, although it is the ancestor of the modern tree sloths in South America. There were several genera, one of which, *Megatherium*, was as large as an elephant. *Mylodon* was one of the smaller genera, yet it weighed close to a ton, as much as a large horse. *Nothrotherium* was a still smaller genus. Shaggy, slow-moving creatures with claws as large as hammer heads, these sloths tore down branches with their powerful forearms and claws, feeding on the twigs and leaves. As part of their food, analysis of deposits in Gypsum Cave identified Joshua trees, various rushes and grasses, and saltbrush. Stupid, slow and heavy, many of the sloth family blundered into bogs and tar pits to leave a fossil record from which paleontologists, with considerable authority, have reconstructed their appearance, habits, and range.

Overlooking the glittering salt flats of the Great Salt Lake Desert, Danger Cave was carved from the limestone Desert Hills by the waves of pluvial Lake Stansbury. The floor level is now 112 feet above the level of Great Salt Lake. The cavern is 120 feet deep and averages 60 feet wide; the cultural deposit extended back from the entrance about 10 yards. During centuries of occupancy the debris on the floor had built up to a depth of 12 feet. Originally it was called "Hands and Knees Cave," for so choked had the entrance become with talus from above that only a small tunnel remained by which it could be entered. The name was changed to Danger as a result of a rockfall that nearly caused a tragedy for some early excavators.

During 1949-51 and 1953, crews from the University of Utah, under the direction of Dr. Jesse D. Jennings, worked the cave.

The data and material they recovered were worked into an unusually well-written and illustrated report (Jennings 1957) that formed the basic concept of the Desert Culture. For access to the cave, a deep cut was made by machine through the talus in front of the cave, forming a gallery through which the spoil dirt could be removed. Excavation was by natural levels; the material was removed in the layers in which it had accumulated instead of in arbitrarily measured levels.

The floor of the cave consisted of clays and gravel and a fossil beach of an ice-age lake; upon this material lay a cemented beach sand stratum a few inches deep containing artifacts. From a bit of wood in this sand, which Dr. Jennings called Structure D1, an age of 11,000 years was determined by the C14 method; and from a disturbed sand layer above, containing signs of campfires, dates from 9,000 to 11,000 years were taken by the same method. Stratum D1 was on the original floor of the cave. Man had entered and lived there as soon as the receding waters permitted, and thenceforth the occupation was continuous, although probably seasonal, for about 10,000 years.

Overlying Stratum I was a cultural deposit a foot or more thick designated Stratum II, the age of which was not determined. However, it started to accumulate about 9,000 years ago. It was here that baskets, milling stones, and other evidence was uncovered showing the great antiquity of the Desert Culture. A total of 122 milling stones, or fragments thereof, were found in Stratum II. This deposit, containing a large portion of ash, showed heavy occupancy during a moister climate than the present; probably both plant foods and game were plentiful.

Above D11 there was a band of roof scalings without the presence of either fiber or guano. Dr. Jennings believes this deposit accumulated during a dry period when the area was deserted by both animals and man. Above this band was an accumulation of ash, dust, and kitchen midden two to four feet thick, designated Stratum III, rich in artifacts and features. The surface was much disturbed, showing removal of material from the living space to the side walls, to give more room, as previous layers had restricted overhead clearance. Many large fires had been kindled, some of which consumed the organic material in the midden. This stratum was evidently laid down during a wet period when ample vegetation provided a relatively numerous population with both a hunting and gathering economy. Quantities of pickleweed chaff and stalks were interpreted as evidence of use of the seeds of this plant for food. No dates were secured in this layer, which eventually built up to block the entrance, but it is believed to range from 7,000 to 5,000 years ago.

Humboldt Cave is a narrow, deep, fault-formed cave on the southwestern tip of the Humboldt Range, about four miles from Ocala Cave. The length is 49 feet, the width only eight. There were about five feet of deposit consisting of trash, dust, guano, and a small amount of cultural material, showing that the cave had been used only occasionally as a living site. Debris from the bottom gave a date of about 2,500 years, basketry from one of the caches about 2,000 years.

Despite the paucity of midden within the cave, it proved to be a rich source of well-preserved artifacts, for it had been used by the prehistoric residents of the area for hiding their valuables. No fewer than 31 caches were uncovered. All were lined with portions of worn-out baskets; some had been opened by the original owner and the contents reclaimed, but the basketry lining of the pits had been left in place.

The cave was excavated in 1936 by Robert F. Heizer and Alex D. Krieger, and they collaborated on the report (Heizer 1956). The caches, having been dug into the deposit, could not be correlated with the excavation levels for relative dating. Over 4,000 artifacts were collected; about one-half were basketry fragments. Some of the pits contained most interesting material. One appeared to be the paraphernalia of a shaman, with such magic-makers as bunches of feathers, a robe of bird skins, a bone-sucking tube, pitch, mineral paint, small stones, and a duck head. All were dusted or painted with red ochre.

The three lines with attached hooks in Figure 80 were found in one cache together with several other hooks. The bundle of line was in another containing modern clothing, an iron and a stone arrow point, and a bundle of eagle feathers.

The largest cache contained nearly 600 specimens; most were basketry fragments but there were a digging stick, arrow fore-shaft, paint, and a few other items. Another pit contained flat-tened pieces of mountain-sheep horn which, from their shape and evidence of wear, Heizer thought to be sickles, and when used proved to be efficient tools to cut either green or dried stalks. Grass cutters made from mountain-sheep horn are known to have been used by the Basketmaker and Pueblo cultures. Another type of cutter was made from the scapula of a large game animal, possibly an antelope. This type of instrument is widely distributed in North America. The thin edge of the blade is worked into a saw-tooth configuration and sharpened.

Heizer and Krieger concluded that the later material found in Humboldt Cave could not definitely be connected with the mod-ern Northern Paiute, nor could that of Lovelock Cave. Certain types of basketry, round, flat, coiled trays; curved mountain-sheep horn sickles, and L-shapped scapula awls are not characteristic of the Northern Paiute, and cultural materials common to them were not found in the cave. However, there were enough similar-ities in the modern and the cave material to indicate that the cave was occupied by the Northern Paiute in the later years, as was Lovelock Cave. Humboldt and the Late and Transitional in Lovelock appear to be from the same culture, a reasonable conclusion in view of the similar dates and the proximity of the caves, only 12 miles apart and both overlooking the same sink.

In the mid-1800's and later, Humboldt Sink contained a lake and a vast expanse of marsh. Water and marsh mean waterfowl and it is evident that the occupants of the nearby caves exploited this source of food, for duck decoys and other evidence were found in them. The sink receives the discharge of Humboldt River, once called Mary's River. Modern irrigation projects now use most of the water from the river, and the marshes have decreased to a small area.

Fort Rock Cave is perhaps the most famous of all the Great Basin caverns because of two historic events in which it played an exciting part. As caves go, Fort Rock would be considered medium size, being about 45 feet deep and 25 wide. The roof at the rear is too low for comfort but ample in front where the southern exposure invites the warm rays of the sun to penetrate the interior. It was carved from a basaltic outcrop by the pounding waves of pluvial Fort Rock Lake, which once covered the adjacent basin to a depth of 75 to 100 feet. The original floor of the cave is covered with shingle—gravel worn flat as the Pleistocene waters sent them sliding about over the stone bottom. Centuries of accumulation of debris from occupancy by men and animals mixed with windblown dust and roof fall had built a deposit over the shingle to a depth of four feet and over. The cave acquired its name from the adjacent semicircular remnant of an ancient volcano, worn to a stub by wave action. The cave and volcano, a gift of Reub Long, are now a State Park.

In 1938, Dr. L. S. Cressman and his crew excavated a portion of Fort Rock Cave, one of the first of many endeavors that have released the secrets of the past. Stone and bone artifacts were few. Scrapers, a few projectile points, seven drills, manos, and awls were recovered from deposits divided by a well-defined layer of volcanic pumice. A few basketry and wood fragments were found, but the outstanding discovery was a large number of sagebrush bark sandals—between 75 and 100—beneath the pumice, all charred as though from the hot ash. It was the sandals from Fort Rock Cave that marked the second of the historic events when they were dated by the then new C14 method and found to be 9,000 years old, thus verifying the antiquity of man in the new world. The important discovery was widely publicized. Even yet, more than 20 years later, it is one of the few Early-Man dates obtained from an actual artifact. Most samples sent for analysis are charcoal, associated animal bones, and the like.

In 1966, Steve Bedwell, under the supervision of Dr. Cressman, dug to bedrock in the cave and tediously gathered specimens of charcoal from the very earliest campfires. These were sent to the C14 laboratory and results were eagerly awaited. Finally they came—the specimens had been lost! The next year the project was repeated, and the issue was well worth the effort. The first fires were built in Fort Rock Cave at least 13,600 years ago, 4,600 years before the sandals were made and worn by a still very early people.

Of the first of the great historic events there is no record save that reconstructed from the geologic evidence. About 6,600 years ago, the scattered residents of Fort Rock Valley witnessed one of the greatest of the Pleistocene cataclysms, the explosion of Mt. Mazama and the birth of Crater Lake. About 4,000 years earlier, other men witnessed another spectacular event of violence without parallel when a dam formed by a projecting remnant of the Ice Age gave way, releasing 500 cubic miles of water from Lake Missoula to rush across Idaho and Washington, filling the Columbia River gorge to the brim and sweeping all life before it. But that was beyond the confines of the Great Basin and not pertinent to this text.

Mt. Mazama towered some 30,000 feet, an eroded cone supporting glaciers several miles long. Beneath its icy cap for centuries the pressure of pent-up magma and gas—mostly steam— had been increasing until finally the huge mound could no longer bear the burden. In one vast explosion the entire mountain and all the imprisoned forces beneath were released, covering the country for miles around with the hot material ejected. What terror must have struck the peaceful inhabitants of the valley! Hot ash propelled by expanding steam roared down the valleys in flaming avalanches. The glaciers and snow, instantly flashing into steam, would have blotted out the sky, only to condense again and deluge the area with mud flows, releasing part of the energy in a violent lightning storm. The sound of the explosion would have carried for 2,500 miles and the floating dust would have obscured the sun for months, as happened when Krakatau exploded in 1883. After Mt. Mazama ejected its giant projectile, the muzzle filled with rain and snow water to become beautiful Crater Lake.

The layer of pumice in Fort Rock Cave was not from Mazama but from nearby Newberry Crater, a less spectacular but still impressive eruption that occurred 2,600 years ago. Deposits showed that the cave was again occupied soon after the ash fell; life went on as usual after the interruption.

Fort Rock was but one of a complex investigated by Cressman (1940, 1942). Others in the vicinity were Roaring Springs, Paisley Five Mile Point Nos. 1, 2 and 3, Plush, and Catlow caves. In all, Early Man had left his trace and in two of them the remains of Pleistocene animals were found. The Northern Great Basin was once rich in the huge animals. From Fossil Lake, not far from Fort Rock, have been taken quantities of fossil bones. Such bones can still be picked up as they emerge from beneath the drifting sands.

Part Two

The Stone Industry

8. Projectile Points

The most familiar Indian artifact and the very symbol of all things Indian is the projectile point, the common arrowhead. It does not seem to matter that these bits of chipped stone were the least used of all instruments about an Indian camp or village; they are still considered to be most representative of the savage race. There are innumerable collectors of these mementos of a vanished and romantic period and people, enthusiastic searchers who enjoy an esprit de corps not exceeded by that of members of any other avocation. Whenever arrowhead hunters gather around a sagebrush fire of an evening to listen to the coyotes and refind their treasures, they relive the old life in the desert, when the stars shimmered in the great lakes filling the basins, and firelight glowed softly at the cave entrance.

Projectile points are practically immune to the elements. The glittering piece picked up from the sand may be several thousand years old or only a few hundred as far as one can judge from the appearance of the stone. They are found throughout the world in countless shapes, many types of stone, and many degrees of workmanship and finish. Some are exquisite bits of colorful stone deserving to be displayed on a jeweler's velvet tray, an emblem of pride of handicraft and testimony to the skill of the long-ago hunter.

The term "projectile points" should be used for these stone-age implements for most of them are not arrowheads at all but dart or javelin points, spearheads, knives, perhaps even fish gorges. Then there are chipped drills, scrapers, awls, gravers, bunts, and sometimes even ornaments. Major J. W. Powell (1961) records in his journal, "Their habitual costumes were loincloths, paints and necklaces of tiny arrowheads made of bright-colored agates and carnelians strung on snakeskins." Figure 21 shows some chipped pieces, from the Luke and Miller collections, that may have been worn as ornaments, judging from the shape of the stems. All stone projectile points were made by flaking or chipping except in a few areas where there was no stone suitable for flaking—for instance in Alaska where slate is the most common material and is ground to shape. Where native copper was available, it was sometimes hammered into projectile points and knives.

Like fossils, prehistoric arrow and spear points were once considered to be of supernatural origin not only by the peasantry but sometimes by the intelligentsia. In some languages they were called lightning or thunder stones. In Scotland they were known as "elfin bolts" and were worn as a charm against the spirits. Sick domestic animals were thought to be elf-shot and fakirs engaged to treat the animal would palm a point which they produced at the proper time—after feeling over the animal —as a token of their efficiency. Samuel Pepys records in his diary, "I remember my Lord Tarbut did produce one of these elf arrows, which one of his tenants took out of the heart of one of his cattle that had died an unusual death." In Japan, arrow points were placed as objects of veneration in chapels. The Greeks considered them to have a more practical virtue and "were thought by the magicianes to be verie necessarie for those that court fair women." The superstitions once attached to stone-age implements picked up by the peoples of many countries, (except the Americas) have been considered as proof of their antiquity.

The oldest industry in the world is flint knapping, started perhaps half a million years ago and not yet extinct. Only a few years ago it was a thriving industry in France and England, but principally in England because of the plentiful supply of superior flint found there in Cretaceous chalk beds. The product was gun flints, and a few are still being made for devotees of the flintlock rifle. These flints were once made in enormous numbers. The Turks placed an order for 11,000,000 of them just before the Crimean war, and from one small community in France the knappers sold 300 tons of the spark-laden little stones to the French army. The price per flint was about one tenth of a cent; the Hudson's Bay Company's price to the Indians of the Columbia District was a dozen for one beaver skin worth three to five dollars. In the Americas there is still considerable clandestine flint knapping—producing "genuine" arrowheads for the tourist trade.

Ancient methods of chipping stones into needed instruments have always appeared a mystery to some people. The present writer has seen more than once in print the fallacy that the method was to heat the stone and drop water on it with a straw, the sudden cooling causing a chip to fly off. Many think the art has been lost, but actually it is well known and is quite simple, yet requires a high degree of manual dexterity—and the skill of the operator is obvious in the quality of the product.

Stone used for flaked implements must have certain qualities. There must be no grain so that the stone can be fractured in any direction suiting the purpose of the craftsman. A crypto-crystalline material—one consisting of submicroscopic crystals—like chert or obsidian is best and the best of these is obsidian; common bottle glass is also good. Obsidian is a natural glass, a volcanic product with the same chemical composition as granite. It is really a rhyolite, ejected as obsidian under special conditions not too well understood. Basically, it starts as very hot rhyolite containing water in the form of steam under great pressure; the steam makes the rock fluid. As the hot brew rises to the surface the pressure decreases, causing the steam to expand and leave the mixture. The loss of water makes the mix more viscous, and rapid cooling prevents crystalization of the dissolved minerals. Ordinary lava, if cooled quickly, does not become obsidian. Much of the lava that is ejected from the bowels of the earth rises beneath the surface of the sea or lakes where it cools rapidly but does not change to obsidian.

Chert designates all types of mineral quartz precipitated from water. It includes flint, jasper, chalcedony, carnelian, agate, and many other generic names. All are more or less pure silicon dioxide. Most chert is produced when silicon dissolved in sea water replaces carbonate sediments of the ocean floor; a similar process replaces wood fibers with mineral to make petrified wood. Chert forms into nodules a few feet beneath the surface of the sediments. After millions of years the mud becomes very deep and the great weight compresses and turns it into sandstone, limestone, mudstone, or one of the other sedimentary rocks. Later, digestive convulsions within the interior depths uplift the chert-bearing rocks into mountains where the nodules are exposed by erosion or mined like coal.

Chert nodules occur in beds several hundred feet thick in some places where they have accumulated by erosion. If the chert is shiny, semitransparent, well colored in shades of grey, brown, or yellow, and cleaves cleanly, it is called flint; the color is due to enclosed carbonaceous impurities. If the chert lacks luster and has a dull whitish or brown color, it is called simply chert. All varieties of chert are harder than steel.

The use of the word flint to indiscriminately cover all chipping or chipped stone is wrong. Flint occurs only in limestone, dolomite, or chalk, as does the greatest quantity of chert. The best-known flint beds are those in the Cretaceous chalk of England and France; these have been mined for thousands of years. There are large flint beds in the eastern part of the United States but the mineral is rather rare in the West.

Agate is a banded form of chert that occurs mostly in lava. When pressure is relieved by the rise of lava to the surface, steam and other gases expand into bubbles that find their way to the surface and vent to the atmosphere if the molten rock is liquid enough. As the stone cools it stiffens and the bubbles are entrapped to form cavities. Over the ages, mineral-laden water enters and precipitates silicon dioxide in the hollows in a way that is not well understood. The penetrating water leaches from the rock impurities that emblazon the silicon dioxide with the many beautiful colors so dear to the heart of the rockhound. Jasper is a red, green, or yellow opaque chert, colored by oxides of iron. Chalcedony is a semitransparent grey or white chert, with a waxy luster. Carnelian is a glowing red. There is no sharp line between any of the different cherts, and many local names are applied to the pretty stones.

Certain kinds of basalt can be flaked, though not easily. Beautiful chipped specimens are occasionally made from agatized wood, but it has a grain and does not fracture easily in all directions. Some men have learned to knap stone and are as skilled as any of the prehistoric artisans they imitate. In Central Oregon there once lived a man who for one dollar an inch would make an arrowhead of any length, even up to three feet. Some beautiful specimens are made from red railway signal light lenses and green bottle glass. Most of the lovely effigies, odd branching forms, and many arrowheads for sale in curio shops were fashioned in a short time by someone in his basement, using a nail set in a block of wood for a tool. Most fake chipped pieces are easy to recognize; they have a shiny, new appearance and frequently a character not in keeping with forms found in the local area. If the faker chooses, however, he can chip out and age a point that cannot be differentiated from the genuine.

The unique quality possessed by chert and obsidian that makes it possible to manipulate into such exquisite artifacts is the way it fractures. When a piece is struck on the edge with a hammerstone it does not shatter but a chip breaks away with a conchoidal fracture. If properly done, a slab struck in the center will expel a slug that has just about the shape of a pear, and there will be a very tiny hole in the slab where it was hit. A blow on the edge will remove a flake having the shape of half a pear. The fracture is caused by a traveling pressure wave and its ripples can be seen on the surface of the fracture. By manipulation of the striking tool, long, thin, slightly curved flakes may be struck from a blank. These small flakes are called microliths and can be used for cutting without further preparation. They are extremely sharp but the edge is brittle. Primitive farmers made sickles for cutting grain by setting microliths in a rib or wood handle. The block remaining after a series of flakes have been removed from it is called a core and looks like part of a small, fluted column (see Figure 24). Cores have been found surrounded by a multitude of flakes, each of which could be replaced in its former seat.

To make an arrow or dart point, the early craftsman would select a block of material and strike off a number of flakes with sharp blows of an elongated pebble. By manipulating his tool he could dislodge flakes of about the desired shape and size. Selecting one to suit his taste, he perhaps further dressed it down with light blows of his stone hammer. Dislodging chips by a blow is called percussion flaking, and this was the only method used for thousands of years. (On the desert, ancient village sites can be located by the flash of myriads of discarded flakes glistening in the early morning or evening sunlight—detritus from the hammer of ancient knappers.) After the blank was sized to suit his purpose, the workman used a tool made from an antler tip or a sliver of bone set in a handle such as the specimen shown in Figure 26. By pressing on the edge of the work piece with his tool, and with a deft twist at the right moment, he could expel a flake.

The flaking tool must not be too hard; it needs to take a "grip" on the stone; a hard point will tend to slip. Modern knappers generally use a soft metal such as a piece of copper or a nail set in a wood handle. If a faker takes his work seriously and wants to avoid detection, he will use a piece of bone or antler because metal will leave a mark. Note the chipping tool attached to the end of the handle of the atlatl in Figure 51; the ancient hunter had his sharpening tool as ready as does the modern hunter with a whetstone in his knife scabbard. A skilled worker could cause a flake thin as paper to be removed clear across the piece.

A chip must always be started from the edge, never from any other place. The flake is not removed by shearing (as a punch removes a metal blank); nor by cutting (as a chisel cuts wood), but by a pressure wave, the same as pieces struck from a core. Look at the track of a long chip and you can see the ripple marks left by the traveling wave; these are clearly shown on the knives in Figure 38. The craftsman continued his flaking, working around the piece until it was complete. Sometimes a series of extremely fine flakes was removed along the edges to sharpen it and improve its appearance; this extra effort is called tertiary flaking.

The art of chipping with a bone tool is called pressure flaking and was a wondrous invention by some long-forgotten genius. The improved weapons and implements increased his mastery over his environment, another forward step in the long journey toward civilization.

In the "Report of the National Museum for 1897," Thomas Wilson quotes an observer who watched the procedure and wrote in his journal, "Possibly, had I not witnessed the operation and had been at the time one of the first Europeans with whom they ever had any communication, the idea would have remained undisputed that they owed their formation to the stroke of the hammer. Being a working amateur mechanic myself, and having practiced in a very similar manner on glass with a penny piece in 1815, I was not at all surprised at witnessing the modus operandi. Selecting a log of wood in which a spoon-shaped cavity was cut, they placed the splinter to be worked over it, and by pressing gently along the margin vertically, first on one side and then the other, as one would set a saw, they splintered off alternate fragments until the object thus properly outlined presented the spear or arrowhead form, with two cutting serrated edges."

There are other methods described in literature on the subject, such as laying the work piece on a stone anvil and forming the edge all around by sharp strokes from a stone hammer, with one man holding the work piece in place while his partner wielded the hammer; or, removing flakes from a core with a stick having a crossbar bearing against the worker's chest, and so on. The details may have varied but the method was to strike a flake, work it down to rough shape by percussion, and then pressure flake it into final form. While on the subject it might be well to say that a workshop is the poorest place to find arrowheads, in spite of the widespread belief to the contrary, because all the points that are found have become lost by their owner in some way and one is not likely to lose them while in the process of manufacture. A workshop was a quarry or place where the only activity was tool making.

The notion that artifacts are found in workshops probably originated in mistaking an ancient village site, strewn with chippings amongst which an occasional arrow point can be found, for a workshop.

On Glass Buttes, near Burns, Oregon, on the northern edge of the Great Basin, there is an ancient workshop. In ages past, a flow of obsidian issued from the flank of the buttes, beautiful red and black, candy-striped, golden sheen, and rainbow obsidian of gem quality, a variety selected for the finest ceremonial knives and showy war points. Evidently Indians from great distances traveled to this source of supply, for their refuse lies feet deep in places—spalls and blanks that were broken in the process of being roughed out. With patience it is possible to find pieces that can be fitted together. No finished points are found, nor usable unbroken blanks. The partly finished pieces were taken to the distant villages for completion into points, knives, scrapers, or drills, and every one of them still lies somewhere on or under the surface of the desert (or in some collection), awaiting the shifting sand to reveal its presence, for they do not deteriorate although they do break.

The popular notion that any place where arrowheads are found is "an old battlefield" is also a fallacy. Conflict between the Indian tribes was rare until the white invaders began forcing them from their hunting and foraging grounds into the territory of others, inspiring warfare of conquest and defense. The natives were not politically organized to engage in full-scale battles. Most of the chipped artifacts come from old camp and village sites, a few from burials; many more are found at random in the desert or on the old lake beds where they were lost during hunting, or where a wounded animal died.

Chipped artifacts are good fossils, and it is surprising that so simple a tool as a flaked point can occur in so many distinct, well-preserved, and beautiful styles. Fortunately they were made in relatively great numbers and therefore are found frequently enough to be useful, although never frequently enough to satisfy either the scientist or the collector. Because the various types peculiar to a specific culture have been segregated and classified, the culture can generally be recognized wherever the points are found—though the profusion of sizes and types and the graduation of one into another make some of them extremely difficult to classify. But there are several key types of very old points that the collector will want to recognize; they are listed here in the order of decreasing age.

The Sandia

Sandia projectile points, first found in Sandia Cave, New Mexico, may be the oldest of all but the dating, over 11,000 years, has not been confirmed. This point is two to four inches long and characterized by a single shoulder and basal grinding (edges of the stem ground so it will not cut the binding). There are two types; one has a rounded and the other a straight base.

The Clovis

The Clovis is one of the characteristic fluted points of the Big Game Hunters. "Fluted" means the removal of a long flake from each side at the base, leaving a channel or flute. The reason for this extra effort is not known. Some think it was to leave an opening to permit more copious bleeding from the wound, others that it made binding to the shaft for efficient, or lightened the projectile. The Clovis has been dated at 11,200 years, and archeologists think it must be at least 15,000 to have such widespread distribution (Krieger 1964). It has been found associated with the mammoth, bison, horse, camel, and musk ox, and in every one of the continental states and Canada. This point is unusually well built and sturdy, and has basal grinding.

The Folsom

While not the oldest of the fluted points, the Folsom is the most familiar, and the first to be uncovered under controlled conditions. In 1926 a Negro cowboy, George McJunkin, reported to his foreman that he saw fossil bones in an arroyo. Dr. J. D. Figgins, paleontologist with the Denver Museum of Natural History, was notified, and during excavations to salvage the fossils, discovered a chipped point in the matrix. Dr. Figgins immediately notified several prominent archaeologists to view the find. They were at first skeptical, but when more points were recovered, including one in contact with and beneath the rib of an extinct bison, remaining doubts were dispelled and the search for Early Man was released from the dogma that had shackled it for so many years.

Following tradition, the point was named after the locality where it was first discovered, Folsom, New Mexico. Folsoms are masterpieces of the knappers art, thin, symmetrical, balanced, pleasing and efficient in shape. Unlike the Clovis, they are found only with the extinct bison.

The type station was merely a kill site. To learn something of the culture a living area was needed, where sufficient garbage had accumulated to be scientifically rag-picked for its horizon markers. By good fortune an excellent one was found in Colorado, called the Lindenmeier Site after the owner of the land. From the artifacts the scientists determined that Folsom man probably wore some clothing, and decorated himself with paint. No milling stones were found, indicating a strictly hunting economy. It is interesting to note that the scrapers, which were plentiful, can be duplicated in almost any modern site. Folsom points have been dated at about 10,000 years.

The Plainview

The Plainview is not fluted, but the base is somewhat thinned by the removal of vertical flakes, and the base is ground. It is dated at about 9,000 years, and appears to be associated with the Folsom.

The Midland

This distinctive point was found in an Early Man site by an amateur, Keith Glasscock. He had the foresight to notify the profession, and Alex Krieger and Fred Wendorf excavated this important site in Texas. The Midland has the general outline of a Folsom; in fact they were at first called "unfluted Folsoms." Dates obtained were unsatisfactory, but appear to be between 13,000 and 9,000 years.

The Scottsbluff

Scottsbluff points are generally between three and five inches long and one wide. The distinctive characteristic is the long and but slightly indented stem; sometimes the identation is only that from grinding. They are symmetrical and beautifully made, with regular, parallel flaking. Many came from surface finds in Colorado, but the first one to be scientifically excavated was in Nebraska. They have been found in Canada and many of the continental states. The accepted age is 9,000 to 7,000 years.

The Eden

Closely associated with the Scottsbluff is the Eden, more familialrly known by collectors as the Yuma because so many were found in blowouts in Yuma County, Colorado. They are considered the most beautiful of all projectile points, long and slender, with exquisite flaking. There are two types, which are not found together. In the oblique collateral the flake scars are parallel, running from edge to edge at a slight angle clear across the blade. The flaking on the collateral runs straight across to the center of the piece, resulting in a median ridge the length of the point on each side. The Eden was used by the same culture as the Scottsbluff, but does not have so wide a range. Their age appears to be between 9,000 and 10,000 years.

The Gypsum Cave

An unusual type of dart point was found in Gypsum Cave. It is rather crudely made with a small tapering stem, and would have been very difficult to haft securely. They seem to be limited to Gypsum Cave although points somewhat resembling them are found throughout the Great Basin. They have not yet been firmly dated but apparently are between 10,000 and 8,000 years old.

The Pinto Basin

This point has been found on the surface only, and the type locality is the Pinto Basin in Riverside County, California. They are about 1.5 inches long, thick, and usually percussion flaked; some show pressure retouching on the edges. A few are serrated, and they have straight or slightly tapering stems and concave bases. This unlovely point has not been dated but is associated with the Pleistocene lakes.

The Lake Mojave   The Silver Lake

The remains of ancient Lake Mojave now consist of two barren playas separated by a ridge. The northern playa is called Soda and the southern Silver; Fr. Francisco Garces passed these sinks on March 9, 1776. On the highest terraces of the lakes, ancient stone knappers left a variety of tools including choppers, scrapers, gravers, knives, crescent, drills, and some crude but distinctive points; no milling stones were found. Most of the artifacts were percussion chipped with pressure retouching. The Silver Lake is a crudely made point, looking somewhat like a poor specimen from anywhere in the Basin. The Lake Mojave, however, is unique, and the type was found in Lind Coulee, Danger Cave, Cougar Mountain Cave, and several other early sites.

The Meserve

The Meserve point is closely associated with the Plainview. They have been found with the extinct bison, and in Graham Cave, Missouri, where uncovered in levels dated between 8,800 and 9,700 years ago. They have basal grinding and thinning, like the Plainview.

In the Great Basin considerable work has been done on projectile point typology but there still exists a great need for a method of differentiating between a dart and an arrow point. Were this possible it would be much simpler to segregate the different phases of the Desert Culture. Many years ago Dr. Cressman realized the importance of this problem and attacked it by utilizing material from caves in the Northern Great Basin (Cressman 1942). He grouped all the points collected from Roaring Springs Cave into nine types (see Chart No. 2). Each of these was then divided into a small (0.4 to 2.0 grams), a large (2.0 to 6.2 grams), and an intermediate group, the latter to take care of the overlaps. The groups were then tabulated by the frequency in the upper and lower beds of the cave. As shown by the chart, some points readily fall into a certain small or large category.

Cressman postulated that the larger points were for the atlatl dart, and the grouping tends to bear this out, the heavier points predominating in the lower levels, which were older than the bow. Types 2 and 5 were not found in the lower bed, and the small Type 1 exceeded in number all the other types together in the upper bed. The large points continued into the upper bed as would be expected, since it is known that the atlatl was used as well as the bow in the late period. The classification did not establish any clear-cut demarcation lines but did indicate a trend. Note that nearly all barbed, stemmed Type 1 and all Types 2 and 5 were small and in the upper levels of the cave, the period of the bow; and all Types 8 and 9 and most of Type 7 were large and in the lower beds, the period of the atlatl. Type 7 is the most common form of known atlatl points from the Southwest.

John Cowles in his delightful little book *Cougar Mountain Cave* (Cowles n.d.) illustrates projectile points in the order of their presence in the deposit and therefore by age. Mr. Cowles is an amateur who spent 63 days excavating the cave, located in the Northern Great Basin about eleven miles north and east of Fort Rock Cave. Figure 31 shows a representative sampling of point types taken from the cave. "A" was the only type of projectile point or knife in the bottom layer of the midden; the same type was found throughout but gradually became shorter and wider. From the top of this same layer, 5.5 feet below the surface, a sandal was tested by C14 and found to be 8,500 years old, corresponding closely with one found in Fort Rock Cave that was abandoned 9,000 years ago. Type "A" was also found in the Haskett Site in Idaho (Butler 1965), the Dalles (Cressman 1960), and in great numbers of surface finds. (Where sites are given here, it does not mean that they are the only ones having the type point; they may come from others but only enough are mentioned to show their distribution.) It has been shown that in the oldest deposits some of the chipped artifacts are made from basalt; a basalt point of this type would almost certainly be several thousand years old.

"B" is another widely dispersed type. It first appeared at the one-foot level. (Cowles reverses the normal level sequence. This one-foot level is at the bottom and his 6.5-foot level is at the surface.) "B" resembles the Agate Basin points except that the base is not ground, a characteristic of the Big Game Hunting culture. Similar ones were taken from the Haskett and The Dalles excavations and in the Lind Coulee Early Man site in Washington (Daugherty 1959). One specimen (W9 in Jennings report) was in the lowest level of Danger Cave in Sand I, a layer dated at about 10,000 years B.C.

"C" is another form of "B," from the same horizon in Cougar Mountain Cave and seemingly wherever "B" occurs. If these are dart points, and there can be little doubt, this style has the marked advantage of being able to be keyed into the shaft by leaving a small crescent projection in the slot in the foreshaft, to fit the projectile point base. It will thus remain parallel to the shaft instead of slipping sideways; in Figure 57 note how one of the hafted points has slipped. This useful feature appears in many points obtained from the later sites.

"D" style points were between the 1.5- and 2.5-foot level. Dr. Daugherty uncovered them in Lind Coulee and noted that the shoulders are different, one sharp and the other rounded. "E" came from the same layers as "D," and also from Lind Coulee, and Layers DII and DIII at Danger Cave (specimen W12). They are also found in considerable numbers around The Dalles, Oregon, in what appear to be the older deposits.

Triangular specimens like "F" were first encountered at the 2.5-foot level and continued to the surface but decreased in size in the upper levels. They were most plentiful at the 3.5-foot mark. This type is discussed further under "stemless points."

From the 3-foot level Cowles took the first notched points, "G," and they far exceeded in number all other types between the 3- and 4-foot levels. They were large at first and gradually decreased in size between the 3-foot mark and the surface. The same style point was in Horizon DIII of Danger Cave (specimen W16) and above. Horizon DIII was not dated but is believed to be between 7,000 and 5,000 years old. Type "G" came from all levels in Roaring Springs Cave, but only two in the lower compared to over a hundred in the upper bed.

One of the more peculiar and individualistic forms is "H," also shown in Chart No. 2 as Type 8. They were scattered throughout

Roaring Springs Cave; Cressman says these were used exclusively for darts. Cowles does not show them from Cougar Mountain. A similar and perhaps the same type comes from Horizon DIII and above in Danger Cave (Specimen W10, right). Type "H" projectiles are common in surface finds about Malheur Lake and the Northern Great Basin.

One and a half feet below the surface of Cougar Mountain Cave there was a layer of pumice 4- to 6-inches thick. The material has never been analyzed so the source is unknown. If it is from the final expulsion from Newberry Crater it would be about 2,000 years old. It might be from a local eruption of unknown age; or if it is Mt. Mazama ash, it would have been deposited about 6,600 years B.P., but this is highly unlikely. If the cave deposit accumulated at the same rate—and that would be a rare occurrence indeed—it would be about 1,400 years for each foot and the pumice would have been laid down about 2,000 years ago, a time in the range of the Newberry eruption. But all levels of Cougar Mountain Cave must remain undated except the bottom and the surface.

Chart No. 3 shows the sequence of the cultural remains in the cave.

The chipped artifact shown in Figure 33, left, is called a stemless point. These are found in considerable numbers on the desert wherever projectile points appear. They are often called war points on the theory that, being stemless, the binding to the shaft would fail to hold and the tip would remain imbedded in the stricken warrior when he removed the shaft. We have never seen any ethnological data to support this conclusion and consider it to be one of the many tales that achieve through repetition the status of a fact. That they were used for war is certain. The present writer once took from what was unquestionably a grave (although no skeletal material was present) four beautiful agate barbed and stemmed points and five of the stemless—the arsenal of a primitive warrior. In the same site were found thousands of stemmed points but very few stemless or triangular.

Since the points occur in such quantities in the desert—where people were too busy warding off starvation to indulge in warfare—they are considered to be knives if wide and large, and projectile points if small and with no sharp demarcation line between them.

Some collectors refer derisively to obsidian as "that old black stuff" and regard Great Basin collections as monotonous. Because obsidian is obtainable in quantity in the Basin (although for some tribes it meant a long, tedious journey to obtain a supply), and because it possesses superior flaking qualities, it was used almost exclusively to other stone. However, artifacts made from agate and other colorful material are sometimes found in the desert, and they rival in form and beauty the famed Columbia River gem points. The Luke family of Fallon, Nevada, has a superb collection picked up during nearly half a century of roaming the desert; the Lairs of Reno also have an assortment of beautiful points, as do many others.

From the Humboldt Valley come some superior points made from an opaque white stone that are a pleasure to behold. Simpson (1876) in his journal records, "The inferior bands of this tribe, especially the To-si-witches (White Knives), inhabit the Humboldt River—who take their name from a beautiful white flint, which they procure from the adjacent mountains, and use as knives in dressing their food. . . ."

9. Knives

Knives were of course one of the most useful implements that the natives possessed. It is surprising how sharp an obsidian or agate knife is, especially obsidian, and nearly all Great Basin knives are made from this practical material. The edge is very brittle and the knife must be used with caution because it will dull very quickly against any hard substance such as bone, but

it will slice through hide and flesh with an ease that was satisfactory to the natives until the more serviceable steel blade was
introduced.

Chipped knives could not only be carried on the person ready
for instant use but in an emergency could be quickly fashioned
from almost any handy stone. Occasionally in the desert foothills
one might find a few percussion flaked splinters of basalt or
obsidian, perhaps left by an ancient hunter when he made an
instant knife to dress his trophy. Lewis and Clark record in their
journals, "many of them made use of flint for knives, and with
this instrument, skined the animals they killed, dressed their fish
and made their arrows; in short they used it for every purpose to
which the knife is applyed. This flint is of no regular form, and
if they can only obtain a part of it, an inch or two in length that
will cut they are satisfyed. They renew the edge by flecking off
the flint by means of the point of an Elk's or Deer's horn."

Figure 25 shows flaking debris that can be found on the surface of thousands of the old village sites in the Great Basin.
Many of the flakes and spalls were used as knives without any
dressing down after they were struck from the core. The edge
will dull if used on anything tough but then another can be easily
struck from the core. Knives can sometimes be differentiated
from a discarded spall by the slightly ragged edge, and occasionally one is found that has been touched up by pressure flaking, but usually it is impossible to tell which of the innumerable
pieces lying about were used to cut up a rabbit or trim a basket
and which are merely chipping debris.

Knives occur in many forms, and there is no clear-cut category in
which they can be placed so that all can be distinguished from
projectile points. In all likelihood no distinction was made by
the ancient workman either; if no knife was handy, an arrow or
dart point would serve very handily for cutting. Long blades
such as those shown in Figures 36 and 38 are undoubtedly knives.
Some of them were handled by wrapping part of the blade with
buckskin as shown in Figure 34. The agate specimen in Figure

36, lower left, from the Johnson collection, is a rare form; it has a tang for attaching a suspension cord. It was found in the Fort Rock desert. The handled knife in Figure 34 also has provision for suspension, a loop in the buckskin used for wrapping.

Triangular and ovoid stemless pieces as shown in Figure 35 may be either points or knives, and are called both. Dr. Heizer considers a hafted point like the one in Figure 28 to be a knife; other equally distinguished archaeologists call them atlatl dart foreshafts, because the handle is tapered to fit the main shaft of the dart. The cache of seven, Figure 57, supports this as it seems more credible to possess seven foreshafts than seven knives. Some of the points are of the triangular, stemless form.

Many triangular pieces are too large to serve efficiently as projectile points but would make good knives; some have been found with a haft or handle in place. But the cache shown in Figure 57, from the same cave as the atlatl foreshafts, shows both triangular and barbed points in the ratio of two to one, indicating that they were dart points and not knives, especially since four knives were found in the same pouch.

Most, if not all, of the extremely wide points such as the one in Figure 35 (right) are knife blades. Similar ones with handles have been found in caves (Guernsey 1921). If the stem is over half an inch wide, you can be sure that it is a knife blade or spear point, for the base would be too wide for an arrow or dart shaft. Any triangular piece showing consistent and repeated sharpening is a knife. Some blades were rechipped so many times that they assumed almost a diamond-shaped cross section and were no longer efficient.

The long, beautiful blades flaked with precision and attention to symmetrical form are generally believed to be ceremonial or show pieces rather than utilitarian. They are too fragile for any but the lightest use, and they do not show any re-chipping. Beautifully worked knives were a favorite article for grave offerings, not only in the Great Basin but throughout the world.

Because knives are sometimes found in caches, experienced relic hunters, chancing upon a blade gleaming beneath the sage, almost ignore it in their frantic search for the promised cache. Some have been amply rewarded. Howard Galbraith used a bed spring from an abandoned cabin to strain out 21 triangular specimens near Fort Rock. Mrs. Jake Brown received a rare Valentine gift when she uncovered 42 perfect blades up to eight inches long on Valentine's Day, near Bishop, California. Paul Praetorius found eight long, beautifully chipped and formed knives in the Fort Rock Valley. The 46 shown in Figure 37 were found in the Great Basin but unfortunately the data and name of the finder are lacking.

The three splendid pieces shown in Figure 38 were found near Thorn Lake, Oregon, by Mrs. Malcolm Loring, while on an Oregon Archaeological Society field trip; the longest measures 11.5 inches. Mrs. Loring was returning to her car for a drink of water after a long, fruitless search of the desert when she spotted the tip of one protruding from the sand.

When caches are found, the blades usually are stacked side by side on edge like crackers in a barrel, and appear to be the work of the same craftsman. Perhaps certain gifted or industrious artisans engaged in a form of primitive private enterprise, operating a factory producing an article of commerce, and in return received a bit more of the better things of life.

10. Scrapers

Next to projectile points, the most numerous of all chipped artifacts picked up from ancient village sites are scrapers. They had innumerable uses — fleshing hides, working bone, decorticating branches, dressing wood; for nearly everything we would employ a file, gouge, rasp, plane, chisel, or draw knife. Some are beautiful relics, chipped from colorful stone and artistically shaped. They make excellent specimens, mementos of the everyday life of an industrious people, but collectors generally ignore them; we have never seen scrapers framed and displayed with the pride they deserve. The projectile point was used only for hunting and warfare, but the scraper was an instrument that was always about the lodge, always handy to perform its alloted task.

Figure 39 shows various types of scrapers, most of which fall into seven or eight more or less separate groups. No. 1 is a "spokeshave," which has a markedly convex blade. Spokeshaves were useful tools for dressing down arrow or dart shafts, game counters, skewers, deadfall parts, or any of the many small round instruments made from twigs or wood (see Figure 62). There are some handsome specimens of this instrument, with a blade chipped into a perfect semicircle, sharp and even.

No. 2 is a "sidescraper," the most numerous of all. It is characterized by a long edge chipped in a nearly straight line on one side of the piece. Some of these probably were knife blades or both knife and scraper. The blade of a sidescraper is relatively wide and thin. No. 3 is a graver, used for incising bone, scraping out narrow grooves or notches in wood, or making slots for inserting the projectile point in a greasewood shaft. On most gravers the point is very short because for working green bone it had to be strong. A "burin" is a tool used for the same purpose as a graver but it has a point like a chisel; instead of being chipped out to resemble a short, tiny drill, it is merely a sharpened corner. Break off one inch from the right end of No. 2 and it would be classed as a burin.

"Snubnosed" scrapers are No. 4. The center one is on its side, with blade at the bottom to show the working edge. It is chipped at a steep angle with the under surface. Sometimes these are called "keeled" scrapers because the working edge is reinforced by the thick shank. This is a common and useful variety because the blade is strong enough for work on hard material like bone and mountain mahogany—yet it can be easily pressure flaked to resharpen the edge. These scrapers are always narrow and sharp and among the most handsome of all the scrapers.

No. 5 is a "turtleback," a form which might be described as a snubnosed scraper with a continuous edge (see Figure 40). They are not plentiful and probably were made from a stone that just happened to have a shape that could be sharpened all around.

Pieces like the tiny No. 6 are called "thumbnail" scrapers because they are about that size; the edge is usually convex. "End" scrapers, No. 7, can be found in any size from thumbnail to huge specimens four or five inches long and two or more wide, the larger ones sometimes being called "planes." An end scraper has a relatively thin blade, in contrast to a snubnosed scraper. The larger ones were occasionally used with a handle. Even to this day, Indian women prefer them, hafted to a long stick, for dressing down deer hides for moccasins for the tourist trade. One Indian woman was recently photographed using this tool on a skin stretched over a frame placed in the shade of her new Mercury sedan.

11. Drills

The chipped stone implements called drills were used to perforate wood, bone, and shell, to make pipes and drill beads and pendants—in fact, for anything that needed a hole. Some perforators were used to puncture leather or textile. These are slim with a sharp point and do not show the wear of the harder working drill. Chipped drills would perform only on the softer stones such as serpentine. Figure 104 shows marks from the stone drill used in making a pipe. A tool for this purpose is more correctly called a reamer. It would be wide and short, somewhat like an arrowhead. Stone drills could either be hafted or held in the fingers.

Hard stone like basalt, granite, and marble was perforated by pecking or abrasive drilling. The holes in net sinkers were "pecked"—which means continual striking with a harder stone. Circular holes were drilled with a rotating wood shaft or hollow cane, using sand and water as an abrasive. The sand does the cutting, and the soft stick or cane picks up and holds each grain as a tiny bit. Generally, if wood is used, the hole will taper as the sides of the shaft wear away. If a hollow cane is the tool, a core will be left and less stone needs to be removed, thus reducing the labor. The hole will be the same diameter all the way through.

Drilling stone was extremely tedious. Experiments indicate that it takes about 60 hours to drill a hole one inch deep by primitive methods.

12. Crescents

A peculiar object picked up in considerable numbers from the sand blows in the Great Basin is the crescent, Figure 42, an attractive winged artifact of unknown use. The edges and corners are often extremely sharp. Nearly all show careful workmanship, the chipping being reminiscent of the splendid knapping of the fluted-point tradition. Such craftsmanship could indicate that the crescents were not strictly utilitarian. The stone is often colored in areas where the points are consistently obsidian. In Figure 42, the one in the lower left is a beautiful, translucent green material, one of the finest chipped artifacts.

There are three variants of crescents according to Tadlock's classification (Tadlock 1966). Type I, the "quarter moon," is illustrated by the specimen in the lower left of Figure 42. The convex and concave edges are evenly flaked and the wings are sharp and pointed. Type II, the "half moon," is similar except that the upper edge is straight across instead of concave. The classic "butterfly," Type III, is the specimen on the top left. These crescents are characterized by a recurve on the convex side;

frequently there will be a short nipple or projection on each side of the recurve, like little pegs staking the corners.

Crescents occur only in the western states—Oregon, California, Nevada, Idaho, Washington, and Utah; and most come from the Great Basin.

Crescents seem to be limited to the proximity of lakes and rivers and the coast, and surface finds are sometimes associated with fluted and other early points (Tadlock 1966). It is certain that they are very old, at least 9,000 years and perhaps more. Whether their use was limited to the early cultures is conjectural. They are found on the surface in association with later type desert points, but then both early and late point types are frequently found together in the blows and washouts of the Great Basin.

These interesting specimens had some special use but what it was may never be known. Some of the guesses are fish knife, ceremonial piece, amulet, bangle, scraper, tattoo knife, net measure, template for drawing symbols, and scarifier for mourning rites. Whatever their purpose, these ancient and intriguing mementos of a long vanished race are found in considerable numbers in the deserts of the Great Basin.

13. Perforated Stones

Not all perforated stones are fishing-net weights. A particularly well-made and puzzling type is shown in Figure 43, top; identical specimens have been found along the Columbia River. They are often called donut stones because of their resemblance to that bit of modern culture. Although their use is unknown, most collectors beieve they were used in some sport.

Stewart Culin, in the 24th Annual Report of the Bureau of American Ethnology, describes and illustrates a great number

of games played by the Indians of North America. One of the
most popular was known as the stick and and hoop game. While
the paraphernalia and regulations varied somewhat from tribe
to tribe, essentially the purpose was to cast a pole so that it
would strike a rolling hoop and cause it to fall on the pole; the
position in which it came to rest would count points according
to the rules. Women were not allowed to view the contest because they would distract and annoy the players. No weapons
were allowed to be carried or even to be in the vicinity, and the
field was at a distance from the village. Large sums were bet on
the outcome of this game of skill. Another version of the game,
though not so popular, differed in that arrows were shot at the
rolling hoop, either to penetrate the hole or to cause it to fall
on the arrow as when the pole was used.

The hoops illustrated in the report are made from wood or
leather, frequently highly decorated, from six inches up to over
a foot in diameter. A few rings or hoops made of stone are
illustrated but they are discs or discoidal and not like the donut
stones; however, this does not rule out the possibility of their
being used for the hoop game. Catlin, in his "Letters and Notes
on the Manners, Customs and Conditions of the North American
Indians," describes the hoop game as follows:

"The play commences with two who start off upon a trot,
abreast of each other, and one of them rolls in advance a little
ring of two or three inches in diameter, cut out of a stone; and
each one follows it up with a stick of six feet in length, with
little bits of leather projecting from its sides of an inch or more
in length, which he throws before him as he runs, sliding it along
upon the ground after the ring, endeavoring to place it in such
a position when it stops, that the ring may fall upon it, and receive one of the little projections of leather through it, which
counts for the game one, two or four, according to the position
of the leather on which the ring is lodged; if either fails to receive the ring it is a forfeiture of the amount of the number he
was nearest to." The fact that "donut stones" are so well made

and frequently polished supports the theory of use in some sport or ceremony.

The stones shown in Figure 43, bottom, are also of unknown use. The writer has seen some like the one on the left (with a pecked hole about the size of a pencil) internally highly polished, and has been told that they were used to dress down rawhide thongs; the thong was stretched between two trees after inserting it through the hole, and the stone was run back and forth over the thong, being pulled sideways to bring pressure to bear on the edge of the hole. This is a perfectly plausible theory; cowboys stretch and dress the thongs for a rawhide lariat, or the finished lariat, by wrapping it once around a bottle which was then run back and forth while the cord was stretched tight. The polish on the edges of the hole could have been acquired from rubbing the thong.

A stone as well balanced as the one on the right of Figure 43— especially since the hole is drilled circular—could have been used on a pin for a top-and-whip game, known to have been played by the Klamath, Paiute, and Shoshone. Or, it could have been a spindle for an up-and-down drill, an ingenious invention used by many primitive people and still part of the tool kit of modern Eskimo carvers. It operated on the principle of momentum, and a flywheel was necessary. A wood shaft about a foot long, with a stone drill bit in the lower end, was inserted tightly in the hole of a balanced weight. Each end of a cord about two feet long was fastened to the extremities of a short stick and the center was tied to the top of the shaft, which was then turned until the draping strings wound about it. Holding the drill in a cupped stone or wood bearing, the operator grasped the short stick, now horizontal, and pulled it down sharply, causing the string to unwind and rotate the shaft. The flywheel provided enough momentum to rewind the string for another stroke, the shaft then turning in the opposite direction. Balanced, drilled stones are often considered as proof that the up-and-down drill was used. For the bow drill, the spindle was not necessary. Instead of a cord and stick as described above, the shaft was turned by wrapping a bow string around it and sawing the bow back and forth.

Figure 44 shows some other types of perforated stones from the Great Basin. The top specimen on the right has a cylindrical hole drilled straight through. The amount of work required to shape these perforated stones indicates some ceremonial or status symbol function. In the East, drilled specimens have been found that are known to be atlatl weights but these Basin stones are too large and heavy for that purpose. We consider them to be war-club heads. John Cowles found a specimen in Cougar Mountain Cave similar to the top left, Figure 44. It was beautifully shaped and polished; the hole was perfectly cylindrical. Half of another was picked up on the Fort Rock desert, and some have been obtained from the Columbia River.

There seems to be no ethnological support to the contention that banded stones were used as hafted mauls in the Great Basin. A stone bound to a stick is an unwieldly instrument at best, and there was very little driving or hammering to be done. With a nomad people a stone maul would have been an unnecessary burden; a pebble held in the hand would serve very well for what hammering was necessary. The people of the Northwest did a great deal of hammering on elk horn and wood wedges to rive out boards, work trees into canoes, and split firewood, yet they used no hafted hammers, only a stone mallet held in the hand. In the O'Shea collection, however, is one that may have been used for hammering (Figure 44, right). It looks exactly like the two-handed "pile drivers" that are found on the Northwest Coast. Similar specimens from the desert are on display in the Klamath County Museum, Oregon. The natives around Klamath and Tule Lakes had permanent winter villages where such heavy instruments could be left while the residents were away foraging. Furthermore, as the Klamath built houses over water, a heavy instrument for setting the piling would have been useful.

14. A Handled Container

Carved stone containers similar to the one in Figure 45 are occasionally seen in collections of desert cultural material; usually the bowl shows signs of heat or smoke. Sometimes these are called frying pans, sometimes lamps. There would have been no use for a stone frying pan, and there is no present evidence that lamps were used. However, lamps would have been very helpful in the dark holes of the Klamath winter lodges. Kroeber (1953, Pl. 16) illustrates a similar instrument made by the Yoruk from steatite. He calls it a salmon grease dish, which would be much more appropriate to the coastal country than to the desert. This specimen is blackened around the rim in the same manner as a burning fiber or moss wick lying against it would have darkened it. If one must judge by appearance this is a lamp—but appearances can be deceiving. It came from the Klamath area.

15. Charmstones

An exceptionally well-made artifact for the desert region is the charmstone or plummet; Figure 46 shows some samples from the Luke and Lair collections. These pieces have been investigated for many years but there seems to be no positive evidence of their function, though the following uses have been suggested: sling bullet, sinker, game piece, metal working tool, ornament, ceremonial, level or plumb bob, weight for weaving, spindle, idol, and ice pick. None of these except the ceremonial seem acceptable. Loud (1929) says he was told they were made to peck holes in the ice on lakes, for fishing holes. While this use might be seriously questioned, the upper piece in Figure 46, from the Sanford collection, would be an ideal tool for that purpose.

Yates (1889) quotes an Indian informant: "The sorcerer arranged twenty of these stones, the proper number, in a circle, pushed them violently together, sprinkled water over them and smoke issued from them. . . ." Yates illustrates more than 30 of these strange objects, some of them similar to those in Figure 46, except for the pointed end. Two show, on the point, a nubbin with a small notch, but it appears to be transverse rather than longitudinal. It is interesting to note that there are some Type II atlatl weights in his illustration; their use was not suspected when Yates did his work.

Those shown here have a uniquely formed end: a semi-ring and a pronounced groove, as though they were intended to be pushed through something a certain distance and then a cord inserted through the groove—the way a marlin spike is used to splice cable. Another suggestion sometimes heard is that the groove and ring were intended to aid in lashing a feather in place, for which it would have been well suited. Or, it may be some type of reamer. As far as the author is concerned, the actual use of charmstones continues a mystery.

16. Artifacts Made from Bone

Awls are the most plentiful of the instruments made from bone and are found in even the oldest sites wherever conditions were suitable for their survival. Splitting bones to extract the marrow would have left sharp splinters, a natural tool that needed only a little grinding on the point to make an efficient instrument. An example is shown in Figure 47 "F." These are called "splinter awls" and are among the oldest and most consistently used of the tools. They are found in very ancient as well as recent sites.

The Desert Culture made some beautiful instruments and ornaments from bone, grinding them out on a sandstone or scoria abrasive slab. Awls were the most useful, performing innumerable duties such as perforating hide for sewing with sinew or thongs, assisting in weaving baskets, and making mats; in fact, anything for which we would use a needle or awl or ice pick. A needle has an eye, an awl none, and very few needles are found in the desert. The use of eyed needles is not a recent trait. One was found in Cougar Mountain Cave at the 1.5 foot level, and they have been recovered from other caves in small numbers. They really were not much more useful for coarse sewing than an awl. Needles are shown in Figure 47 "B."

The instrument "H" is unique; it has a hook instead of a hole. This specimen from the Johnson collection is 4.75 inches long and polished until it glistens like ivory. It may have been used in net making, in the manner of a crochet needle.

Typical well-made bone awls are shown in Figure 47 "E," fashioned with pride and used with pleasure. The L-shaped awl, "A," is normally made from the scapula (shoulder blade) of an antelope, deer, or elk; a scapula from a large animal was required. This distinctive type is widely distributed throughout the West; in Danger Cave it was used at least 4,000 years ago. The instrument shown in "G" is an uncommon type: a tiny, highly polished splinter of bone about the size of a ballpoint pen filler is bound to a wood handle. If the ancient people of the desert did any tattooing this would have been a perfect instrument for the painful process, but it was probably only the favorite awl of a neat housekeeper. The awl specimen "C" is an unusual type: a tiny bird bone ground to a beveled point and inserted in a larger hollow bone that serves as a handle. Ruth and I have seen this style only on the Klamath.

"J" is an unusual tool for the desert. Found in a cave near Paisley, Oregon, it is made from elk antler and is similar to instruments used by the Plains Indians for fleshing hides, and like those found at Klamath Lake by Cressman (1956); he too calls them fleshers. This one, however, shows battering on the end from being struck with a maul, so it was used as a wedge for splitting wood. Antler wedges are common along the Northwest Coast and the Columbia River and were used by the Klamath.

Two specimens of another uncommon-type tool (from the Gienger collection) are shown in Figure 48, center. Both are gouges; the points are ground smooth and sharp and show evidence of considerable use. The bottom piece, eleven inches long, shows much care in workmanship and finish and is decorated with incised lines and geometric designs. The end of one of the two slots has been split and patched by drilling a hole on each side for a thong lace. It is probably an ornament. All seven of the objects at the top of the figure are decorated bone whistles, sometimes called flageolets, but they are not true flutes or flageolets because there are no finger holes. These specimens were found together near the Klamath Lakes. Bone or cane whistles are found throughout the world.

Bone is an organic material subject to deterioration. Sometimes bone in excellent condition will be found in a midden. Occasionally it is very fragile or has entirely disappeared, depending primarily on the acid content and moisture of the environment. In a dry cave, bone will be preserved indefinitely. When it is moist or wet, it will still last several hundred years if no acid is present. Rainwater, though, is slightly acid from carbon dioxide in the air, and many sands and soils are acid. The larger the quantity of bone, the longer it will take the small amount of acid in the soil or water to consume it. Either an ash pit or a shell heap offers excellent conditions for preserving bone as either will absorb acid. Ruth and I have found bone tools deep in centuries-old shell that were as hard and bright as when new.

Part Three

The Atlatl and Other Weapons

17. The Atlatl

It is probable that the first contrivance ever developed by man that could be called a machine was the atlatl, a device by which a spear or dart could be hurled with more force than by hand alone. The axe, knife, spear, and scraper were not machines. They were tools or weapons, manipulated by the hands and an end unto themselves. The atlatl was a machine, a "device that transmits or changes the application of energy," as defined by Webster. It performed no function by itself; only when it was employed in conjunction with a dart was it useful.

The world owes a debt of gratitude to the long vanished and unknown inventor of the atlatl, the first of the inventions that started man on the long road toward civilization. With it he had more control over his environment and was better able to protect himself and furnish his family with food and fur. In some caves it has been noticed that there was a sudden increase in the number of animal bones in the litter—an increase that might have been due to the appearance of the atlatl. The only other machine which might compete for first place with the atlatl is the fire drill, another device which must be considered as one of the greatest inventions of all time. These two inventions may well have ad-

vanced the emergence of civilization by many centuries, or even
millenniums. Except for them the world might yet be in the stone
age.

The other tools and weapons of prehistoric man can be considered improvements rather than true inventions. The first chopper or knife must have been a rock already sharpened or shaped
by nature, perhaps a flake from a flint nodule fractured by pressure of boulders in a glacial moraine, or a splinter of basalt from
a talus slope. The art of flaking a stone to improve its shape, to
increase its effectiveness by sharpening its edge, or to create a
tool where no natural form existed, could have been patterned
from natural phenomena—possibly from observing a flake struck
from a stone accidentally dropped, or while using a hammer
stone. The bow may have been the result of the accidental loop-
ing of a string from the ends of a supple stick by some individual
capable of recognizing the possibilities. However, anyone who
has seen an atlatl and understands its use must realize that the
device is not just a chance combination of events. The throwing
stick had to arrive full blown. The throwing motion is far from
simple, and one must be filled with admiration for the long-
forgotten genius who conceived the device and perfected the
skill necessary for its use.

The atlatl, in effect, lengthens the arm of the user, thereby
imparting more speed and force to the projectile. It consists of
a stick or board about 24 inches long, with one end handled and
the other hooked. The handle end is grasped and the device held
horizontally over the shoulder, with the dart shaft steadied by
the fingers of the throwing hand. The butt of the dart, slightly
cupped for the purpose, is engaged on the hook or spur at the
far end of the atlatl. With an overhand throw and a sharp snap
of the wrist at the moment of release, the dart is sped on its way.
The use of the atlatl puts extra stress on the elbow and wrist,
and it has been noted among the Aleuts that their throwing muscles have been developed to compensate for the added effort. It
is also interesting to note that some ancient skeletons found near

Tranquility, California, and examined by J. Lawrence Angel, showed evidence of arthritis of the elbow in one arm, which he called "atlatl elbow," a defect caused by the exertions of using this weapon.

There is no doubt that the atlatl is an ancient device; how ancient is unknown. Evidence of it has been found in late Paleolithic Magdalenian sites in Europe, generally considered to be at least 15,000 years old. The elaborate development of the specimens, carved of bone or ivory, indicates a long tradition, perhaps dating back to the Solutrean culture (Harrington 1933). Although archaeological evidence of the atlatl occurs only in Europe and the Americas, it probably had extensive distribution. Its use is recorded in historic times in Australia, some South Sea islands, the Arctic, and Asia (Kellar 1955).

The time that the atlatl was introduced into the Americas is not known. Perhaps the best indication of its antiquity in America came from the Roadcut site on the Columbia River near The Dalles, Oregon. Here Cressman (1960) found an atlatl spur in levels 28 and 22, both older than 8,000 years. In Gypsum Cave, dart shafts and foreshafts were beneath sloth dung that dated more than 7,500 years. Apparently the weapon was well established in the culture prior to 8,000 B.P., and survived until quite recently—in fact, the spear thrower is still used by the aborigines in Australia. A section from the broken atlatl shaft shown in Figure 56 was submitted to the University of Oregon for C14 analysis and the test indicated an age of about 1,500 years. At present this is the only date obtained from an actual atlatl or dart from the Great Basin.

Eskimos used the spear thrower historically—and had been for centuries before the white invasion. They were remarkably skillful with it. It is known that some Northwest Coast people used the atlatl. Forced by the Russians to brave the stormy waters of the western coast in search of the sea otter, the Aleut or Tlingit hunters in their skin kayaks carried the spear thrower as far south as the Columbia River, where it was seen in 1812 by Robert

Stuart (Spaulding 1953): "The boards used in throwing these darts are very judiciously fixed, in semblance of a gutter, which enable the natives to cast them with great exactness to a considerable distance." It was a weapon much feared by the Spanish in the conquest of Peru and Mexico, where it was used very effectively by the natives. The world "atatl" is from the Aztec language.

There are three general types of atlatls, according to Kellar's classification. There are those with a hook (either integral or attached) that projects above the upper face of the atlatl shaft to engage the butt of the javelin; these are called "male." The "female" has no hook; instead, they have a deep groove and the butt of the dart rests against the end. There may be a projection to engage a cup in the base of the shaft, or the rounded end of the dart may rest in a depression at the base of the groove. The third type is the "mixed," which has the groove and also the projecting point. Most Great Basin atlatls are the third type. Such a classification segregates and identifies atlatl shafts from different cultural groups for they tend to follow one type.

Atlatl shafts were sometimes carved from bone and ivory and even jade, but wood was the usual material. The shape varied considerably in details, although basically it remains the same. The Great Basin atlatl, from the few specimens found, is similar in construction to the Basketmaker type. Guernsey and Kidder (1921) took two complete specimens and three fragments from burials in White Dog Cave in Arizona, a Basketmaker site. They are made from oak, carefully worked down nearly flat, with rounded handles and sides. At a distance of 3.5 inches from the handle end there is a rounded notch on each side, forming the inner surface of two leather finger loops bound to the shaft. The hooks are integral with the shafts, and each has a groove, though on one it is little more than a notch. One of the complete specimens has three small weights set in pitch and lashed to the handle end; above the handle are weights made from a fossilized tooth of a prehistoric animal. One of the fragments also has three small weights, and another has lashing scars showing that a stone had once been attached.

There are two methods of forming the hook or spur which engages the butt of the projectile. One is to carve it integral with the shaft; the other is to attach—on a seat at the hook end—a separate spur made from wood or bone, sometimes even stone. Figure 53 shows some of these attachable spurs, picked up on the Nevada deserts or found in caves. Figure 51 shows one attached to the Nicolarsen atlatl. The separate spur had the advantage of being replaceable. If one of the integral hooks broke in service, it might well render the shaft useless, and it was a real task to scrape a new one from the hard mountain mahogany with only a chip of obsidian. However, the attached spurs were not without fault; it was difficult to mount one with sufficient rigidity to withstand the force required to catapult a five-foot dart.

At present, only seven complete atlatl shafts have been reported recovered in the Great Basin and its periphery, though numerous fragments have been found. One was found in Lovelock Cave, but it has been lost and only a drawing survives to show what a splendid specimen it was. A fragment was found by Cressman and his crew in Plush Cave, near Plush, Oregon. Later, the missing section of the shaft was found by Mr. and Mrs. Ralph Patrick of Lakeview and given to the University of Oregon to complete the specimen. It is a type very similar to those found in Basketmaker sites in Utah and New Mexico. The finger notches (see Figure 51) may be intended to accommodate or replace finger loops of cord or thong, a characteristic of Southwest atlatls. Above and below the notches are grooves that could serve to secure the loops. The hook is integral with the shaft, and there is a channel in which to lay the dart. The specimen is nearly 22 inches long.

Two complete shafts were uncovered by Dr. Cressman's crew in Roaring Springs Cave in Catlow Valley, Southeastern Oregon. When excavated, they were facing each other and about three inches apart, well down in the fill and about half way from the entrance. The larger of the two is 20 inches long; the shorter only a little over 16. Both are made from the mountain mahogany, *Cercocarpus ledifolius,* a hard, reddish wood from a common shrub along the top of the rimrocks in the Great Basin. It is just different enough from juniper so that at a distance it can be readily identified. It is not a true mahogany but a member of the rose family. The wood is so dense that it will not float. The author once brought home some dried limbs of this beautiful wood, intending to make a duplicate of an atlatl, but quickly became discouraged with its resistance to blades of even the most modern tools. What patience the ancient artisans must have had!

The handle of the larger of the Roaring Springs atlatls is wrapped with skin, and both have been painted all over with red ochre; the smaller is decorated with rows of white dots. As shown in Figure 51, the atlatls are similar in design. There is a handle, then two finger notches and a wide, flat shaft terminating in a hook reinforced on the back with a keel. The smaller specimen has a very small hook, incapable of engaging a dart of the usual size. It differs from the Plush Cave atlatl in that the finger notches seem to be complete in themselves, not needing the looped thong or cord.

A large number of carved stone objects about which there had been considerable controversy and speculation (Butler 1959) have been found in the Great Basin and the Plateau, especially along the Columbia River where several hundred were collected. These strange loaf-shaped or elongated pieces were called atlatl weights because of their similarity to prismoidal stones from the Southwest, some of which had been found attached to atlatls (Harrington 1933). But professional archaeologists do not make bold statements assigning a function or age to any artifact without solid proof, either archaeological or ethnological. It is indeed fortunate that the science so disciplines itself, for if it did not, only confusion and distrust could result. The same situation now exists with Early Man sites. Several have been found with evidence of the presence of man in the Americas about 30,000 years ago, but as yet there is no universally acceptable proof.

Atlatl weights from the West fall into three classes called Type I, II, and III by Butler (1959) (see Figure 55). The Type I is loaf shaped with a transverse perforation to hold the binding. Nearly all of them are made from the lead ore galena, but occasionally from stone. Type II is an elongated semi-spherical stone tapering toward each end, where there is usually a notch to hold the lashing. Type III is also loaf shaped and has a transverse groove for the chord. This type is generally made from colorful stone, beautifully shaped, and polished. Quite often they are found in pairs, either with another Type III or with a Type I. Sometimes two Type I are found together.

Since there was no proof that the stones were atlatl weights they were called that for convenience only until a young amateur, Bill McClure, made a remarkable discovery. He was exploring a cave east of Condon, Oregon, near the northern boundary of the Great Basin. Noticing a packrat's nest and knowing the peculiar habits of that interesting animal, he started to disassemble the large pile of sticks and trash piece by piece. A foot or so below the top of the nest he uncovered the remarkable atlatl shown in Fig. 56. This specimen had a Type III stone weight attached to it, irrefutable evidence of its function. Further search revealed another similar, damaged shaft (Fig. 56). No weight was found with it, but it has a seat for a weight, similar to that of the complete specimen. Like the Roaring Springs atlatls, both are made of a dark, red wood, probably mountain mahogany, but not yet positively identified. The stone weight was lashed to the shaft with two-ply cord (now broken) and the seat for the stone coated with pitch.

The handle is made from mountain sheep horn, transversely drilled. The wooden shaft is tapered to fit the hole, and the two are cemented together with pitch. One finger hole has partially decayed away; the other had been broken and its owner had fitted in a piece of wood or antler, binding the patch securely with two-ply cord. The number of hours of patient labor expended on this instrument—scraping down the wood, grinding out and drilling the antler handle, forming and decorating the stone weight, and gathering and spinning the material for the cord—can only be conjectured, but one must admire the patience and skill of the ancient craftsman. But, for what purpose on this particular specimen? It is too slight, too delicate to cast a dart; the handle is too small to grasp and the holes are unfit for inserting the fingers. Reason can assign no other function for this atlatl than that of a symbol of rank, or an object upon which to expend an artistic expression.

Archaeological proof that the Type II stone was actually an atlatl weight was discovered by Mr. and Mrs. Jack Nicolarsen, who found a hafted specimen (Figure 51) in a Nevada cave. This atlatl is the simplest type, although just as functional as the most elaborate. It is merely a section of a limb with a minimum of dressing. The handle is embellished with a series of grooves, which may have been to improve the grip rather than to decorate it. The separate wooden or bone hook is bound to the shaft with sinew, as is the weight. Type II weight is the most common variety found in the Great Basin. Nearly every collector has one or more, although he does not always recognize its use—that it may have helped its prehistoric owner to dine on a camel, horse, or even an elephant.

Whether the use of a weight on the atlatl shaft is beneficial or not is a subject of some dispute. (It should be noted again that the weight is attached to the atlatl—not the dart). Experiments with weighted and unweighted atlatls have been conducted by Malcolm Hill (1948), Orville H. Peets (1960), and Campbell Grant. Mr. Hill constructed ten different atlatls, each a form corresponding to those known to have been used by the natives, and tested them with and without weights, using darts of different lengths and weights. He found that darts failed to soar well without the balancing effect of a stone projectile point; that short darts of about 30 inches wobbled and tumbled in flight. He also found that untrimmed feathers were as efficient as trimmed ones, and that the atlatl with weight was no more efficient than without, and even less with some types of atlatl shafts. The longest throw Mr. Hill made was 216 feet. Mr. Grant used the Basketmaker type atlatl with and without weight; his 16-year-old son Douglas cast a dart 240 feet with this atlatl.

Mr. Grant's final conclusions were the same as those of Mr. Hill—the stone weights had no advantageous effects and must have been used as a good luck charm or fetish. Mr. Peets experimented with a replica of an atlatl that was found in the Baylor Rock Shelter in Texas. He observed that the weight did not add force to the throw but did serve to balance the dart when the weapon was in a horizontal position ready to cast. If the weapon is held in throwing position for some time—as it might be in stalking game—the force required to hold up the end of a dart adds considerable stress to the wrist and arm muscles and tires them.

From a strictly engineering standpoint, the extra force required to accelerate the weight, which may be heavier than the dart, could better be used on accelerating the dart. There may, however, be a mental advantage, a feeling of increased stability, of greater control, like that from the exertion required to turn the steering wheel of an automobile — a task that could easily be made effortless. The present writer used the atlatl both with and without the weight and experienced a more confident attitude from the firmer feeling of the weighted shaft.

Some of the atlatl weights are beautiful. The stone, carefully chosen for its pleasing color, was formed, decorated, and polished with precision. Some have been found sculptured into zoomorphic forms, and the exquisite bird and banner stones found in the Midwest are considered to be atlatl weights. Those used for grave offerings are nearly always beautifully made and polished. Still, there are found many of the grooved stones, especially in middens, that are only functional — merely a pebble slightly flattened on the bottom and a rough groove pecked for the lashing.

As the atlatl was replaced by the more efficient bow, it may have become a status symbol, a mark of distinction and affluence, a ceremonial object upon which to lavish an artistic urge—like an antique automobile today. Fortunately a large number of dart fragments from atlatls have been found, and some complete specimens, so their construction features are well known. The mark that separates an atlatl projectile from an arrow is the construction of the butt end. Instead of the nock that is used on the arrow to straddle the bow string, the atlatl dart has a cup—a depression to engage the hook of the spear. For the female type, which does not have a hook but a cup in the far end to engage the dart, the butt will be rounded. The difference between an arrow and dart shaft is unmistakable if one has the butt end. With the other end, identification is not so simple, depending mostly on the size and length, the dart shaft being both longer and larger than the arrow as a general rule.

18. The Bow

Just when the bow was introduced (or invented) in the Americas is not known, but it is thought to be fairly recent. The bow is very old in Europe, between 5,000 and 6,000 years (Lowie 1963) and perhaps much older if smaller points mean the bow and arrow rather than the atlatl. It is certain that the bow is much older in the Old World than it is in the New. Wilbur A. Davis (1966) writes: "At some time between 1000 BC and AD1 the bow was introduced." Davis is basing his statement on the archaeology of Lovelock Cave, where only atlatl dart shafts appeared in layers about 3,000 years old, dart and arrow shafts in a 2,500-year layer, and arrows only in the deposits above.

In Cougar Mountain Cave, Cowles found a bow fragment in the 3.5-foot level, just below the pumice layer. In Basketmaker caves the bow and arrow replaced the atlatl during Basketmaker III and probably was introduced in Basketmaker II (Kellar 1955.) In the upper levels of DIV in Danger Cave, dated by interpolation as 3,000 or 2,000 years ago, there was a marked and sudden increase in animal bones, nearly three times as many. Davis (1966) thinks this increase might reflect the improved hunting success coincident with the introduction of the bow and arrow. Both arrows and bow fragments were found in level DV, supposed to date from about the first century. From these and other data it appears that the bow and arrow came to the Great Basin about 2,500 years ago. In level DIII of Danger Cave, Jennings found a foreshaft which, because of the size, he believes to be for a dart although the small stemmed point ". . . would probably have been, if found alone, called an arrow point." Two other probable foreshafts without points came from this level, dated about 7,000 years ago. This illustrates the pitfalls one must avoid in assigning isolated points to dart or to arrow by size alone.

Replacement of the atlatl by the more efficient and simpler bow was gradual. It took many hundreds of years, and in some places the bow never did completely displace the atlatl. Great Basin bows did not attain the refinement of the splendid specimens of the Plains, partly because of the much less advanced culture and partly because bows were not of great importance, rabbits being the usual game animal—though deer and mountain sheep were important. Lt. Henry L. Abbot describes the bow and arrow seen during explorations for a railroad route to the Pacific:

"They are armed with bows and arrows, which they make with great skill. The bows are sticks of soft wood, about three feet in length, backed with deer sinew. The bow string also is of sinew. The arrows are made in three parts. The head is generally of obsidian, which abounds in portions of the valley. It is carefully shaped into the usual barbed form, and lashed by deer sinew to one end of a small stick of hard wood about ten inches long. The other end of the stick is inserted into the extremity of a reed and also lashed with sinew. The reed is tipped with feathers, attached by some kind of fastening. This weapon inflicts a dangerous injury; as the blood immediately softens the sinew, and, on attempting to extract the arrow, the reed separates from the hard wood stick, and that from the arrow head, which thus remains at the bottom of the wound."

19. Dart and Arrow Shafts

The normal atlatl dart was made in two parts. For the main shaft, about five feet long and half an inch in diameter, cane or light wood was used. The near end was rounded or cupped as required for the atlatl type, and generally feathered to stabilize the flight. The far end was mortised to receive a foreshaft like those in Figures 28 and 57. Foreshafts were made from some strong, tough wood like catclaw, mesquite, greasewood, or screwbean and might be a few or several inches long, and smaller than the main shaft. One end was tapered to fit the socket in the main shaft; in the other the projectile point was inserted and bound securely. The mortise in the main shaft was wound with sinew or cord to prevent splitting from the wedging action of the foreshaft; sometimes the butt was reinforced to withstand the thrust of the atlatl hook by inserting a wooden plug. Cressman once found part of a dart that the prehistoric craftsman had fitted to the atlatl spur by cutting out wedge-shaped sections and then reducing the diameter to the proper size by drawing the edges together with binding. A tinsmith reduces the size of a downspout to fit the elbow in the same manner.

Arrow shafts were made similar to darts, but of course were much smaller. Both arrow and dart shaft were frequently painted.

The reason for making atlatl darts—as well as arrow shafts—

in two pieces is not clear. Archaeological reports carefully de-
scribe the shafts but refrain from citing any reason for expending
the considerable amount of extra effort to form and fit the two or
sometimes three parts. Baron Karl von Loeffelholz wrote in
1850: "A small cleft is cut out in the wood at the end of the
arrow. The point sits in this depression. It is then tied to the
arrow with fine threads or tendons. Wounds made by these saw-
like arrowheads do not heal easily. To make deep body wounds
still more dangerous, the Indians make an arrow the tip of which
is fixed to a short, thin piece of wood, which is stuck into a hole
in the actual arrow. When the arrow is pulled out of the wound,
the tip remains in the body" (Heizer 1952). This theory is doubtful as the point could readily be made detachable in other and
better ways. A point without notches will easily slip off in a
wound because the sinew binding it to the shaft will quickly
soften and lose its grip.

Lewis and Clark, while on the Columbia River during the
winter of 1805-1806, described the arrows of the local Indians
"The arrow is formed of two parts tho' sometimes entire; those
formed of two parts are unequally divided that part on which
the feathers are placed occupyes four fifths of its length and is
formed of light white pine reather larger than a swan's quill, the
lower extremeity of this is a circular mortice secured by sinues
roled around it; this mortice received the one end of the 2nd part
which is of a smaller size than the first and about five inches long,
in the end of this the barb is fixed and confined with sinue, this
barb is either stone, iron or copper. the shorter part of the arrow
is of harder wood as is also the whole arrow when it is in one
piece only. as these people live in a country abounding in ponds
&C and frequently hunt in their canoes and shoot at fowl and
other anamals where the arrow missing its object would be lost
in the water they are constructed in the manner just described
in order to make them float should they fall in the water, and
consequently can again be recovered by the hunter." The present
writer made an arrow from cedar, 25 inches long and a quarter

inch in diameter, with a chert point of normal size, and found that it would float easily; even when broken in half, the pointed end would float. Cedar was the usual material for making arrow shafts on the Columbia River, and perfectly straight slabs 20 feet long could be easily split from the log. This would seem to refute the assumption of Lewis & Clark.

The reason for using the compound shaft in the desert probably was that suitable material was not easily obtained. The long, straight cane Phragmites met the requirements for the shaft but lacked the strength to hold the point or to withstand the thrust of the atlatl. Therefore a foreshaft of more durable material was used; one that would not break on impact and in which the point could be securely bound.

In Danger Cave, solid shafts of willow and service berry were found; and compound shafts of Phragmites and elderberry. The cane Phragmites was favored for compound shafts. This lovely plant with the showy plumes decorates the margins of most of the bogs and marshes of the Great Basin. It looks something like rye grass except much larger. The author once measured a stalk growing straight and strong eleven feet high. Stabilizing feathers were sometimes split before attachment to the shaft and sometimes not. They have been found with a wood plug in the quill, presumably so it would not be crushed by the binding cord.

Not all arrows and darts were tipped with stone points. Sometimes the wood shaft or foreshaft was pointed and perhaps fire-hardened—a technique with which the Indians were familiar—forming a very efficient point although one not so damaging to tissue as the ragged stone point. Figure 61 shows a human ilium or hip bone in which an untipped shaft has penetrated over a quarter of an inch after passing through the abdomen; the tip is still in place in the bone which shows no sign of healing—the wound was fatal. This specimen was found in a Nevada cave. Cressman (1940), while discussing materials found in caves in the Northern Great Basin, noted: "In the upper bed, projectile points are exclusively of obsidian, insofar as flaked points are concerned, while foreshafts without stone heads enter as a new form. The latter are from 10 to 25 cm. long, pointed at both ends, and were doubtlessly socketed into the projectile shafts. This trait has a wide distribution in the Great Basin, and is of interest here since it was probably absent in the lower bed."

The tools required for making an arrow shaft (as well as the atlatl dart shaft) were a knife for cutting, scraper for debarking, wrench or straightener for removing the kinks, and a smoother for dressing down the shaft (see Figure 62). The latter three are strictly arrow-making tools, specimens of which are in many collections. The knife and scraper were always at hand. Paul Schumacher tells how arrows were made in the 1870's in "Archiv fur Anthropologie," Vol. VII:

"The aboriginal warrior was well aware of the advantage of a straight arrow-shaft over a crooked one, and when, therefore, nature did not provide the desired perfection, ingenuity was resorted to, by which it was attained. The way it was accomplished I learned from living witnesses, and by the many implements found which were used for the purpose of straightening the arrow shaft. The twigs were cut to the proper length, worked by scraping into the desired thickness, and were left to dry in the shade. When partially dry such bends and crooked parts which restricted the common practice of straightening were subjected to the action of the arrow straightener. This utensil is made of steatite, a rock that well resists the destructive power of the fire to which it is subjected during the process of straightening the shafts, and retains the heat long. It is usually oval in shape, and slopes towards both ends and sides, and has a flat base, upon which it rests when in use. Across its ridge passes a groove (sometimes two and even three), corresponding in its width to the thickness of the arrow-shaft, while in depth it varies, often twice its width, according to the service is rendered, by which the grooves are deepened and its width enlarged. Into the groove of the heated implement the crooked part of the shaft is pressed, and by heating, or steaming, the wood becomes very flexible, and is easily bent and straightened, which position it will retain when cooled off. It is the same principle now employed in the manufacture of furniture, wagon wheels, etc., of bent wood, brought into almost any shape by the process of steaming."

The Wheeler report carries some arguments against the process by heating. However, along the Columbia River a number of the same type of arrow-shaft straighteners have been found, showing evidence of having been strongly heated. Kroeber (1953), in describing straighteners used by the California Indians, says "The joints were warmed in the groove and bent by hand or on the ridge after the stone had been heated; the groove was also used for smoothing."

The process of steaming wood to bend it was well known to the Indians. The Coastal tribes, after hewing out a canoe, would fill it with water and boil it by tossing in hot rocks, until the sides of the canoe were supple enough to widen and flare; boxes were made by steaming and bending boards. Campbell Grant, author of *Rock Art of the Chumash* and *Rock Art of the American Indian* and a keen student of Indian lore, says: "While I was doing the atlatl research, I tried straightening some cane shafts on a steatite arrow straightener I made from a big nodule found in the Santa Ynez Range. I got the stone very hot in the oven—then held the joint I wanted to straighten in the hot slot until the fibers 'relaxed' —then held in straight position until cool—it really worked!" The grooved arrow-shaft straightener is not common in the Great Basin and may be a recently imported trait. The fact that most of them are of steatite, a stone much used on the Coast, supports this conclusion.

The usual arrow-shaft wrench is a piece of flat bone, antler, or horn with a hole in one end. In use, the arrow shaft is slipped into the hole until it is opposite the bend, then by bearing down on the wrench, pressure is brought to bear on the side of the bend until it is straight. It works just like the "hickey" an electrician uses to bend conduit, or like a claw hammer, which tends to bend the board from which a nail is being withdrawn. The horn wrench is listed as a Desert Culture trait by Jennings (1957); they were found in both Danger and Humboldt caves. Cressman (1956) shows a perforated stone four inches in diameter and about two inches thick which he calls an arrow wrench, since it is similar to a Klamath ethnographic specimen. The hole is conical, 0.4 inches in diameter on one side of the stone, and a little over one inch on the other. It would have been used in the same way as the horn wrench. The "donut stones" shown in Figure 43 are considered by many collectors to be arrow-shaft wrenches, but they are not adapted to that purpose.

Arrow-shaft smoothers are made from scoria, sandstone, pumice, or similar abrasive stone. Down one side runs a semicircular groove of the same diameter as the desired arrow shaft. It is used by sliding the stone back and forth on the straightened shaft to reduce it to a uniform diameter and to polish it. They are sometimes used in pairs, face to face on the shaft, the groove slightly less deep than one half of the shaft diameter, so that pressure can be applied. Arrow-shaft smoothers were found in Danger Cave and in the Klamath excavations, and are picked up from the old campsites. Straighteners and smoothers would have been most useful on one-piece arrows; their scarcity indicates that the compound shaft was more popular with the desert culture.

20. The Sling and Spear

The sling, the ancient weapon with which David slew Goliath, must be listed along with the atlatl and the bow as part of the Desert Culture complex. The sling was used historically in the Basin (Heizer 1952) both as a weapon and as a toy. Examination of some specimens, long after they were uncovered in Lovelock Cave by Loud and Harrington, revealed a sling still wrapped in the Olivella shell necklace with which it had been placed in a child's burial. No date could be assigned though, because it was an intrusive burial, but it would have been many centuries old. The pocket of the sling measures about 3.5 by 1.5 inches; the sling cords are fragmentary. Another sling was found in Humboldt Cave (Heizer 1956); it was discovered in a cache and no date could be assigned to it either. The sling was widely distributed over the world and, historically at least, well known in the Southwest, the Basin, and Western California.

Regarding the spear, the author has not seen in reports on excavations or ethnology in the Great Basin any evidence of the use of the spear other than for fishing. It is hard to believe that such a common and useful weapon would have been unknown; none is more natural. It would have avoided the body contact required of a knife—an advantage not to be ignored when facing such a formidable opponent as a cornered bear. There are found large points, thick and heavy, with a wide stem, that would have served admirably for a spear point but are too coarse for an efficient knife. One wants to believe that the spear was used and served as a badge of distinction, carried by the bravest; and that the beautiful pieces such as that shown in Figure 23 tipped such a weapon.

Part Four

The Culture

21. Seed Gathering

The tools used by the ancient rovers of the desert in gathering, preserving, and preparing seeds, roots, and nuts were simple and efficient. Centuries of experimenting had perfected them. Baskets and milling stones recovered from the lower levels of Danger Cave, dated at about 9,000 years ago, are evidence of a long tradition in the preparation of seeds and roots for food. To a gathering economy, the one essential was the basket; without it there could be no harvest, no storage; there could not even be any cooking by boiling. The basket was indispensable and the Desert Culture excelled in its manufacture.

Twined basketry from desert caves is among the oldest dated textiles known to archaeology. It appeared before coiling and the direction of the stitch is thought to be a regional characteristic. The Nevada burden basket in its handsome cone shape is unique in being so closely woven that it will hold tiny seeds and yet be strong enough to carry heavy loads of firewood. The Panamint Shoshone in Death Valley used both willow (*Salix lasiandra*) and sumac (*Rhus trilobata*) for the foundation of their baskets. They gathered the willow in the mountains before it sprouted leaves and kept the peeled bark for stitching. The unfading black and red decoration is from the unicorn plant (*Martynia proboscidea*) and the fire-treated roots of the Joshua tree. The year-old shoots of the aromatic sumac and the long red roots of the tree yucca (*Yucca brevifolia*) were much sought after.

Seeds were gathered in two ways: beating them from the heads into a basket with a seed beater or the hands, and stripping them with the fingers or a tool made from two twigs tied together at one end. The seed beater was usually woven from willow and shaped like a tennis racket; the gathering basket was held in one hand and the beater in the other. The stripper was passed over the seed stalk, one twig on each side, squeezed together, and the seeds stripped from the stalk. It would work only with seeds on stems, like rye grass. Powell (1961) says, "They gather the seeds of many plants, as sunflowers, golden-rod, and grasses. For this purpose they have large conical baskets, which hold two or more bushels. The women carry them on their backs, suspended from their foreheads by broad straps, and with a smaller one in the left hand and a willow-woven fan in the right they walk among the grasses and sweep the seed into the smaller basket, which is emptied now and then into the larger, until it is full of seeds and chaff."

Seed gathering was strictly women's work and they performed their tedious task with pride. The author has talked to aged Indian women whose faded eyes would gleam with pleasure as they told of the old days and the good times they had when they and the children would go to reap the harvest. Gathering was hard work, but there was gossip and merriment. An early explorer said, ". . . there appears a degree of happiness among them, which civilized men, wearied with care and anxious pursuits, perhaps seldom enjoy." This trait contributed much to their survival in this brutal land; most if not all primitive tribes possess it. This pleasant companionship happily supplemented the meager reward at day's end of perhaps a quart or two of tiny seeds.

Seed gathering, however, was not always a pleasant outing. Stansbury (1852), while in the Great Salt Lake Valley, wrote: "During our ride through the valley we suddenly came upon a party of eight or ten Indian women and girls, each with a basket on her back, gathering grass-seeds for their winter's provision. They were of the class of 'root-diggers.' The instant they discovered us, an immediate and precipitate flight took place; nor could all the remonstrances of our guide, who called loudly after them in their language, induce them to halt for a single moment. Those who were too close to escape by running, hid themselves in the brush and grass so effectively, that in less time than it has taken to narrate the circumstance, only two of them were to be seen. These were a couple of girls of twelve or thirteen years of age, who, with their baskets dangling at their backs, set off at their utmost speed for the mountains, and continued to run as long as we could seem them, without stopping, or as much as turning their heads to look behind them. The whole party was entirely naked."

Many times a similar group had been accosted at their work, but in more tragic circumstances. The younger women would be busily gossiping and gathering, the older ones helping as they were able, while the children happily dug in the sand. Suddenly with raucous yells the enemy would attack from the shadows. There would be a moment of frozen horror before frenzied flight—then the flash of guns and the screams of girls and children as they were captured. Stillness would then descend again over the desert until the mourning wails rose from the village. The raiders would be pleased with their catch; the wealthy ranchers to the south would pay handsomely for such slaves as these.

As many as 40 different varieties of seeds were harvested, ranging from the plump, sticky wokas to tiny grass seeds that were almost invisible. Later, the seeds were first cleaned of extraneous material such as sticks and leaves by winnowing on a tray or sieving in an open weave basket. Then the hulls were cracked and loosened by lightly rubbing the seeds on a stone platter called a "metate" with a flattened stone, a "mano," held in the hand. In order to crack the hulls on some grains it was necessary first to parch the seeds by placing live coals with them in a winnowing basket and skillfully toss them so that none were burnt but all were properly roasted—a process that required much practice. Powell says in his journal:

"Then they winnow out the chaff and roast the seeds. They roast these curiously, they put seeds and a quantity of red-hot coals into a willow tray and, by rapidly and dexterously shaking and tossing them, keep the coals aglow and the seeds and tray from burning. So skilled are the crones in this work they roll the seeds to one side of the tray as they are roasted and the coals to the other as if by magic." Some seeds were parched after hulling, as certain varieties were too soft to grind into flour otherwise. After cracking the hulls, the seeds were tossed in a winnowing basket, the wind carrying away the chaff while the heavier kernels fell back into the basket.

There were three types of milling implements: grinding stones, metate and mano, and mortar and pestle. The first to appear were grinding stones, flat rocks on which the seeds were ground with a rotary motion of a stone held in the hand; these have been found in sites dating back 10,000 years. Both stones were usually unworked except for the effects from many hours of use at the mill. The grinding stones evolved into the metate and mano. The metate (a Spanish word meaning platter) was a shaped, flat stone upon which the mano was used with a back and forth motion for either hulling or grinding the seeds into meal. Powell observed women at this work:

"Then they grind the seeds into a fine flour and make it into cakes and mush. It is a merry sight, sometimes, to see the women grinding at the mill. For a mill, they use a large flat rock lying on the ground, and another small cylindrical one in their hands. They sit prone on the ground, hold the large flat rock between the feet and legs, then fill their laps with seeds, making a hopper to the mill with their dusky legs, and grind by pushing the seeds across the larger rock, where they drop into a tray. I have seen a group of women grinding together, keeping time to a chant, or gossiping and chatting, while the younger lassies would jest and chatter and make the pine woods merry with their laughter."

Metates are found in many forms, from a simple unworked slab to beautifully shaped platters. Being large and easily seen even if partially buried, most of them have been picked up long ago. Some conception of the enormous number of individuals who lived out their lives in the Great Basin may be gained by viewing some of the collections of cultural materials that have been gathered from the surface by searchers like John O'Shea of Tule Lake or the diligent Luke family of Fallon. The Lukes have carried home enough metates and mortars to construct a fence around their lawn and enough manos to fill a truck.

One especially beautiful metate design is that built like a trough (see Figure 66). They are very rare and extremely difficult to photograph so that their true form will show. Most metates are simply thin slabs of basalt, scoria, or sandstone shaped into a rounded rectangle. After years of constant use they assume that pleasant utilitarian look associated with any useful tool. Milling stones are the cultural remains that truly personify the Great Basin. They are the horizon markers of the Desert Culture and from these, more than from any other artifact, one can vicariously associate with the ancient ones who for so many thousands of years survived in the Great Basin.

Manos are generally blocks of basalt or sandstone dressed into a loaf shape that fits the hand—the two opposite sides flattened and polished from performing the office of crushing and grinding seeds on the metate. Some are shaped so that the hands can grasp them firmly, thus permitting more precise control of the pressure exerted on the grist. The flat mano is held by the fingers and pressure applied with the heel of the hand. One form of modified mano, peculiar to the Klamath area, is the horned muller (see Figure 66). By grasping one horn in each hand the operator could lift or press to exert exactly the pressure required by the work. Most of them are beautifully made. Some were used so long that only a thin sheet remains of the once plump poll. They were greatly valued by their owners. Cressman (1962) tells about seeing an aged Indian woman hold one lovingly to her breast, stroking it gently and softly talking to it in her native tongue. It was, perhaps, the only treasure remaining to link her with a cultural heritage from which she had been so violently uprooted.

Manos, but a few years ago, could be picked up on any of the thousands of ancient campsites in the Great Basin. When we first began to search the sands of the desert for its mementos we ignored them except for some unusually fine specimen, as our storage space was limited. Once we did fill an apple box to set out at home and let friends take their choice. Now even the broken ones are being carried away by the many seekers for the curiosities of the Broken Land.

The other stone instruments used in food preparation were mortars and pestles. The mortars of the desert, in some areas, were objects upon which a great amount of loving skill was lavished. Tall, graceful, ground and polished, they are a sensitive portrayal of a deep desire to fashion an object of beauty. The writer has never been fortunate enough to find one protruding from the sand beneath a sagebrush but has seen the remains, shattered to small fragments, of mortars that stood possibly three feet high with no part thicker than two inches; they seemed to have been deliberately destroyed, perhaps to prevent use or desecration by an enemy.

There are two general types of mortars, the flat and the pointed bottom (see Figure 66). The pointed bottom was for stabbing in the sand for stability, while the flat could rest on hard ground. When they were used for preparing seeds, a quantity was placed in the mortar and reduced to flour by pounding with a stone, or possibly wooden, pestle. One interesting bowl-and-pestle combination was the roller, a hard, heavy pestle rotated in a bowl. The bottom was seated in the mortar, the top grasped and swung in a complete circle against the sides of the vessel. Eventually the combination became an efficient instrument with perfect contact between the mating surfaces.

Sometimes a hopper mortar was used. The hopper was a wide, stiff basket with sides sloping inward, and no bottom. It was placed over a flat rock and held down with the legs of the operator; the grist was confined within the hopper while being milled with a pestle on the rock. The stones, with a shallow depression beaten out by use, are found on the old camp grounds. A hopper could be easily transported, and a flat stone could be found almost anywhere—to be discarded when camp was moved. This was not always, though, for there are hopper mortars with the basket securely cemented to the stone with pitch. A hopper is sometimes not recognized for the purpose it performed; it can be mistaken for a basket with the bottom broken out.

One of the more interesting traces of a vanished people is the bedrock mortar, of which a great number have been found in the range of the Desert Culture. There is at least one place where they are so large and plentiful that a farmer uses them for feeding his hogs, but it was necessary first to partially fill them with concrete to bring their capacity to a useful level. On an ancient terrace of Summer Lake there are several (see Figure 6). They are in forest and field, desert and mountain—artifacts that will be preserved for thousands of years unless they stand in the path of the bulldozer. However, the pestles, once so plentiful, have all disappeared.

The shaping of a mortar was a tedious but relatively simple process. It was formed by pecking, a method universally used in the shaping of stone. By continually striking the work piece with a harder stone, it is gradually worn away, each blow removing a few grains. The worker, though, must be careful not to strike hard enough to fracture the piece and lose his labor. Pestles were laid on a bed of sand or soil while being worked to help absorb the shock. After pecking the tool into the desired shape, a careful workman polished it with scoria, sandstone, or sand and water. The careless would leave it rough, eventually to develop a glistening polish from the clasp of a dusky hand.

While some of the Desert Culture mortars are exquisite specimens of symmetry and form, their pestles show no special care or elaborate decoration like the splendid examples from the coastal country of California. These latter are true works of art, formed and carved and polished with precision. Long ago the author saw an umbrella stand full of them at a curio shop, some of which were nearly four feet long. Their unbelievable length is illustrated by an experience of Dr. H. H. Stuart of Eureka. Digging on the beach with a friend, he uncovered a delicately carved stone zoomorphic head in the bank. While carefully removing the surrounding sand with brush and trowel, he was astounded to see it suddenly disappear down a hole—his friend in a nearby excavation had found the other end of a long pestle and jerked it out.

The two principal gathering crops of the western edge of the Desert Culture range were the acorn and the pine nut. Oak trees grow among the foothills of the Great Basin and for those within reach of the groves, acorns were an important food. To the west, they were the staple of the residents of the pleasant California valleys. Several varieties of oaks bear edible acorns. They were gathered and soaked in water overnight to split the shells, or were cracked with a stone. The kernels were then dried and ground into flour. In order to utilize acorns it is necessary first to remove the tannic acid. This was done by leaching, a tedious process for which the natives devised several ingenious methods. Basically the process was to allow water to flow through the meal until all the acid was removed; the difficulty was to make a sieve that would confine the flour. Baskets lined with various grasses and leaves were used, and structures hollowed in sand.

After removing the tannin the flour was dried, and if not eaten immediately, it was stored. Acorns, too, could be kept, even up to two or more years as insurance against a bad crop. The usual method of preparing the meal was to make it into a mush by stirring it in a basket with water, kept boiling by tossing in hot rocks. The porridge of acorn meal was stirred with a paddle. These paddles and lifting tongs for hot rocks, along with baskets, are occasionally found in caves. Leonard (Ewers 1959) desribes the method:

"Their food is composed principally of . . . acorns—the latter are very large and of good quality, which they manufacture into a kind of mush. Their method of manufacturing this is as follows:—They go to a large log and build a fire upon it and burn it half or two-thirds of the way through, which is done by keeping the log wet except about a foot in diameter, where the fire is kept up until the hole is deep enough, and of the proper shape. After the hole is burnt deep enough they extinguish the fire, scrape out the coals and ashes, and have a tolerably well shaped hopper. When this is done they get a long stone which is rounded at one end, and put the acorns in and commence mashing them fine, which is easily done as they are always previously dried by fire or the sun. The meal thus made is then taken out and mixed with water in a basket made almost water-tight—which they broil by making stones red hot and throwing them into the basket. By this process they made a kind of mush with which any hungry man would be glad to satiate his appetite."

All spring and summer the women gathered seeds and dug roots. Family groups were ever on the move, living from day to day on what they could find. How they must have anticipated the fall when the great crop of the year was ready, when they could meet old friends and make new ones as bands from far and near assembled to gather the rich pine-nut harvest! One aged lady who well remembered the time said, "When we come to the pine nut place we talk to the mountain, and ground and everything. We ask to feel good and strong. We ask for cool breezes to sleep at night. The pine nuts belong to the mountain, so we ask the mountain for some of its pine nuts to take home and eat."

Prior to the white invasion, the pinon pine (*Pinus monophylla*

Torrey) covered vast areas of the Upper Sonoran zone of the Great Basin. When the rich ore veins of the Comstock Lode and the many other mining districts were discovered and developed in the mid 1800's, the removal of thousands of acres of pine forests so incensed the natives that they were forced to battle for their existence—a vain fight by a people not addicted to warfare. The remains of huge charcoal ovens like those near Ely attest to the quantity of trees slashed down to make charcoal, essential to the smelting of the refractory ores. Whole mountains were stripped to obtain timbers to reinforce the endless tunnels following the rich veins of ore. The slaughter of the pines was as tragic to the people of the desert as was the slaughter of the buffalo to the people of the plains.

The pinon pine, however, was not a particularly dependable tree. Some years it bore an enormous crop and others it was practically bare; but in general there would be a good crop somewhere and that was where the harvesters would gather—no matter how many miles they would have to walk—carrying their meager possessions and their children on their backs. The men would shake down or knock off the cones from the stubby trees with a hooked pole, and the women and children would gather them into baskets to be carried to a central storage place. One of these hooked poles may be seen at the museum in Independence, California.

The cones were dried in the sun, or sometimes by means of fire, so they would open and allow the nuts to be beaten out. With the ever-present winnowing tray the plump kernels were separated from the dirt and chaff. When there was a good harvest the cones were stored in great piles for future use; the family groups might camp all winter in the vicinity of their food supply. Old photographs show the huge mounds of cones gathered to ward off the ever-present spectre of starvation. The nuts are so saturated with oil that they will not keep for more than about a year.

Pine nuts made a delicious and nutritious food. Fremont (1849) says, "A man was discovered running towards camp as we were about to start this morning . . . he brought with him, in a little skin bag, a few seeds of a pine tree, which today we saw for the first time. . . . We purchased all from him. The nut is oily, of a very agreeable flavor, and must be nutritious as it constitutes the principal subsistence of the tribes among which we are traveling." And again, "A party of twelve Indians came down from the mountains to trade pine nuts, of which each carried a little bag. These seemed now to be the staple of the country; and whenever we met an Indian, his friendly salutation consisted of offering a few nuts to eat and trade; their only arms were bows and flint-tipped arrows."

The only tool that was unique to the pine nut harvest was the hooked pole. This was a simple affair, a sapling cut so that one projecting limb could be lopped off for the hook, or perhaps a short section with a protruding limb was bound to the end of a pole. Figure 71 shows a hook found in a Nevada cave that has been dressed down and bent by steaming, or perhaps a sapling had been tied until it grew into a curve. It may have been lashed to a pole and used for the harvest, but more likely at one time the end made a complete circle and the instrument was used to stir mush made from milled nuts or seeds.

One of the methods of preparing pine nuts for food was to remove the hulls and grind the kernels into a meal for boiling. They also made a delicious and readily portable food with no other preparation than parching them. Pine nuts are still obtainable as a delicacy; but to us the nut is a novelty, whereas to the Desert Culture it was their very existence in those areas where the acorn did not grow.

The handsome horned muller, Figure 66, was essential for the preparation for the seed of *Nymphaea polysepala*, the yellow water lily called wokas by the Indians. A plentiful supply of this nutritious food was available to the people of the Klamath Lakes, an area that must be included in the Great Basin prehistoric culture.

Presumably wokas was a source of food for the residents of

the Great Basin wherever the pluvial lakes offered a suitable habitat for the plant, although the present writer has seen no statements to support this. The vigorous lilies once covered over 10,000 acres of the Klamath Marsh, growing so thickly they smothered all of the usual growth except a few inferior, low-growing species. So plentiful were the seeds that at one time consideration was given to harvesting them commercially for use as a breakfast food (Colville 1904).

Wokas was harvested with dugout canoes. While the vessel was propelled from the stern by poling, an Indian woman sat in the bow and plucked the seed pods as the slowly moving boat passed through the lush green jungle. The seeds were separated from the moist and sticky mass within the pods by two methods. Seeds which were so mature that they had split were kept separate while harvesting, then placed in a pit and allowed to ferment until the seeds could be reclaimed from the rubbish by washing. Pods not completely mature were cooked and then fermented in the same way as the mature pods, or dried and crushed so that the seeds could be winnowed from the chaff. The seeds were dried before storing; and when ready for use the kernels were removed from the hulls by cracking them with controlled, light strokes of the muller on a metate—this is where the horned muller was so useful. After the kernels were winnowed from the hulls and parched in a winnowing tray with live coals, they were ready to eat out of hand like popcorn—which they resemble in flavor—or ground into meal and made into a gruel.

22. Insect Food

Insects formed a small but important portion of the diet of the desert people, important because they offered a variety in the menu not less desirable to a primitive race than to ourselves, and because no food source could be overlooked. Perhaps essential minerals and vitamins were added to the diet, too. Our culture generally revolts at the use of insects for food, and relegates those who do to an inferior status in the same manner as any other native trait differing from our beliefs, yet edible insects may have cleaner habits and be as tasty as some delicacies considered by us a luxury; for instance the oyster.

One unreliable yet at times plentiful invertebrate food was the pupae of *Ephydra hians* and *E. subopaca,* small inoffensive insects commonly called shore flies. Their eggs are laid in salt lakes, and they hatch into larvae that thrive in a habitat so rigorous, so inhospitable that one is filled with wonder that it could be so. They occur in the warm, saline pools at Bad Water in Death Valley and in vast shoals in Great Salt Lake, that fragment of pluvial Lake Bonneville that is up to 28 per cent salt. The larvae, which feed on other organisms equally adapted to the stern environment, metamorphose into pupae which sometimes become the victims of storms that cast them upon the shore in layers that darken the sands. Larvae cases also drift into layers, as do some of the drowned flies, for they hatch in a manner that forms one of the mysteries of evolution—the adults emerge from the pupae under water and arise enclosed in a bubble of air, miniature balloons from which the navigator must immediately take wing as the bubble bursts on the surface—or be entrapped in the briny broth.

Stansbury (1852) says while exploring Great Salt Lake, "Small quantities of bitumen were found on the shore, in the masses of a substance which buried the beach to a depth of six inches, and resembled in appearance the brown, dried seaweed of the ocean. Under the glass, these masses were found to consist almost entirely of the larvae or dried skins of . . . insect[s], adhering together. They apparently had been driven on shore at different periods, some appearing fresher and of a different texture from others, the insects having been of a larger size. The question where these larvae originated presents a curious subject of inquiry. Nothing living has as yet been detected in the lake, and only a few large insects in the brackish springs, which do not at all resemble these remains either in shape or size. That they have existed in almost incredible numbers is evident, as the shores are lined with their skins, and the bottom, in many instances, for a long distance from the shores, is covered with them. This is especially the case in the north-east part of the lake, where they lie on the bottom a foot thick, mingled with the oozy mud, of which they form a large portion."

Leonard (Ewers 1959) writes in his journal, "In warm weather there is a fly, about the size and similar to a grain of wheat, on this lake, in great numbers. When the wind rolls the waters onto the shore, these flies are left on the beach—the female Indians then carefully gather them into baskets made of willow branches, and lay them exposed to the sun until they become perfectly dry, when they are laid away for winter provender. These flies, together with grass seed, and a few rabbits, is their principal food during the winter season."

Fremont also noticed these hardy insects—"Among the successive banks on the beach our attention had been attracted by one of 10 or 20 feet in breadth, of a dark colour. Being more closely examined, this was found to be composed, entirely of the skins of worms, about the size of a grain of oats, which had been washed up by the waters of the lake. . . . Attending to this subject some months afterward with Mr. Joseph Walker, an old hunter, I was informed by him, that, wandering with a party of men in the mountain country east of the Great California range, he surprised a party of several Indian families encamped near a small salt lake, who abandoned their lodges at his approach, leaving everything behind them. Being in a starving condition, they were delighted to find in the abandoned lodges a number of skin bags containing a quantity of what appeared to be fish, dried and pounded. On this they made a hearty supper: and were gathered around an abundant breakfast next morning, when Mr. Walker discovered that it was with these, or a similar worm, that the bags had been filled. The stomachs of the stout trappers were not proof against their prejudices, and the repulsive food was suddenly ejected."

Crickets and locusts were gathered in the early morning, picked like huckleberries from the bushes before the warm rays of the rising sun had released their benumbed bodies from the grip of the cold summer night. Foraging grasshoppers and Mormon crickets were herded with boughs in pits where they could be captured. The busy hands that gathered the hoppers tossed the helpless victims into baskets, then carried them to a pit previously prepared by building within it a hot fire. Over the glowing coals grass was laid and the insects were dumped in; then more grass was piled on and all was covered with earth. After a few hours of steaming the cooked insects were removed and dried in the sun. Considered a delicacy, they could be eaten at once like raisins, or ground into a meal on a metate for a soup that is said to taste as though it were made of dried meat.

Peter Skene Ogden, who spent many years in this inhospitable land, records in his journal written on his trip through the Great Basin in the winter of 1825-26, "on our travels this day we saw a Snake Indian and as it so happened his hut being near the Road curiosity induced me to enter I had often heard these wretches subsisted on ants, Locusts and small fish in size not larger than minnies and I was determined to find out if it was not an exaggeration of late travelers, but to my surprise I found it was the case, for one of their Dishes not of a small size was filled with ants and on enquiring in what manner they collected them in the morning early before the thaw commences the Locusts they collect in summer and store up for their winter, in eating they give the preference to the former being oily the latter not, on this food if such it may be called these poor wretches drag out an existance for nearly four months in the Year, they however so far as we can judge from appearances live contented and happy and this is all they require, it appeared rather strange and the only reason I can give for it is from the poverty of their food on which they subsist that few or no children among them, we have now seen upwards of 30 families and only three children among them so from this before many years not many will be living and ants and Locusts will again encrease" (Davies 1961).

Another source of protein, and one the natives considered a particular delicacy, was the larvae of the Pandora moth, *Coloradia pandora*. These fat caterpillars feed on the needles of yellow and Jeffrey pines and are a serious pest in several of the western states where they infest the host trees in great numbers. The Indians collected them by building a smokey fire under the trees, causing the caterpillars to drop to the ground. They were then picked up and dried, after which they were boiled into a sort of stew called pe-aggie by the Paiutes. The pupae of the Pandora moth were sometimes gathered and cooked by roasting.

23. Hunting

Most of the hunting practiced by the Desert Culture was for small game, chiefly rabbits; but deer, antelope, and mountain sheep were not neglected and of course were the most desired. In many of the hills and rocky canyons of the Great Basin there can yet be seen traces of these ancient hunters—temporary camp sites, many petroglyphs, and remnants of stone fences constructed to lead the larger game into the vicinity of blinds from which they were shot with arrows or darts. Brush fences were used also, although of course no archaeological trace remains. Simpson (1876) says, "I notice a couple of brush fences or barriers converging on a narrow pass, and a large hole in this last portion. Peter says they are to guide deer near the hole, in which the Indian hides himself, and shoots them as they pass with bows and arrows at night, a fire being used as a lure." Early sheepmen also constructed many stone fences and corrals and care must be taken that one of these is not mistaken for an aboriginal endeavor.

The mountain sheep was the most coveted prey, judging by the vast number of naturalistic and stylistic reproductions of this graceful animal decorating the rocks and cliffsides in their range, perhaps imprinted by shamans and hunters indulging in rites to assure a successful chase and an increase in the herds. Atlatls as well as hunters with bows and arrows are sometimes depicted with the sheep (see Figures 54 and 75). The greatest concentration of hunting petroglyphs in the Great Basin is in the Coso Range west of Death Valley, and there are also many leads, blinds, and occupied caves. On at least one of the steep mountains there are yet a few of the elusive sheep, remnants of the once-great bands.

While large game was the most desirable, the Desert Culture's greatest reliance on a source of meat and protein to supplant their diet of seeds and roots was placed upon the rabbit, that symbol of fertility that seems to have been created solely for the purpose of assuaging the hunger of man and beast. Few rabbits ever died a natural death; the end came with slashing fang or piercing arrow. Existence consisted of rapid reproduction, fleeting foraging, and constant vigilance against the inevitable instant of stark terror and torn flesh.

Both jackrabbits and cottontails in several species populate the Great Basin, but the former are more plentiful and in some years inhabit the sage in incredible numbers. Sometimes, driving along a desert road at night, on every side the jacks ride the headlight beams into the darkness like apparitions, or stand transfixed in the glare to test the driver's skill. In 1915, Harney County, Oregon, paid a five-cent bounty on 1,029,132 jackrabbits. They saved many an early homesteader and explorer from starvation. Geiger (1845), while traveling along the Humboldt River toward the California gold fields, said, "Almost every one came in camp at noon with a 'Jack Ass Rabbit.' These animals are at least four times as large as our own. They have ears in proportionate size of the Jack Ass. Some idea can be formed of the size when I tell you one of common size will make a full meal for a mess of six, & who are not bad feeders either, but are generally blessed with good appetites." Geiger was stretching it a bit; an ordinary jackrabbit will weigh five to seven pounds, much less when dressed. They were originally known as jackass rabbits because of their large ears; the word was contracted to jackrabbit about 1870.

Rabbits were tracked in the snow, stalked in the bushes, and throttled by snares in the path, but the greatest dependence was placed on mass destruction in a rabbit drive. Fremont (1849) records, ". . . they seemed to have no other subsistence than the roots or seeds they might have stored up, and the hares living in the sage, and which they are enabled to track through the snow, and are very skilled in killing." Powell (1961) describes a rabbit drive that he saw about 1870 ". . . the whole country abounds with rabbits, which are often killed with arrows and caught in snares. Every year they have great hunts, when scores of rabbits are killed in a single day. It is managed in this way: They make nets of the fiber of the wild flax and of some other plant, the meshes of which are about an inch across. These nets are about three and a half feet in width and hundreds of yards in length. They arrange such a net in a circle, not quite closed, supporting it by stakes and pinning the bottom to the ground. From the opening of the circle they extend net wings, expanding in a broad angle several hundred yards from either side. Then the entire tribe will beat up a great district of country and drive the rabbits toward the nets, and finally into the circular snare, which is quickly closed, and the rabbits killed with arrows." The early homesteaders and townspeople also conducted drives to lessen these denuders of the range. Some writers have described them as a most repulsive exhibition of the pure savagery of which humans are capable, even the little children shouting with excitement as they gleefully clubbed to death the entrapped, terrorized victims.

Fremont (1849) says, "We had scarcely lighted our fires, when the camp was crowded with nearly naked Indians; some of them were furnished with long nets in addition to bows, and appeared to have been out on the sage hills to hunt rabbits. These nets are perhaps 30 to 40 feet long, kept upright in the ground by slight stakes at intervals, and were made from a kind of wild hemp . . .". This statement indicates that rabbit nets were also used in individual efforts, placed across the trails or surrounding a thicket in which the animals were hidden.

The rabbit nets are an example of the technical ability with which the natives were endowed. They were made usually from Indian hemp, one of the finest, strongest, most silky of all fibers. It is the inner bark of the *Apocynum,* a dogbane, rolled into thread on the thigh and twisted into two- or three-strand line. Nets have been made for at least 2,000 years and possibly for 10,000, and many have been found in caves. The early explorers frequently comment on the quality and size of the nets. Escalante said in 1776, "This Indian whom the companions brought to camp was so terror-stricken that he seemed to be insane. He looked in every direction, watched everybody, and was excessively frightened by every action or movement on our part. He carried a net very well made of hemp, which he said he used to catch rabbits."

But rabbits were not the only small game that was hunted; practically everything that swam, flew, crawled, or ran was captured or shot or ambushed. Lizards were withdrawn from crevices in the rock with a stick that had fastened to one side on the end a sharp bone barb sloping backward. Fremont says, "Many of these Indians had long sticks, hooked at the end, which they use in hauling out lizards, and other small animals, from their holes." In the museum at Independence, California, one of these instruments is on display, along with many other tools of the Desert Culture. Gophers, mice, and squirrels were snared in their runways, flooded from their dens, crushed with deadfall, or withdrawn from their burrows by twisting a stick into their fur.

Along the Truckee River, Fremont saw where dams had been built to turn water into burrows to flush out the residents; and

Simpson describes a deadfall, "The rats are caught by a deadfall made as it ordinarily is for a trap, except that, instead of a piece of wood, a string is used, tied, and provided with a short button, which, being brought around the upright, is delicately held in position by a spear of dried grass or a delicate piece of wood, which pressing against the button, rests on the other end against the ground or stone. Traps like this are placed over the hole of the rats, and they, coming in contact with the long or lower piece of the figure 4, bring the stone upon them. They are also speared in their holes by a stick turned up slightly at the end and pointed, and with another, of a spade-form at the end, the earth is dug away until the animal is reached and possessed. The Go-shoots, as well as the Diggers, constantly carry about with them these instruments of death which, with the bow and arrow and net, constitute their chief means for the capture of game."

Waterfowl were important to the residents of the desert if they were fortunate enough to include a lake in their territory, and most of them did for the main geographical feature of the Great Basin is the system of escarpments and basins. Migrating ducks, geese, cranes and swans are yet a spectacular sight in this picturesque region, old-timers describing the blackening of the sky by the great flocks. In the Nevada State Museum is displayed a huge shotgun used to fire into flocks of ducks and geese resting on the lake or wheeling overhead; one shot would bring down dozens for markets in the gold-rush cities. In pluvial times there would have been many more permanent lakes for alighting waterfowl, and marshes in which they could nest. More than 20 different varieties were bagged by the stone-age hunters, as established by the bones found in caves.

There were several methods of exploiting this wildlife resource. Nesting birds could be taken, and eggs and young were considered fair game. Nets were set vertically in the water along the margins of lakes with the top slightly above the surface; the diving birds would become entangled in the mesh when they dove to escape the hunter, or in the search of food. The vast number of arrow and dart points found in the dry beds of the old lakes indicates that hunting was a primary method of obtaining waterfowl. A bird was not only food; its skin and feathers were useful for ceremonial clothing, ornaments and rites. From caves along the lake margins have come feather headdresses, plumes, tassels, bundles indicating a ceremonial use, and remnants of feather blankets.

One interesting method of hunting was to use an arrow with a blob of pitch encircling it a short distance back of the point, the pitch served as a hydrofoil causing the arrow to skip along the surface of the water into a flock of resting birds (Cressman 1962). The wide assortment of sizes and types of arrow and dart points blown out from the dried mud of the old lake bottoms shows the fallacy of the lore that the Indians had different size arrow points for each size game. They used whatever arrow or dart they had on hand when the game presented itself for a shot.

Decoys aided the hunt and their manufacture approached a form of art. Edward Kern in Simpson's report says, "They have some very pretty duck-decoys, made from the skin of these birds, neatly stretched over a bullrush float"; and Simpson records, "The Decoy-ducks they use on the lake to attract live ducks are perfect in form and fabric, and I have obtained a couple for the Smithsonian Institution." Figure 79 shows these very decoys obtained by Simpson, the top and bottom views illustrating both the neatness and method of construction. Duck decoys have been found in Lovelock, Ocala, and Humboldt Caves on Carson Sink and in caves about Pyramid Lake and in the Southwest, indicating that they were widely distributed. They make poor fossils even in a dry cave. The fill crushes the form and insects feast on the feathers; they are so dedraggled when lifted from the dust that they are barely recognizable.

Decoys were made from tule stems bound in bundles of two or three pieces each that were twisted and bent to assume the shape of a duck—an operation that took considerable skill and a good eye for form. Tail, neck, and head were shaped along with the body, and a skin from a duck was stretched over the form just as a taxidermist stretches a pelt over his plaster model. Sometimes, instead of using a complete duck skin, only a few feathers were glued on. The specimen from Humboldt Cave was made this way, but this was a slipshod method. Duck decoys are considered to have been used for at least 2,000 years.

24. Fishing

The Great Basin lakes were famous for the size and quality of their fish; and the quantity of net sinkers, hooks and other fishing equipment found on the shores and beds of the old lakes show that this resource of food was vigorously exploited. Large handmade copper lures with wire leaders capable of landing the 40-pound lake trout are sometimes picked up in the bottoms—lures lost by white fishermen supplying the early gold camps.

Many of the lakes are now gone, their source of water diverted into irrigation canals. The balance between supply and evaporation has been delicate since the pluvial, and beheading the inlet streams tipped the scales in favor of evaporation. Now vast playas have water in them only in the spring. We have sometimes marvelled at the depth of water in the remnants of the ancient lakes; it appears to be substantial but when the shore birds alight their toes project above the surface. So flat are these beds that such a nebulous film of water will cover acres. Not the least of the pleasant sights to be enjoyed in the desert are the antics of the birds on the shallows and nearby marshes; the redwinged blackbird with its beautiful trill, the yellowhead that with tremendous preparation and effort brings forth a feeble squawk, the avocet vaccuum-cleaning the mud, sandpipers balancing on their reflections.

Fremont in his journals writes: "Reaching the groves, we found the inlet of a large fresh water stream, and all at once were satis-

fied that it was neither Mary's River nor the waters of the
Sacramento, but that we had discovered a large interior lake
(Pyramid) which the Indians informed us had no outlet. It is
about 35 miles long, and by the mark of the water line along the
shores, the spring level is about 12 feet above the present waters.
The chief started talking in a loud voice as we approached; and
parties of Indians armed with bows and arrows issued from the
thickets. We selected a strong place for our encampment. The
village, a collection of straw huts, was a few hundred yards
higher up. An Indian brought a large fish to trade, which we
had the inexpressible satisfaction to find was a salmon trout; we
gathered around him eagerly. The Indians were amused at our
delight, and immediately brought in numbers, so that our camp
was soon stocked. Their flavor is excellent; superior, in fact, to
that of any fish I have ever known. They are of extraordinary
size, about as large as the Columbia River salmon, generally
from two to four feet in length. From the information of Mr.
Walker, who passed among some lakes lying to the eastward,
this fish is common to the streams of the inland lakes. He subse-
quently informed me he had obtained them weighing six pounds
when cleaned and the head taken off, which corresponds very
well with the size of those obtained at this place. They doubtless
formed the subsistence of these people, who hold the fishery in
exclusive possession."

Peter Skene Ogden, while in the Klamath country, wrote:
"Friday December 9th 1826. 1 otter from our Traps & 46 dogs
traded also some Carp, the longest of the kind I ever seen measuring 20 inches in length and six in breadth and at certain
seasons of the year are taken in numbers in the large Lakes
ahead of us the natives I am informed take them with nets made
of the inner rind of Furs and it is from the waters alone they
derive their support as for Roots those in this quarter do not
appear well stock'd from the information I have been enabled
to obtain I presume the Clammetter nation 350 men." There
were no carp in those days; what they bought was one of the

suckers that abounded in the streams and lakes. The "inner rind of the Furs" would have been the inner bark of the cedar, a material widely used for the manufacture of the more coarse cordage; but not nets, which were made from *Apocynum.*

Zenas Leonard passed through the Owens River Valley in the Great Basin with Joseph Walker's exploring party in 1833 and describes the native method of fishing: "They subsist upon grass-seed, frogs, fish, &c.–Fish, however are very scarce–their manner of catching them is somewhat novel and singular. They take the leg-bone of a sand-hill crane, which is about eighteen inches long, this is fastened in the end of a pole–they then, by means of a raft made of rushes, which are very plenty–float along the surface of these lakes and spear the fish. They exhibit great dexterity with this simple structure–sometimes killing fish with it at a great distance. They also have a kind of hook by which they sometimes are very successful, but it does not afford them as much sport as the spear. This hook is formed of a small bone, ground down on a sand-stone and a double-beard (barb) cut in it with a flint–they then have a line made of wild flax, this line is tied nearest the beard end of the hook, by pulling the line–the sharp end with the beard, catches, and turns the bone crossways in its mouth."

Figure 80 shows types of Great Basin fishhooks and fish lines found in Humboldt Cave. The photograph was furnished through the courtesy of Dr. Robert F. Heizer who, with Dr. Alex D. Krieger, excavated the cave. In the top left is a composite hook showing how the bone points illustrated in Figure 83 were used. The beveled side of the point is laid against a formed wood shank and securely bound together with cord set in pitch. The three hooks on the right use barbed points and the shank has a bevel groove to seat the point. They are also bound together with pitch and string. The bone points are about two inches long. These would have been used for the large lake trout and the materials needed to be not only strong but securely made or the heavy fish would escape. In one cache in Humboldt Cave, seven of these assembled hooks were found, and one point without shank. *Apocynum* cord was used for line and binding on all fishhooks.

Lower left of Figure 80 shows a set line that when untangled was found to be 120 feet long and had 183 hooks attached at regular intervals of eight inches, with leaders 2.5 inches long. The hooks were distributed over the full length of the line. The bone points are unbarbed, sharp, and ground from a bird bone splinter about half an inch long. The same type hook was found in Lovelock Cave and described by Loud: "A twig of tough wood, 2 mm in diameter, is split in half and folded over the blunt end of the bone. The extremities of the twig are brought together, pinching between them a cord. The cord then spirals about the two halves of the twig, securely binding them to the bone by several half hitches." The wrapping line extends out and becomes the leader.

See the detail of this type of hook in Figure 82—a line found by Mr. and Mrs. George Luke while looking through a Nevada cave. It has never been unwound. The string looks as strong and the hooks as bright as when they were first made, perhaps centuries ago. The inventor must have been endowed with extraordinary perception to design such an ingenious instrument for we still cannot visualize how it would possibly catch and hold a fish. These lines were probably baited and staked out in the water, then occasionally visited to remove the catch.

The use of fishing nets and canoes presupposes the use of net weights and canoe anchors and indeed they were used. Many have been found on the margins of the fossil lakes, now dry playas, playgrounds for the dust devils. On the shores of variable level lakes such as Pyramid they still show up occasionally as the waves wash them out of the deposits or receding water exposes them. These net weights and canoe anchors were perhaps lost in a sudden storm, or by a fisherman who failed to pay proper attention to his knots.

Along the Northwest Coast, net floats are eagerly sought by

a growing group of collectors—floats that leisurely ride the Japanese Current across the Pacific only to be thrown unceremoniously ashore by the storm-tossed waters. Amos Wood, in his *Beachcombing for Japanese Glass Floats,* tells about them and where to find them. But, as to what sort of floats the Desert Culture used to hold their nets, the archaeological record gives no clue. They would have been simple, a piece of driftwood perhaps, or a bundle of tule; perishable material that left no trace. The ropes used to bind them and the sinkers to the nets, though, do occasionally appear in the mud along the shore, preserved by continual immersion since the day they were cast adrift.

The net weights were manufactured from sterner stuff, made in a variety of forms that fall into four classes: the perforated, notched, banded, and bi-pointed. Very little work was required to peck out a notch on a piece of rock sufficiently outlined to hold the tie to the net, and there are plenty of rocks that would serve with no alteration. But like the modern fisherman, the Stone Age fisherman had to have the best equipment. Beautifully made sinkers were sculptured from such refractory material as limestone, dolomite, and basalt. Perhaps the primitive mind rationalized that the fish would not be reluctant to sacrifice himself to such a pleasing image, or at least its spirit would be placated and the species increase; there is plenty of ethnographic evidence of such beliefs, especially in connection with whaling and the buffalo hunt.

Most sinkers are grooved or bi-pointed and weigh less than a pound. Nets used in the quiet lake do not require such heavy weights as those in swift waters such as the Columbia River where, not many years ago, banded sinkers weighing one to three pounds could be picked up by the dozen along the banks. Perforated sinkers, too, were heavy and sometimes found in caches of half a dozen up to 40 or more in the old village sites along the lower Columbia, where the ancient fishermen buried them at the end of the fishing season.

Figure 84 shows some typical net weights found in the Great Basin. The perforated sinkers were made from a flat pebble by pecking a hole through it either at one end or in the middle; the pecking was done from each side so that the hole is tapered toward the center. Occasionally one is found broken in half with the hole only partly finished—fractured in the process of manufacture. Sometimes the stone was trimmed or reworked to give it a more pleasing form or possibly to make it lighter. Perforated net weights would have been more easily attached to the net than the banded.

Grooved sinkers are found in two forms, the notched and the banded; the difference is probably academic because on the notched sinker the groove is on the end, but on the banded it is in the center. The groove, like the hole in the perforated weights, was made by pecking. One should be careful not to file all grooved stones under the sinker label, though; they may have been atlatl weights, bolo stones, fetishes, pendants, or club heads. Their use must be judged from the general form and workmanship as well as the particular site where the piece was found.

Canoe anchors were also banded and may weigh 15 pounds or more but usually they are smaller. Along the Columbia River they were used to moor away from shore to avoid damage to the frail craft from beating on the beach; it is assumed the desert anchors were used in the same way on the ancient Basin lakes. A tule raft could easily be run up on the shore and is not susceptible to damage. The presence of anchors indicates the use of dugouts. A carefully made anchor (the size of a football) from Tule Lake is shown in Figure 85. The groove was pecked and then the surface away from it relieved so there is an even ridge all around the rock on each side of the groove, like miniature mountains flanking a Lilliputian valley.

The use of the bi-pointed stones shown in Figure 84 has been somewhat conjectural. Originally they were considered to be gambling stones, but now are believed to be sinkers because of recent finds in the vicinity of Pyramid Lake. Great numbers of them are found on the old fishing sites. They occur only in the vicinity of lakes and streams. Mr. and Mrs. Leroy Gienger of Chiloquin, Oregon, avid searchers for traces of Early Man in the desert, said that they once found five of these objects lying neatly spaced in a circle, eroded from the sandy beach of Clear Lake as though they had been left from a net lost there and long since decayed away.

The Southwest Museum has a different version of their use. In a display showing the manufacture of rings and hooks from abalone shells, they state that these bi-pointed stones were used to ream the hole to size after drilling; some of the stones are shown with shells in different stages of the process. The present writer has never seen any with marks showing they were reamers in any of the collections examined, but they would have been an ideal instrument. West (1934) shows similar objects made by the Northern California Indians from sand cemented with lime. They were bound to a drill shaft and used to ream pipe bowls. In the Great Basin there are far too many bi-pointed stones to consider that they were used as reamers only. Those found in the Great Basin are now called sinkers (Tuohy 1968). Just how they were fastened to the net is unknown.

Another type of stone net weight occasionally found in the desert, at least in the Northern part, is a flat slab of lava or sedimentary rock about one-quarter to one-half inch thick, two wide and three long, with considerable variation in these dimensions (see Figure 86). They are percussion chipped into a rectangular form, and sometimes have a light notch pecked out on the edges. Personal experience indicates that they are found in piles of two or three or perhaps a dozen, seldom singly.

Dr. Douglas Osborne (1957) illustrates similar artifacts; in the section, "Net Sinkers," he says: "Under this heading are two types. One is the usual 2- or 4-notched flat cobble sinker so common on the Pacific Coast. The second is a type which, to my knowledge, has not appeared previously in the literature. It is not possible to be wholly certain that it is a sinker, but this seems the most reasonable assumption. They are rather like chipped geological specimens. Local collectors call them fish scalers, whether from accurate information or not has not been ascertained. . . . Twenty-four specimens were found. They are the typical flat cobbles of the beach that have been chipped and battered into roughly rectangular shape. The chipped edges may extend around the whole piece or, and usually, one or both ends retain partly the unchipped surface. Usually the edges have been battered until thoroughly dulled. In only a few specimens do the edges appear to be as sharp as those of the choppers. This is one of the facts that has led to the belief that they are not chopping or scraping tools."

These sinkers were made like those from the desert except from washed river cobbles or shingle instead of flat rock. Perhaps they represent the work of a resident of the desert who migrated to the river and refused to give up his traditional method of shaping net weights. Typical Desert Culture artifacts are sometimes found along the Columbia River, indicating that the desert people visited that river for its plentiful supply of salmon.

25. Shelter

A wandering people cannot have permanent housing as can those fortunate tribes that populated Western California and the Northwest Coast, with its rich natural heritage. Nor can they, without beasts of burden, transport the material for even temporary shelter. What protection from the elements they get must be constructed from the material on hand, and there was only the juniper and the sagebrush. Fremont (1849) says, "Riding quietly along over the snow, we came suddenly upon smokes rising among the bushes; and, galloping up, we found two huts, open at the top, and loosely built of sage, which appeared to have been deserted on the instant; and, looking hastily around, we saw several Indians on the crest of the ridge near by, and several others scrambling up the side. We had come upon them so suddenly, they had wellnigh been surprised in their lodges. A sage fire was burning in the middle; a few baskets made of straw were lying about, with one or two rabbit skins; and there was a little grass scattered around, on which they had been lying. Eight or ten appeared to live together, under the same shelter; and they seemed to have no other subsistence than the roots or seeds they might have stored up, and the hares which live in the sage." Later Fremont writes, "Where we camped on the black, sandy plain, the Indians had made circular enclosures, about four feet high and 12 broad, of artemisia bushes."

Such was the summer and winter habitation of many of the tribes of the Desert Culture when on the move, a simple wind-break of sage with no roof overhead. Fortunately for archaeology, however, caves were inhabited whenever they were convenient to the food routes. Without the screenings from the rubbish of these natural shelters our knowledge of the desert people would be poor indeed. No characteristic of the ancient people is more appreciated by the archaeologist than their untidy habits. A permanent winter habitation of substantial construction was utilized in more friendly areas where a sufficient supply of food could be laid by for the winter; yet for many of the desert people there was no home but a sagebrush windbreak. Even for the fortunate residents of winter villages there were hunts and intertribal visits and excursions for salt or obsidian when temporary shelters must be built. Sometimes the brush lodge was covered with tule matting, a tremendous improvement; but it was impossible to carry and was confined to areas where the mats could be stored and reused, such as a village site. The tule mat house was well established on the Columbia Plateau. The mats were rolled up and cached whenever the lodge was unoccupied, but the stick frame was left standing. Rolls of matting were laid away in the campgrounds at the close of the season, and traces of them are sometimes uncovered while excavating the old habitation sites.

The winter house, when used, was sometimes earth covered. A pit was dug from two to four feet deep, perhaps as much as six feet, and ten or so in diameter. In the pit, four posts were erected to support poles over which rafters were placed, then brush or grass, and finally the whole was covered with earth. The apex was left open for an entrance and smoke hole. Pit houses looked like enlarged mole hills; they were seen and described by many of the early desert travelers. The odor in one of these tight, warm, crowded lodges was a solid wall to repel the white invader; had it been visible like smoke, no ray of light could have penetrated.

Lieutenant Williamson, while surveying for a railroad in 1854-55, passed a Klamath village and noted: "We soon reached a collection of Indian huts built near the edge of the water but recently deserted. Large quantities of food, consisting mostly of seeds of plants and dried fish, several canoes made of hollowed logs, many baskets formed of reeds curiously woven together, and other valuables, were scattered around in wild confusion. The fires were burning in front of the huts, of which there were three distinct kinds. The summer lodges had vertical walls supporting flat roofs. They were composed of a framework of sticks, covered with a matting of woven tule. The winter huts were shaped like beehives and made of sticks plastered with mud. We noticed only one of the third kind, which was apparently used for a council house. A hole, about four feet deep and ten feet square, had been excavated, and the earth heaped up around the sides. Large sticks planted in this mud wall supported a roof made of cross poles covered with earth. The entrance was a flight of mud steps that conducted to the roof, from which a rude ladder led through a hole to the floor below." The Klamath were fortunate in that they did not have to wander so much to find subsistence as the other people of the Desert Culture.

Peter Skene Ogden, in the winter of 1826-27, after an especially trying day in the vicinity of Malheur Lake in the Northern Great Basin, observed the desert people in their winter habitations: "Thursday 2nd November 1826 . . . it is almost incredible the number of Indians in this quarter we cannot go ten yards in any direction without finding their Huts generally made of wormwood or grass and of a size to contain from 6 to eight persons and I am fully of opinion there is no Indian Nation so numerous as they are in all North America—in this alone I include the upper and lower Snakes—the latter are as yet as wild as the animals of the plains and so far have not acquired any information or knowledge from Indian Traders and in their present stage of ignorance would be fit subjects for the Missionary Society who could bend, twist and turn them in any form they pleased . . . they informed us from the severity of the weather last year they were extremely reduced for want of food . . . miserable unfortunate creatures to what sufferings and cruel privations are you not doom'd to endure but the allmighty has so ordained it what an example is this for us, when we are as at present without Beaver and reduced to one meal a day how loudly and grieviously do we complain, but in truth how unjustly and without cause when I consider the Snakes sufferings compared to ours many a day do they pass without food and still without complaint or murmer and in this wretched manner do they pass their *lives*."

Escalante says: "Their habitations are chozas or little huts of willow, of which they also make nice baskets and other necessary utensils" (Bolton 1950). These little huts offered no protection except from the wind and sun, a service they performed very efficiently if well constructed. In the desert and along the river my wife and I have sought shelter from many a wintry blast behind rocks, beneath and behind cliffs, and in the hollows, but to no avail—having encountered only gusts and eddies more uncomfortable than the wind itself.

However, in the lee of a willow grove or juniper thicket there is shelter; the wind is neither deflected nor directed but entrapped and lost in the branches, reduced to a gentle breeze by friction. Many of those little huts were reinforced with a semi-circle of stones around the base. These incomplete rings are encountered by the thousands scattered over the Great Basin. Today's traveler, driving through, snug in an air-conditioned jeep with provisioned ice box and a comfortable motel within easy driving distance, is in marked contrast to early desert travelers—a contrast almost too great for the imagination to grasp.

26. Clothing

"In the matter of dress they are very poor. The most decent clothing they wear is a buckskin jacket and long leggings made from the same material. These Indian women were so poorly dressed that they wore only some pieces of buckskin hanging from their waists, which hardly covered what cannot be looked upon without peril." So wrote Fray Silvestre Velez de Escalante in 1776 of the Indians in the vicinity of Utah Lake. Never could men of the cloth, nor most explorers, realize that to the natives of the Great Basin, clothes were an unnecessary burden, worn only for ceremonial or decorative reasons, or during the severest weather and sometimes not even then. Leggings and jackets, when worn, were as much for protection from the sharp, grasping twigs and thorns as from the weather. Their bodies were inured to the cold, their feet hardened almost like hoofs. Lewis and Clark tell with chagrin about issuing an extra garment to the men for protection from the approaching winter's chill, and immediately thereafter meeting a war party clad only in breechclouts.

Paul Kane, in *Wanderings of an Artist,* records meeting Indians traveling on the ice and snow barefoot—"and when they sit down to rest they put them (moccasins) on and wrap their feet in furs." The white men in those rugged times were also considerably inured to the cold. The same Paul Kane fell through the ice "about noon. Luckily I got out easily enough, but I was wet through . . . I pushed on in my wet clothes . . . the freezing of my leathern trousers made me very uncomfortable. We encamped after a hard day's work."

Early explorers comment on the miserable appearance of the natives of the Great Basin. Well clad, generally in government-issue clothing, well mounted, with an entourage of packers and pack animals numbering in the hundreds, and laden with tents, blankets, food and drink—it is no wonder that the travelers considered the naked savages to be miserable. Simpson (1876) says: "We have today seen a number of Go-shoot Indians. They are most wretched looking creatures, certainly the most wretched I have ever seen, and I have seen great numbers in various portions of the country. Both men and women wear a cape made of strips of rabbit skins, twisted and dried, and then tied together with strings, and drawn around the neck by a cord. The cape extends just below the hip, and is scant protection to the body. They seldom wear leggings or moccasins, and the women appear not to be conscious of any impropriety in exposing their person down to the waist. Children at the breast are perfectly naked, and this at a time when overcoats were required by us."

And Fremont (1849) records: "The Indians had only the usual scanty covering, and appeared to suffer greatly from the cold. All left us except our guide. Half hidden by the storm, the mountains looked deary; and, as night began to approach, the guide showed great reluctance to go forward. I placed him between two rifles, for the way began to be difficult. Traveling a little further we struck a ravine, which the Indians said would conduct us to the river; and as the poor fellow suffered greatly, shivering in the snow which fell on his naked skin, I would not detain him any longer; and he ran off to the mountain, where he said there was a hut nearby. He had kept the blue and scarlet cloth I had given him tightly rolled up, preferring rather to endure the cold than to get it wet." And again Simpson tells us, "Quite a heavy shower of rain has been falling, but, although it came down cold and chilly, these Indians seemed to take it as if it was not an extraordinary experience."

Clothing is one of the least essential of human requirements, except in the severest weather such as that experienced by the Eskimo, most skilled of all native tailors. Human beings existed for many thousands of years before they had even a fire to soften their existence. The first evidence of the use of fire appears in caves in China, evidence that has been geologically dated at about 250,000 years ago. Clothing probably came much later; it never arrived for some people. Many natives live out their lives with little or no clothing or shelter, even those at the tip of South America where the weather is far from favorable.

The lack of clothing cannot be attributed to lack of ability to prepare it but simply to the fact that it was neither needed nor desired. The want of proper materials would have discouraged the development of clothing—buckskin trousers and a jacket of sagebrush bark add little to human comfort. The eagerness of the tribes to acquire manufactured clothing at the time of the white invasion was due to decorative appeal and gain of prestige —not for protection from the elements. The Indians were willing to let those have clothes who could least support the want of them.

Archaeological evidence of the existence of clothing must rest to a great extent upon bone implements used for sewing and a few materials and fabrics found in caves. Most of the perishable materials long ago vanished. In White Dog Cave, Guernsey (1921) recovered aprons, one of which was made from strings of Indian hemp (*apocynum*) looped over a belt of human hair. It was about twelve inches long and a little less in width. Another was made from yucca fiber twisted into cord. In a cave near Fort Rock a buckskin breechclout was found, and there is scattered evidence elsewhere. From the archaeological and ethnological record it is evident that clothing styles did not change significantly, if at all, for thousands of years: for the men of the desert culture, the usual clothing was not a stitch, for the women a short apron.

In the winter a robe made from rabbit skins, or more rarely from the skins of mud hens, was worn to ward off the cold; and a tule cape or animal pelt sufficed to turn the rain. However, none of these were habitually worn. By far the most common garment was the rabbit-skin robe, a covering with the properties of the most expensive sleeping bag. In fact, rabbit skins are still used and enjoy some favor with mountain climbers and arctic explorers as a light, warm sleeping cover.

Rabbit-skin robes are frequently mentioned in the journals of the early explorers of the Great Basin. Daniel Potts, while on the Sevier River, wrote: "This river is inhabited by a numerous tribe of miserable Indians. Their clothing consists of a breech-cloth of goat or deer skin, and a robe of rabbit skins, cut in strips, sewed together after the manner of rag carpets, with the bark of milkweed twisted into twine for the chain. They call themselves Pie-Utaws." These "miserable Indians" were clever enough to ambush and slay the Gunnison exploring party near Sevier Lake in 1853.

Peter Skene Ogden says, "They had all Blankets made from Feathers and from a distance had rather a strange appearance, they are certainly entitled to some credit in devising such warm clothing."

To make a robe, the rabbit skins were cut spirally into long strips about an inch wide with a stone knife held in the teeth (Price 1962). The strips were wound, with the fur out, around twine usually made from sagebrush bark. The ends of the strips were lapped, sewn, or tied. A rectangular frame about four feet by five was constructed and the prepared strip — now many feet long — threaded back and forth between two sides of the frame as the warp. Two weft strings were used, crossing at each warp strand. The weft was made from sagebrush bark or—for an especially fine robe— from *Apocynum*. Smaller blankets were made for infants' cradles. The weaving was always done by the men.

Rabbit-skin robes were excellent garments but too fragile to wear on the hunt, and they were useless in the rain. They served as a cover while sleeping but were never slept on; a bed of grass or perhaps a mat or animal skin was the mattress. The robes were worn while idling in camp in the winter; and because they were donned even in summer for meeting important visitors, were considered a mark of prestige. Perhaps this use was more important to the primitive owner than protection from the weather. Simpson says, "They wear their rabbit-skin capes summer and winter, and on such a hot day as this I would suppose the warmth of it would be insupportable." The robes were a favorite mortuary offering and a number of them have been recovered in archaeological excavations, although in a fragmentary condition.

The aboriginal protective covering that is best known to the public is the sandal because of the widespread publicity given to its scientifically important discovery and dating by Cressman. No less than 75 complete or incomplete specimens were uncovered in an ancient cobble shop in Fort Rock Cave, and perhaps as many more have been unearthed by amateurs. The sandals were among the first archaeological specimens tested by the newly discovered Carbon 14 method, and the date is still one of the few determined from an actual artifact. The world was astonished at the antiquity of this footgear of a people who inhabited Fort Rock Valley at least 9,000 years ago. They were living there when one of the greatest of the volcanic eruptions occurred, the explosion that transformed Mt. Mazama into Crater Lake. The mountain top vanished in an instant, releasing several cubic miles of hot ashes to scorch the countryside to a cinder.

Sagebrush as a material for sandals seems to be peculiar to the Fort Rock area as far as archaeological findings are concerned; elsewhere they were made from tule. Fremont (1849) says of the Klamath, "Their shoes were made of straw or grass, which seemed well adapted to a snowy country." Ray (1963) says that the Paiutes of Northern California made sandals from both tule and sagebrush; the former would last 10 to 20 days of ordinary wear, the sagebrush bark much longer, but tule was preferred because it was so much easier to prepare and weave. These fiber moccasins were worn in winter as a protection from the cold and were lined with grass or fur. Because such fragile footwear would last no longer than a cheap tire on the sharp rocks of the desert, they were not used for traveling. Even leather moccasins had but a short life. Lewis and Clark made 358 pair of "mockersons" during the winter at Fort Clatsop in preparation for the return journey. Pitch was sometimes smeared on the bottom of the bare feet as a protection (Malouf 1964).

27. Fire

Few things are as cheerful on a winter evening as an open fire in the living room. Even a false blaze like that of an electric or gas log dispenses a considerable degree of comfort. Imagine, then, what the warming flame must have meant to the primitive dweller in a dark and chilled cave or brush shelter. Without matches or an electric starter, they kindled their fires by means of friction. Some long-forgotten aboriginal engineer discovered and perfected this simple mechanical process. No monument honors that ancient scientist, but surely his contribution must be included with the atlatl as two of the greatest inventions of all time.

There are several methods of starting a fire with the heat generated by friction; they differ only in application, not in principle. The tools used in the Great Basin were the fire drill and hearth. Simpson (1876) records: "He had with him his appliances for making fire. They consisted simply of a piece of greasewood, about two feet long, and of the size or smaller than your little finger in cross-section. This was rounded at the butt. Then a second piece of the same kind of wood, six inches long by one broad by one-half thick. This second piece had a number of semi-spherical cavities on one of its faces. With this piece laid on the ground, the cavities uppermost, he placed the other stick between the palms of his hands and with one end of the latter in a cavity, and holding the stick in a vertical position, he would roll it rapidly forward and back, till the friction would cause the tinder, which he had placed against the foot of the stick in the cavity, to ignite. In this way I saw him produce fire in a few seconds."

Bruff, along the Humboldt River in 1849, also described the art of making fire: "The fire sticks, are 2, in number,—one about 10 ins: long, and one ¾ in: square, drilled full of conical holes, about ¼ in: in diameter and depth. The other stick is about 18 ins: long, cylindrical, ¾ in: diameter, and pointed at each end. These they carry in their quivers, I saw several, on the route. To produce fire, the Indian lays down the square stick, holding it with his feet, inserts the end of the round stick, in one of the conical holes, drops in a few grains of fine sand, and some crumbs of dry rotten wood, then rapidly whirls the cylinderical stick around, with his hands, by rolling it with the palms, and then applies the wisp of dry straw, and in a few seconds has a blaze."

Lieutenant Henry Abbot, while investigating possible railroad routes to the West in the early 1850's, saw fire being made: "Several Indians came into camp in the afternoon, and I saw one of them kindle a fire by rubbing two pieces of wood together. A block of cedar, about six inches square and one inch thick, perforated with a small hole, formed the lower piece. One Indian held this firmly on a horizontal rock, having placed a little tinder under the hole. A second took a round stick, apparently of elder, about six inches long and a quarter of an inch in diameter, and, inserting one end in the hole, rolled it very rapidly between the palms of his hands. In a few moments sparks of fire fell down upon the tinder and ignited it."

Figure 92 shows one of these hearths and the drill point, found in a Nevada cave. The point is made to be inserted into the end of a cane; this method was sometimes used instead of making the drill in one piece. Heizer (1956) says: "It is surprising to find so many hearths, with almost no fire drills. There were eleven hearths [in Humboldt Cave], made of various materials: cottonwood (5), willow (3), sagebrush (2) and split and bound cattail rush (1)." Only one solid fire-drill stick was found. Perhaps the point type was used; the points would easily become lost in the debris. Of "Danger Cave" Jennings says: "The fire drills themselves were evidently of compound construction. At least the only presumed fire drill tip is a charred cone of rabbit brush with a spirally rasped point which resembles the roughened tip of the dart foreshafts and was presumably set in a hollow cane drill shaft." Cressman (1942) found both simple and compound fire drills in Catlow, Paisley, and Roaring Springs caves in the Northern Great Basin. The compound was the more plentiful. There were 13 of the foreshafts found and two of the one piece or simple type. Perhaps the point type was the more popular because the hearth, which was a valuable instrument, and a point would be much easier to carry than would a hearth and a two-foot drill shaft. Or perhaps it was found that a certain wood that could not be found in long straight pieces was more efficient in starting a glowing spark.

Some materials are better than others for creating fire, for not only must the heat of friction be sufficient to reach the kindling point but a bit of wood dust be generated at the same time to start the glow. A small amount of dry, shredded sage bark or similar tinder, sometimes carried along with the hearth in a pouch, was placed alongside the hearth at the end of the small notch in the drill hole (the hole is always placed close to the edge of the hearth as shown in the picture). The rapid twirling of the drill ground out a little dust that dribbled onto the tinder through the channel, and when enough heat had been generated the dust started to smoke, then burn, and the tinder caught fire. As soon as there was a glowing spark in the tinder, twirling was stopped and by gentle blowing the spark was coaxed into a flame, and soon the camp was cherry with the fire. The fire-maker's hands, rapidly spinning the drill back and forth, gradually descended to the bottom of the shaft from the downward pressure, but by a quick movement were shifted to the top with barely a pause in the rotation. A bit of sand was sometimes used to increase the friction and generate more wood dust.

The ease of kindling a fire with the drill depended to a great extent on the weather. If the humidity was low and dry tinder available, a fire could be kindled with ease by the "Boy Scout" method. But if everything was damp it was practically impossible to start a fire. The white pioneers were not so restricted; with flint and steel and gunpowder they could start a blaze under very adverse conditions. The Indians, whenever possible, carried fire with them. There are a number of materials that will smoulder for hours, notably pulverized, rotten wood. Only one family of a group needed to carry the fire, but ethnological reports indicate that anyone who had to borrow fire in order to make camp was considered just a bit of a bore. Some insist that the large tubes such as that shown in Figure 102 were used to carry fire—and they would have served admirably for the purpose, but Ruth and I have not seen any evidence either archaeological or ethnological to support this contention.

28. Personal Adornment

From earliest times, the urge to decorate their persons has been indulged in by the natives. In the Lindenmeier site of the Folsom people were found ornaments and paint. Perhaps the first and certainly the most consistently used bauble for beautification was the bead. These are found all over the world in archaeological sites—beads made from a wide variety of materials ranging from a simple, notched bird bone through decorations of shell, wood, seeds, ground stone, and the precious metals. In the desert, bone tube beads are found; stone rarely. One of the favorite materials from which to fashion beads was shell, obtained by trade from the Pacific Coast. In 1776, Fr. Francisco Garces tells in his journal of meeting Mojave Indians in the desert on their way from the coast with a load of shells. They carried neither food nor water on the four-day journey so they could bring back more of the precious shells.

The large, thick shell beads were made from the Pismo clam, *Tivella stoltorum*, found off the coast of California. The prehistoric method of manufacture was to break the shell into pieces, drill them, then dress the edges down with an abrasive stone while the beads were strung on a stick. It took about half an hour to make one bead. Later they were made by white men with machinery. An old bead will have a hole tapering toward the center from each side, whereas a machine-made bead will have a cylindrical hole all the way through. Small, thin disc beads were made from the shell of the Washington clam, *Saxidomus nuttalli*. The small cup-shaped beads are shown on the string in the upper right of Figure 93 are from the "saddle" of the Olivella shell.

A popular bead was made from the Olivella shell with no other preparation than grinding off the apex so that a string could be passed through. Sometimes these beads were decorated with incised designs, as shown in Figure 93. There are two sizes of Olivella. The large shell is *Olivella biplicata*, which grows all along the Pacific Coast, and the small shell is *O. batica*, which occurs from Point Conception on the California Coast to the Gulf of California. Olivella shell beads are widely distributed over the desert and are found both on the surface and in caves. One from Danger Cave was in a layer dated possibly 8,000 years ago. In Cougar Mountain Cave they were only in the upper layers.

The Abalone (*Abalone haliotis*) was a very popular shell because of its pearly luster. It was cut into a variety of ornaments that must have been dear to the primitive heart—glittering bits of iridescence to be treasured and enjoyed. Another popular shell was the Glycymeris, a small clam-like shell from the Gulf of

California. It was made into beads by drilling a hole near the apex. All shell beads and bangles weather and deteriorate rapidly, especially if the soil is acid. In clean, dry sand they will retain their luster and hardness for many decades.

A very rare bead in the desert is Dentalium, a thin, tubular marine shell averaging a little over one inch in length; it appears in the upper left in Figure 93. The Dentalium comes from the vicinity of Vancouver Island, although it occurs off the coast of California, but only in deep water. The North Coast Indians gathered the shell by lowering into the water a long pole with a number of sharp splints projecting from the end. If the fisherman was lucky, one or two splints might penetrate the upright growing mollusks and bring them to the surface.

This shell was the standard of value, used for money up and down the coast. The very long ones, about 2.5 inches or more in length, were extremely valuable. An instance has been recorded where one was refused in exchange for a gun. The very short ones, an inch or less, were of low enough price so that they could be used for beads. They, like the Olivella, were sometimes decorated with incised lines, red feathers, and snakeskin. Ornaments and bangles were made from the abalone shell and beads from clam shells. The latter were used for money more than the Dentalium in the interior regions. Shell beads and pendants, though widely distributed, are far from plentiful, as could be expected in a culture lacking material wealth.

Other materials beside expensive imported shells were used by the ingenious natives to fashion into ornaments. One of the simplest was the pine nut. Great numbers were used in the manufacture of beads not only in the Great Basin but wherever the pinion grew. Carbonized by the heat of cremation fires, they will be preserved for centuries. Pits of fruit such as the wild plum were used, as well as other seeds. A variety of the freshwater clam is found in most of the permanent Basin streams. Although the shell is fragile it can be cut into bangles. Bone beads were not difficult to make and were considered quite handsome, they have been found in all stages of manufacture (Cressman 1942, Fig. 65). Selenite crystals were perforated and worn (Harrington 1933), and even chipped stone was used for decoration (see Figure 21). Stone beads are rare in the Basin although plentiful in many other areas. They require much tedious labor to fashion, and a supply of workable material such as steatite. The stone may have been available to the Desert Culture—but not the leisure for working it.

Figure 94 "A" shows a bangle about 2.25 inches in diameter found on a Nevada desert by Gene Favell. It is made from one of the serpentines, and has a hole for suspension. Stone rings used for pendants also come from the Columbia River but they do not have suspension holes; the thong was passed through the center or in a groove inscribed around the circumference. Plain stone pendants are shown in "D," "E," and "G." The pendants "B" and "C" are made from white marble or dolomite; "C" is a splendid example of the capabilities of a few of the Desert Culture artists. The zoomorphic motif is drawn from the hard rock with skill and a feeling for form. It may be a fetish rather than an ornament.

A truly superb and artistically decorated pendant is illustrated in "H." It is highly polished, perhaps from constant use. The material has the same color and texture as fossil ivory. It was in the pouch shown in Figure 57.

No one knows what ornaments of feathers, fur, hair, and other perishable materials were made and worn, only to disappear without a trace. Feather plumes from Lovelock Cave have already been mentioned, and bits of fur and bundles of feathers were frequently found that might have been decorative. One article of dress that must be mentioned is the basket hat, shown worn by the women in many of the early photographs. These caps were made of beautifully woven and decorated basketry and must have been ornamental rather than functional.

29. Spirit Quest Cairns

While wandering about the desert one occasionally encounters piles or mounds of rocks that have every appearance of being arranged by hand. They may be a slender column of stones as neatly placed as apples at a country fair, some pebbles carelessly heaped, or merely a succession of flat slabs laid one on the other, ranging from large to small. Many of them are of Indian origin; and many were made by the white invaders as claim or corner markers, or to anchor a fence post long since gone to dust. Some can be identified as recent because of their location, but it is difficult to distinguish from their appearance whether they are Indian or not. As with petroglyphs, there have been many speculations about the purpose of these mounds; they are frequently called "Indian Post Offices."

While in the Klamath country, Lieutenant Abbot wrote in his journal ". . . we noticed, in many places, large stones laid one upon the other, forming piles from two to six feet in height. Some of the party thought that these were trail markers to show the trail when the ground was covered with snow; but the vast numbers of them sometimes found within a few feet of each other, and their frequent proximity to trees which could easily have been blazed, rendered this hypothesis rather improbable." Dan DeQuill (1947) says that, in the desert, stone monuments were made by the Indians with one long stone pointing to water. However, since the wandering desert people must have known their territory as intimately as a farmer knows his fields, my wife Ruth and I do not believe that the rock piles were made to be direction markers of any kind, but that there were several reasons for their construction or accumulation.

One reason was their use as a supply of stones for the sweat bath. Water was sprinkled on hot rocks from the fire to make steam within the sweat lodge. Since this cleansing custom was widely practiced throughout the Americas, there should be many accumulations of the stones—but they quickly became scattered from trampling by stock and by weathering. Another reason for the mounds was that, in accompanying puberty rites, both boys and girls would go to some distant place to fast and perform some task; gathering and piling stones was one of the least imaginative. Ray (1963) says the puberty ritual sought a prophetic and satisfying dream and "This was achieved by engaging in energy-consuming but economically worthless activities." Cressman, in his report "Klamath Prehistory," shows a picture of one of these spirit quest cairns in the Klamath country. Another task was breaking and piling brush, all trace of which has vanished.

The aboriginal custom of a traveler adding a stone to an ancient pile along a trail—in the same manner as people today add a penny or two to a wishing well—was a primary source of artificial heaps of rocks. The donor hoped to attain good luck, freedom from fatigue and sickness, or perhaps he just wished to appease the spirits. The stones in these piles will be small since their addition was a symbolic invocation and not a task. One of the prayers quoted was "You see me give you something. I bring this rock to you. Help me now to have the luck to get anything I want" (Ray 1963). Rogers (1966) calls these accumulations of offerings "trail shrines" and says some of them are not on trails or where trails were convenient. These would be shrines for petitions not necessarily connected with traveling. Ray gives a sample: "My good helper, stone pile, you give me good luck. I am going out to hunt now. Help me to have good luck hunting deer. That is what I want you to do."

Some shrines became very large, about the size of a grand piano. The most spectacular stone pile Ruth and I ever saw was on Hart Mountain near the edge of a cliff; a spire about seven feet high and one foot in diameter was piled up from rocks as though by a professional stone mason. There is no way of knowing whether it was Indian or not, but it was a long way from civilization. It is known, though, that sheepherders constructed

a great many rock cairns. In one place in the desert there are
several in a row, some so high it would have been necessary to
have been on a horse to place the cap rock.

30. Gambling and Games

Prehistoric Indians, as well as many of the historic, were in-
veterate gamblers. Many of the early travelers mention the
colorful excitement prevailing during a gambling session. Simpson, in describing such a session, notes, "They are so infatuated
with this arrangement that I have known parties of them to refrain from eating or sleeping for twenty-four hours at a time, and
gamble, with but little intermission."

While there were many different games (the 24th Annual
Report of the American Bureau of Ethnology, 846 pages, is
entirely devoted to them), the universal favorite was the "hand
game." It seems to have been played in one form or another by
all the tribes. Essentially the contest required two sides numbering from one up to six or more each. Participants seated themselves in a line facing each other a few feet apart. The leader
of one side had two objects; one was marked and the other not.
These he rapidly and adroitly passed from hand to hand with
many strange and confusing motion, his partners meanwhile
loudly singing and beating time with sticks on a plank in front of
them to confuse the opponents. At a signal, the leader suddenly
stopped and crossed his hands in front of his chest. The leader
of the opponents then guessed which hand held the marked
piece. If he guessed correctly, his side got a counter and the
pieces; if incorrect, the other side got a counter and kept the
pieces for another try. When one side had won all the markers
they divided the stakes which had been wagered before the
game started.

J. K. Hillers, who was with the Powell Expedition in 1869-72,
describes the game: "It is called ne ang-puki, meaning to kill the

bone. The banker takes two bones, one with a string wound round the middle and the other plain, and places his hands behind his back. His side then chants for a minute or two, during which he shifts the bones from one hand to the other. On 'call' he brings both hands to the front, and crosses them on his breast. The callers now begin their chant. Suddenly one will extend his arm and point to the hand in which he thinks the banker holds the marked bone, at the same time hitting his breast with the other hand. If the guess is correct, the guesser takes the bones after the 'rake down,' and the game continues until one side or the other has all the counters." Small polished bones two or three inches in length and one half or one inch in diameter—one marked with a strip of leather wound around the middle, or carved—were the usual instruments. Cleaned and painted sticks were the counters, normally ten or twenty. The counters and bones are frequently found in caves.

Another object often called a hand-game piece is the curious bi-pointed and shaped bit of stone or baked clay found in quantity in the Great Basin (see Figures 84 and 96). In the 24th Annual Report of the American Bureau of Ethnology, Doctor Dorsey says: "In connection with the hand game there should be mentioned a lozenge-shaped stone measuring 2¼ inches long and 1½ inches in breadth and an inch in thickness. This stone, with several others similar in shape, was found at Klamath Falls, near the foot of Klamath Lake, and was obtained by me from a merchant as I was leaving the reservation. The person from whom I procured the specimen said that a number of Klamath Indians had seen the stone and had unanimously declared that it was formerly used in playing the hand game. It was not possible for me to verify this statement, but from the shape of the stone and from my inability to see to what other use it could have been put, I am inclined to the belief that it had been used in the hand game." (See page 148 and Figure 84)

Figure 98 shows a collection of 15 perfectly formed and graduated stone balls found in a cache by LeRoy Gienger in the Northern Great Basin. Stone balls are also found in the Coast and Plateau country. So far no one knows their exact use although almost all guess that they were for some type of amusement. The 24th Annual Report of the Bureau of American Ethnology lists many ball games played by the natives. One of the favorites and most exciting was called ball racing; each side had a number of players. To start, one man from each side stood at the starting line with a small stone or wood ball resting at the base of his toes; the rest of the players scattered out ahead. At a signal, each starter kicked the ball as far as he could. The first one of those ahead to reach the ball belonging to his side did the same. Meanwhile the others were running ahead as fast as they could to be ready to pass on the kick. No one was allowed to touch the ball with his hands. The race continued over a course that might extend for miles across country. Betting was heavy and the excitement intense.

Other games in which stone balls were used included juggling and many different types of throwing and rolling games. In one of these, contestants threw or rolled a stone ball at a hole in the ground. If one fell in and that of the opponent did not, the opponent had to carry the successful player to the opposite end of the course on his back. This was one of the few games played for amusement only; most of them involved betting.

Another theory is that the stone balls were used for grinding, in place of a mano or pestle. Without a mating stone slab it is difficult to see how they could have been used for this purpose. Nor can one conceive of any advantage they would have over the mano or pestle.

A favorite diversion of many primitive societies throughout the world, one that did not involve gambling, was the ball and pin game. A ball of fiber or hard material like stone or bone with drilled holes was attached with a cord to a wood or bone pin. The object was to cast the ball in the air and impale it on the pin when it came down. Sometimes balls of tule or similar material are found in caves; a number of holes where it was pierced by the pin will identify it as part of the game. The penalty for using a hard ball of bone or stone was that the player got a severe rap on the knuckles if he missed catching it on the pin.

31. Pipes and Smoking

The use of pipes and tobacco was a custom of nearly all the Indian tribes of North America. In South America, too, tobacco was used, but mostly in the form of snuff; chewing apparently was not customary as there are very few references to it in the early literature. Pipe smoking among the Indians was more of a ritual, practiced on ceremonial occasions or by the shaman in his liturgy, rather than the pleasant pastime that some consider it to be today—although it was smoked also for pleasure. Perhaps one should say that smoking was also a test of physical endurance, when one considers the potency of a harsh weed afire in a stone tube.

Many early writers tell about the natives inhaling from their pipes until they fell over senseless. Lewis and Clark record in their journals ". . . in the act of smoking they appear to swallow it as they draw it from the pipe, and for many draughts together you will not perceive the smoke which they take from the pipe; in the same manner also they inhale it in their lungs untill they become surcharged with this vapour when they puff it out to a great distance through their nostrils and mouth; I have no doubt the smoke of the tobacco in this manner becomes much more intoxicating and that they do possess themselves of all its viertues in their fullest extent; they frequently give us sounding proofs of its creating a dismorallity of order in the abdomen."

Since the most ancient times, tobacco and many other plants and gums have been sprinkled over fire as an incense in social or ceremonial occasions. Herodotus mentions: ". . . a fruit of a peculiar kind, which the inhabitants, when they meet together in companies and have lit a fire, throw on a fire, as they sit in a circle; and that by inhaling the fumes of the burning fruit that has been thrown on, they become intoxicated by the odor just as the Greeks do by wine; and that the more fruit that is thrown on, the more intoxicated they become, until they rise up to dance and betake themselves to singing."

Plutarch says: "In Thrace near the Hebrus there grows a plant which resembles the origanum; the inhabitants of that country throw the leaves on a brazier and inhale the smoke, which intoxicates them." Pliny records: "Sandarach, taken in the form of fumigation, also with cedar, has a remedial effect" and by "inhaling the fumes of chameleuce at the mouth thereby diminish the volume of the spleen." The Aztecs mixed herbs and pleasant-smelling gums to make an incense for sprinkling on burning coals, and the use of incense in temples is known throughout the world.

But the custom of smoking seems to have originated in the Americas. The early explorers were astonished when they saw the natives indulging in the practice. Columbus was the first to mention it; he "found a great number of Indians, men and women, holding in their hands little lighted brands made of herbs, of which they inhaled according to their custom." Other writers refer to this practice of using a sort of cigar or cigarette. Las Casas, bishop of Chiapas, mentions a firebrand, "a kind of musquitoon packed in a dry leaf, which the Indians lit at one end while they sucked it or inhaled it from the other. Those musquetoons were called Tabacos." Thus originated the word tobacco, a term that was not applied to the smoking ingredient until late in the seventeenth century. The custom was so peculiar that it was frequently described by early chroniclers of the Spanish conquest, though never clearly enough to indicate the details of either the equipment used or the herbs smoked. The habit was well established with the aborigines and also adopted by the Spanish soldiers. Las Casas says that when they were admonished for indulging in the vice of smoking "tobacos," he was told that it was not in their power to leave it off and he adds, "I do not know what savor or profit they found in them."

Tobacco was endowed with wondrous properties by the Europeans when first introduced from America and was prescribed by the physicians to cure and prevent disease. The plague in England created an enormous demand for the weed which was thought to be a powerful fumigant—a situation that gladdened the hearts and filled the purses of the Virginia planters. Joseph D. McGuire, in *Pipes and Smoking Customs of the American Aborigines* (the Annual Report of the Smithsonian Institution for the year 1897, from which most of the information for this section on pipes and smoking was taken) says that during the reign of Charles II, the worst floggings received by the boys of Eton were for refusing to smoke.

Nicolas Monardes, in *De Simplicibus Medicamentes*, in 1574, says: "The name tobacco was given to it by the Spanish from the island of the same name, and while only the use of the leaves of the plant is advised, seed was at times utilized when the leaves were not available. These leaves were strung together, hung in the shade and dried, and used whole or powdered, and were considered good for headache, lockjaw, toothache, coughs, asthma, stomach ache, obstructions, kidney troubles, disease of the heart, rheumatism, the poisoning for arrows, carbuncles, polypus, consumption, etc."

The scarcity of pipes among the Desert Culture indicates that smoking was not a prominent vice, a normal situation with a people compelled to spend a major portion of their time just to exist. The pipes found in the desert are rather crude, although in some areas they were beautifully made, laboriously created from an obstinate element upon which great skill and care were lavished. A few pipes from areas peripheral to the Great Basin are masterpieces of creative art and control of technique. The Klamath produced some exceptional tubes—long, slim polished specimens such as the one shown in Figure 100. A feature of these pipes is the raised ring around the stem. This type of tube pipe is complete with bowl and mouthpiece; some of the shorter tubes were made to be used with a bone or cane stem. The very finest of pipes, treasured by collectors and museums for their delicate shape and beautiful finish, were made by the Hupas from wood with an inset stone bowl.

Some of the specimens called pipes were not for smoking at all, but were sucking tubes used by the shaman in his healing rites. Sickness was believed to be caused by evil spirits who either resided in the body or inserted some foreign object such as a stone or worm. The shaman alone possessed the power to overcome the spirit. With mask and mantle and magnificent contortions he conquered the phantom; then by applying the tube to the affected area he sucked out the evil. If it was an object, he would display it to the multitude gathered to assist in overcoming the hostile specter by tremendous noise. The object, cleverly palmed, was overwhelming proof of the efficiency of the shaman. The specimen shown in Figure 100 may have been a sucking tube.

Spier (1930) says the tube pipe was unknown among the Klamath. Gene Favell, a collector from Klamath Falls, says that many short tube pipes have been found in Klamath territory and some long ones like that shown, but he has not seen any of the latter that show signs of having been smoked.

In his *Ancient Tribes of the Klamath Country*, Carrol Howe describes "the longest known straight pipe found in the Klamath country. It is sixteen and a half inches long and had been broken into seven pieces when cast into a cremation pyre by a mourner. The pieces were scattered in a range of about twenty feet. Over the years each piece took on the color of the particular soil or ash in which it was buried. While pipes were often used for cremation offerings, they were not always scattered about. It was common practice in house-pit cremations to place the pipe upon the chest of the deceased."

Among the North American Indians, smoke was often blown over the patient by the shaman, and it must have been endowed with a virtue potent enough to subdue the stoutest demon, judging by the herbs used to produce it. Large tube pipes are called "cloud blowers" because it is believed that the user placed the lightened end in his mouth to cause the healing vapors to emerge.

Figure 103 shows an unusual form of pipe from the Great Basin, ground and drilled from stone with infinite patience and skill. This type is not illustrated in either West (1934) or McGuire (1899), each of which shows many hundreds of forms of pipes from all over the Americas. The nearest they come to it is called a "wedding pipe," which has two mouthpieces and a place at the base of the V for the tobacco. The two at the top of the Figure were found and photographed by Jim Thomas of Klamath Falls. The lower of the two is made from green steatite, with deep carving. One hole was drilled off center and ran out the side. The maker inserted his drill through this hole to connect to the one in the other leg; it required a patch to close the hole and make the pipe draw. The total length of this pipe is 22.25 inches. The other one is made from reddish stone and is 18.5 inches long. Both have a definite mouthpiece and bowl, one in each wing.

The pipe at the bottom is from the O'Shea collection; it is about 13 inches long. This one also has a hole at the V; it was perhaps drilled to connect the hole from each arm. It is rounded off to receive a plug stopper.

These pipes are extremely rare. Mr. Thomas says the only place that he knows they are found is on the east shore of Clear Lake, in Northern California. My wife Ruth and I have not seen any in either museums or collections from any other area. They perhaps are another illustration of the imitative trait in human nature—some primitive genius created a new style and others duplicated it.

Figure 101 shows several other types of Great Basin pipes. No. 1 is made from white dolomite or marble, a hard, white stone found in Nevada. It is beautifully made and symmetrically formed, highly polished all over, with a decorated stem end. It it further embellished with inlaid bits of abalone shell, a very unusual specimen for the Great Basin. It was found by Wallace Munk of Lovelock, Nevada.

In a letter dated July 12, 1827, to William Clark, of the Lewis and Clark expedition, Jedediah Smith wrote: "The Pa Ulches have a number of marble pipes, one of which I obtained and send you, they told me there was a quantity of the same material in their country. I also obtained a knife of flint, which I send you." This was the first report of archaeological remains in Southern Nevada.

Another form is the elbow pipe, No. 2. From its form one suspects that it is quite recent. No. 3 is also an elbow, and Nos. 4 through 8 are the usual form of desert pipes—a short tube made from scoria, sandstone, or clay, probably used with a bone or reed stem. They resemble those of the Basketmaker. The tube pipe was derived from the Middle America custom of smoking tobacco made into a tubular form, a primitive cigar. This pipe was very inconvenient to smoke; it had to be held somewhat upright or the user had to lie on his back, else the fiery charge would spill out. When so held the smoker was in danger of inhaling the hot embers. The primitive participant neatly solved the latter problem by inserting a pellet of clay or a pebble at the bottom of the bowl, with a fit poor enough to allow passage of the soothing vapors but good enough to withhold the fuel. Pipes have been found with the pebble still in place.

The tube pipe was known throughout America. In the West and Southwest it was virtually the only type used, but the elbow type was dominant in the East and the Great Plains (Linton 1924). Elbow pipes in the Great Basin are recent and due to influence of contact and trade. However, it is possible, as has happened on the Columbia River, to find an elbow pipe in an old site—a pipe acquired by trade or capture.

Part Five

The Art

32. The Meaning of Art

The creation and enjoyment of aesthetic objects is fundamental in most cultures. Although the degree of artistic attainment varies widely, the degree of enjoyment is of the same order. The ancient owner of the ivory amulet shown in Figure 94 probably derived as much pleasure from the look, feel, and possession of it as does the present owner of a lovely modern piece.

Traces of the artistic impulse have been found in the oldest of the archaeological excavations, but one must not be too hasty in judging the artistic attainments of an ancient people by what has survived; no one knows what wood, shell, ivory, quill, fur, or feather creations have disappeared without a trace over the centuries. Little would remain for archaeologists of the full glory of the Northwest Coast monumental creations in wood, if the natural processes of preservation were depended upon.

Technical skill, of course, is fundamental—to be able to extract the creation from within the medium. The chipped pieces shown in Figure 36, top, are examples of precise control. Pride of workmanship is apparent in these objects, which are only slightly more effective for their function than if they had been haphazardly made. Technical perfection has an aesthetic value. The decorated pottery of the Southwest culture would lose much of its appeal had the potter lacked the skill to achieve symmetry of form and smoothness of surface—both without the aid of the potter's wheel—regardless of the quality of the decoration.

Symmetry is always pleasing to the eye, providing monotony is avoided. Equal right and left halves express symmetry, a favorite theme of the Northwest Coast artists. So does division of two elements by a vertical line. There may be a symmetrical pattern, such as that on the pendant in Figure 94 "H." Bowls and baskets may have a regular decoration, a technique skillfully mastered by some of the desert tribes, especially with baskets. In fact, most of the art expression of the wandering people of the Desert Culture was expended on baskets. The women as weavers were the art interpreters of the Great Basin.

Rhythm is important in art, as it is in music or poetry. A repetition of pattern expresses rhythm—to again use Figure 94 "H" as an example—or it may be acquired with geometric figures. The rhythmic repetition of elements on a basket is pleasing even if the decoration is of the simplest kind; the regular spacing of the strands in weaving has the same effect. Dr. Franz Boas, in *Primitive Art*, says that the ancient people seemed to appreciate rhythm more than do our modern expressionists.

Artistic objects or figures may be realistic or representative. In the realistic style, the subject is delineated in its true configuration, such as a Michelangelo sculpture; the appeal is in the mechanical perfection and association with the viewer's experiences. Representative art is symbolic; the rendition may be in outline only, with details subdued or lacking entirely. This type is most common with primitive people, and is most appreciated by some students as the highest degree of art interpretation, where emotional expression overcomes technical perfection. An example is the anthropomorphic bone carving in Figure 105 "A," where one instantly recognizes the human contour, yet most details are non-existent. Another illustration is the stone sculpture in Figure 105 "B," suggesting one of the amphibians; the form is pleasing and the imagination is stimulated in supplying the details.

Another aspect of representative art may be a mass of symbolic decoration; in the Desert Culture this type sometimes appears on pottery. The motif attained its highest stage of perfection in some Northwest Coast and early Mexican art. In much of the prehistoric art the symbolism may be completely camouflaged to all but the initiated. The pattern on baskets follows this style; the symbol for a dog might be a simple cross, or for a bird a T. What may be another example of symbolic art is the atlatl weight, Figure 55. The atlatl was replaced by the bow and its utilitarian function transferred into the symbolic, a mark of rank and affluence subject to decoration, according to some authorities. The amount of work expended on these pieces far exceeded that required for strictly useful purposes, if useful they were.

Pure formal art is not common in the Desert Culture, the expression tending to be restricted to everyday objects such as baskets. The pleasing form and texture, the complete mastery of the media, and the sophistication of the applied design elevates the basket work of the Desert Culture to a high level of art; specimens are eagerly sought by collectors and museums. Textile decoration is an ancient tradition; basketry excavated from Northern Great Basin caves shows an extremely high quality of technical skill and embellishment (Cressman 1942). Simple twined, plain baskets would have served just as well. Sometimes baskets were adorned with feathers; these too are occasionally found in caves. Where pottery replaced baskets as the chief domestic receptacle, the art was transferred to it in the form of painted designs.

The men also possessed the skill and patience to create art objects from a refractory material. The zoomorphic carving in Figure 105 "D" is one of the finest examples, beautifully shaped from a dense black stone and highly polished. It is pleasing not only to the eye but to the touch. Note all the features of this piece—which is difficult to show to its best advantage in a two-dimension picture. Technical control is complete; the piece has symmetry and rhythm; it is representative and the design elements are perfectly balanced. "B" is an appealing representation; both "E" and "F" are beautifully executed pieces.

Figure 106 shows some typical small bone and stone Desert Culture carved effigies. The well designed and fashioned "A" perhaps represents a turtle; "B" shows lizards, one in stone and one in bone. The small zoomorphic carving "J" apparently served no utilitarian purpose, and, like the anthropomorphic figure "C," seems to have been made for aesthetic pleasure or totemic representation. When viewed in the round, "E" looks very much like a jackrabbit; "J" and possibly "F" are intended to represent grasshoppers. "D" is one of the marked pebbles found in many other areas besides the desert. "K" is a fiber effigy found in a cave in the Northern Great Basin. It may be a toy or a symbolic hunting charm for it appears to represent a mountain sheep.

33. Rock Art

The most plentiful examples of art expression by the peoples of the Great Basin are petroglyphs and pictographs, familiarly known to some as "rock writings." The former is a design carved into the living rock by pecking or abrasion; the word is derived from the Greek "petra" and "glyphe" for rock and carving. A pictograph is a painting and here means a painting on rock. These art forms are of great antiquity, dating back possibly 50,000 years in Europe. The famous cave paintings of France and Spain are about 15,000 years old. Preliminary dates have been assigned to Great Basin rock pictures but they are not considered very old; at the most only a very few thousand years, and some only a few hundreds.

In the United States pictographs or petroglyphs have been reported from all states except nine — Alabama, Connecticut, Delaware, Florida, Indiana, Louisiana, Mississippi, New Hampshire, and South Carolina. In Southern Texas and Southern California there are enormous numbers of pictographs, but relatively few petroglyphs. In the Great Basin the petroglyphs predominate and occur in considerable numbers throughout the area.

Petroglyphs were made by pecking a series of rapid blows with a convenient river pebble or stone—delivered with enough force to remove a few grains from the surface. Sometimes these well-worn tools are found at the base of the panel. It took a tremendous number of taps to complete a design. A few petroglyphs were made by abrading the surface with a rough or sharp stone. In hot, dry areas like the Great Basin, most rock acquires a shiny black surface called "desert varnish." While the exact nature of the process is not known, it is the result of minerals leaching out of the rock by rain water, and then being deposited on the surface as the water evaporates. The mineral is chiefly manganese dioxide, the same mineral that makes the beautiful drapery effects in the red-rock country of Utah and Arizona. By breaking through this layer to the living rock beneath with his hammerstone, the artist could reveal his conception in bold outline against the black surface. It takes many years to form a coating of desert varnish, and those petroglyphs that have been revarnished have considerable antiquity.

The pigments used for pictographs are all natural earths. Red paint is hematite, an iron oxide very similar to rust. It occurs in many places but is usually a dull color, which can be enriched by the action of fire. Most pictographs are made from paint using this mineral as a pigment. Yellow is also an iron oxide, limonite, and the natural color varies widely. White is made from one of the clays such kaolin, or from diatomaceous earth. Black comes from charcoal, manganese dioxide, or from burned graphite. Shades of blue and green are sometimes found; they are made from sedimentary clay deposits or from serpentine. The raw materials were ground on a flat stone or in a cup-shaped depression in a rock, then mixed with vegetable or animal oils and perhaps other substances such as pitch or albumen from birds' eggs. Frequently the raw pigment, after grinding, was mixed with water and pressed into cakes, then dried. These little blocks have been found still bearing the fingerprints of the ancient artisan. When paint was needed, some was scraped from the block and mixed and ground.

Almost anything could be used to apply the paint: a brush made from crushed yucca fibers, a bit of fur, a frayed stick, even the fingers. These mineral paints are surprisingly permanent; the pores of the rock seem to absorb the pigment and it becomes part of the stone itself. If reasonably sheltered from windblown sand and the weather, pictographs will last for many decades, even centuries; that is, unless they are easily accessible. Then they suffer from the hands of the thoughtless. Sometimes heedless hunters seem unable to resist taking a few shots, trusting that the lingering spirits of the departed will be unable to blast back. Campbell Grant, in his delightful book *Rock Paintings of the Chumash,* shows one exquisite painting, photographed in its pristine state in the 1870's, that has since been completely obliterated by rifle fire. Even those who should know better are not without fault; one must castigate the camera artist or archaeologist who robs the creation of its original charm by an assault with chalk.

The interpretation of ancient rock writings has intrigued many people; and there are wild speculations on the meaning of the symbols. Most of the interpretations, though, are mere romantic conjectures.

In 1886 and 1893, Gerrick Mallery wrote extensive reports on petroglyphs and pictographs in the Fourth and Tenth Annual Reports of the Bureau of American Ethnology. He thought that petroglyphs might actually be a form of writing, a method of communication; and he gathered a mass of information on their translation from local Indians and other sources. He found no reliable clues, no logical sequence in the symbols or the legends attached to them. To be effective as a means of communication there must be a series of basic elements depicted with sufficient precision that they can be easily and unmistakably recognized. No continuity of such symbols can be traced in Great Basin petroglyphs. There are certain designs that occur throughout the area; most are found universally. These have been named, but the meaning is not necessarily that intended by the prehistoric engraver. It was done for the convenience of tabulating only, like naming a plant so others will recognize the variety of which the author speaks.

The most common symbols are sunburst, rain, fertility, rake, ladder, dot and circle, and snake. All are the simplest figures and each would eventually be inscribed by anyone, even if merely doodling.

A careful study of design elements of a great many desert petroglyph sites by Robert F. Heizer and Martin A. Baumhoff, reported in *Prehistoric Rock Art,* convinced these scientists that there are no hidden messages in petroglyphs awaiting a Rosetta Stone for their translation. Petroglyphs and pictographs do not carry messages, but they were occasionally used to record events. Some in the Southwest have every appearance of depicting the Spanish invaders, and there are two known pictures there of a new moon with a circle near it that is thought to record the appearance of the supernova of 1054. This death of a star was a spectacular event that the natives would have regarded with superstitious awe, and one which was otherwise recorded only by the Chinese and Japanese. A petroglyph near Dillon, Montana, appears to be of the Lewis and Clark expedition, and there are some in the plains that may record smallpox epidemics.

If not for writing, what then was the purpose of the petroglyphs? Was the primitive artist expressing an artistic urge? Are they spiritual symbols, a task during puberty rites, or merely doodles? According to our opinion, they may be all of these. Certainly the local shaman would have utilized visual representation, creations displayed on the rocks, exposed symbols that would have achieved among the primitive subjects the status enjoyed today by the written word. The shaman was trusted to use his power to communicate with and even exorcise the gods and win their favor to mitigate the struggle for existence and increase the harvest. Such rites are used even today in sand paintings and ritualistic dancing. However, none of the shaman's powers could be wasted on the ordinary, the plentiful.

The Columbia River Indians depended for their very existence upon the salmon, yet of the thousands of extremely fine petroglyphs that once decorated the cliffsides of that mighty river prior to the great dams, less than half a dozen depict the salmon, for it ascended the current in teeming millions and was easily caught. Yet in the Nevada desert, in the dry Massacre Lake area where game was once plentiful, there is the fine fish representation shown in Figure 109.

The mountain sheep is an elusive and wary animal inhabiting the steepest hillsides and remotest canyons. To stalk within range of the atlatl or bow and arrow required superior skill in the hunter and preeminent power in the shaman. Throughout the West, the mountain sheep is depicted in countless numbers far exceeding that of all other animals together—realistic representations on mountain cliff and desert boulder. There is even a ritualistic shorthand—a picture of a sheep, then a large number of the horns only, followed by another sheep; magic secured by sheer weight of numbers like the service of a prayer wheel. In the Coso Range of California, in sites that have been declared national landmarks, the finest as well as most numerous representations appear.

Occasionally there appears among all peoples, however low their cultural level, a person who possesses such natural ability that he rises above the multitude, providing the opportunity presents itself to develop the talent. Such a one must have created the monumental carving overlooking the ancient Indian village of Wishram on the Grand Dalles of the Columbia River, a site that had been occupied for thousands of years. Representations of this monumental carving, which somehow escaped the crushing bulldozer, have appeared over a wide area, including the Great Basin. Such a one must have had the original conception of the "Fremont Men," the elaborate Chumish paintings, and the blanketed figures of the Coso Range.

Artistic creations never did appear in some areas of the Great

Basin. The carvings in general show the same lack of both ability and creativeness and follow the same dull motif of curvilinear lines, random dots, and geometrical symbols. They can be considered no less interesting because of their faults; they are the product of a people low on the cultural scale but high in the ability to survive and even prosper in a forbidding land—and must be so respected. But there are some among the thousands of carvings that show talent and must have been created for art's sake alone. Notice the small lizard beneath the large zoomorphic carving in Figure 107. No modern artist could better achieve movement and depict life than did this stone-age artist. There are many such examples. To religious symbolism must be added art for art's sake.

Modern ethnographers have shown that petroglyphs and pictographs were sometimes made in connection with puberty rites (Grant 1967; Heizer and Baumhoff 1965); something that could not be proved from any archaeological evidence. Boys approaching manhood were required to perform a spirit quest by going to some distant place alone to fast and pray for days until a guiding spirit appeared in a dream, probably more of a nightmare brought on by fatigue and hysteria. The vision, usually some animal or bird, but sometimes a supernatural being, might then be depicted on stone by the initiate. Girls, at the conclusion of their long and elaborate puberty rites, were sometimes required to paint symbols or representations of tasks performed in the rites, and many such pictures have been recorded. Various figures are sometimes considered fertility symbols, or thought to have been engraved as part of fertility rites.

Petrographs have been subjected to but a minor amount of study by scientists, compared to what has been done on archaeology. H. Thomas Cain (1950) studied those in Washington, noting that there was a similarity between those of the Columbia Plateau and the Great Basin, and that there was a marked difference in style between the coastal and interior areas. This stylistic diversity is universal. A serious student of petrographs, if shown a number of representative samples, can tell from what area they came. Cain concludes: "It is obvious that all such aboriginal carvings and paintings were simply a medium for expressing some emotion over spiritual or concrete events. That the primitive artist knew what was intended and his friends or tribal group understood the significance of the pictures cannot be doubted. It is equally certain that they were neither applied for the edification of strange peoples nor intended to provide some permanent record for future generations."

Cressman, after conducting a survey of petrographs in Oregon in the early 1930's, pointed out that the design types are separated, and that characteristics of the Great Basin designs extend northward into the upper Deschutes and John Day rivers. He makes no attempt to explain their function beyond quoting ethnographic authorities that pictographs were made by boys and girls during their puberty rites, and some speculation on possible magic or representative functions.

Julian H. Steward conducted an extensive survey of the petrographs of California and adjoining states and published a report in 1929. He says: "The meaning and purpose of petroglyphs and pictographs can only be ascertained through careful study of art and symbolism of present Indian groups and a comparison of these with petrographic elements."

Dr. Thomas Newman, in 1964, excavated a cave on the South Santiam River in the Cascade Mountains of Oregon. The cave, on one of the few passes through the Cascades, was beside an old Indian trail and had been used as a temporary shelter since 6,000 B. C. by natives passing back and forth between the Willamette Valley and the Great Basin. In the cave were three panels of petroglyphs that are similar to those found in the Great Basin. Newman says: "Since it is impossible to discern the intent or motivation of the artists, the petroglyphs are simply recognized as examples of the art expression of the culture or cultures represented. As such they may be dealt with descriptively and, when justified, treated taxonomically and placed with some precision in time and space. It is not necessary to discover the intent or motivation which produced petroglyphs in order to establish cultural and chronological ties."

The survey by Heizer and Baumhoff covered 99 sites in Nevada out of a possible 300. In bordering states, especially California, there are many more petrograph sites of the Desert Culture, and 42 of these sites were included in the survey. All sites were studied in detail in a concerted attempt to determine the purpose and meaning of these impressions of a vanished people. They classified the design elements in each site and studied their distribution. The report is the most detailed and conclusiv' yet done on this interesting subject, although their conclusi s are not entirely accepted.

My wife Ruth and I believe that the petroglyr out not the pictograph—sites were associated with game ti and had a magico-religious significance, a ritual device to :sure success of the hunt and to increase the supply of game. ' he premise is based on the proximity of most of the sites to known or probable game trails. At several of the sites there were vestiges of blinds and, even more significant, remains of stone fences to guide the animals into ambush. One of these relics can be seen at the Grimes Site near Fallon, Nevada, one third of a mile from and paralleling U.S. 50 on the northwest border of the site. It consists of a series of rock piles. The animals hunted were the mule deer, antelope, and mountain sheep. Mountain sheep representations are the most plentiful of the petroglyphs covered in the survey, there being 259 realistic designs plus 20 more representing the horns only. There are 78 other zoomorphic carvings; in most of them the animal was not realistic enough to be identified.

Hunting by ambush along trails could have been successful only in the spring and fall when the animals were migrating from and to their winter feeding grounds—unless the trail was to water. An ambush at a water hole would not be completely successful because the quarry would quickly grow wary. Most hunting was stalking by individuals, and that is the reason projectile points are so widely scattered throughout the Great Basin. They have been found in the most unlikely places, such as the top of Hart

Mountain. Occasionally there may be two or three together, an unexpected dividend that must have been caused by the escape and eventual death of a wounded animal. Hunting big game was a relatively undependable source of food in the Great Basin, yet it seems to have been an important avocation and attended with considerable ritualistic ceremony. Perhaps hunting was associated with manhood, as opposed to gathering, which was women's work.

Campbell Grant (1966) says, "It seems likely that most of the abstract paintings in the Chumash country are visualizations of supernatural beings or forces to be used ceremonially in much the same manner as the Navajo sand figures." He believes that some of the pictures were stylistic representations of things or ideas known to the local shamans. This theory would account for the area diversity of design motifs. Of all the hundreds of different universal design elements, there is only one found throughout the Chumash area. Julian Steward, in *Petroglyphs of California,* says that because there is a local style, the specific design elements must have had a definite significance; the artist followed the local tradition. Mr. Grant offers proof that some pictographs in Southern California were made by girls during their puberty ceremonies.

No method has yet been found to determine the age of the pictographs and petroglyphs themselves. Some can be dated relatively, that is, if one picture is superimposed upon another, the under picture is obviously older and the difference in weathering indicates greater or less relative age. If some petroglyphs have been re-covered with desert varnish, they are obviously older than those nearby that are not, if the exposure is about the same. Pictures of men on horseback cannot be more than about 400 years old.

Differential weathering is of little significance except with adjacent pictures, for both the weathering characteristics of the rock and the exposure may vary. If the pictures are on the same rock with the same exposure, differential weathering is significant, indicating a marked difference in age, but one that cannot be specifically stated in years. The only way yet found to date petroglyphs is by association with archaeological evidence, and this is not a particularly fruitful method.

Heizer and Baumhoff believe that the pit-and-groove style petroglyphs may be as much as 7,000 years, the pecked style 3,000, and the pictographs 1,000 years old. No other authority that we have found is willing to be so specific as to age except Newman. There seems to be good reason to assign a respectable antiquity to some of them because the Indians have been in the Great Basin for a long time. If petroglyphs are as much as 7,000 years old, it must have been on very rare occasions and by few individuals that they were carved, despite the great number of them.

Dr. Thomas Newman, commenting on the petroglyphs in Cascadia Cave, says, "It now appears probable that a date of 3-4000 B.C. may be justified for both petroglyphs and notched points." According to Newman, Cascadia Cave was first used about 8,000 years ago and abandoned 3,000 years ago with no satisfactory proof of the terminal date, since the upper strata of the cave had been much disturbed by relic hunters.

NOTABLE COLLECTIONS

The following families have extensive collections of Great Basin archaeological material. Although these are but a small number of the many collectors in the Basin, they happen to be owners of the ones which the author examined and photographed: Horace Arment, Ontario, Oregon; Eugene Favell, Klamath Falls, Oregon; LeRoy Gienger, Chiloquin, Oregon; Louis Johnson, Paisley, Oregon; C. D. Lair, Reno, Nevada; George and Alfred Luke, Fallon, Nevada; George A. Miller, Cedarville, California; Jack Nicolarsen, Sparks, Nevada; Johnny O'Shea, Tulelake, California; George Sanford, Sparks, Nevada; and Peter Ting, Reno, Nevada.

The following have extensive collections of photographs and slides of petroglyphs and pictographs: Dr. Dale Ritter, Chico, California; Campbell Grant, Carpinteria, California; and Don Martin, Santa Rosa, California.

Bibliography

Following are some useful books, pamphlets, reports, and magazine articles, in the opinion of the author. Some of the out-of-print publications can be obtained from firms in the re-print business. Names and address of two of these are: Kraus Reprint Corporation, 16 East 46 Street, New York City 10017; Johnson Reprint Corporation, 111 Fifth Avenue, New York City 10003.

Antevs, Ernst
    1948   "Climate Changes and Pre-White Man," part of "The Great Basin," Bulletin of the University of Utah, Vol. 38, No. 20. A valuable reference work on the geology, zoology, and climate of the Great Basin in glacial times.
Arment, Horace
    n.d.   "Indian Artifacts of the Upper Great Basin." Privately printed, Box 455, Ontario, Oregon. 8 pages, many illustrations.
Binns, Archie
    1967   *Peter Skene Ogden: Fur Trader,* Binfords & Mort, Publishers.
Blackwelder, Eliott and others.
    1948   "The Great Basin," Bulletin of the University of Utah, Volume 38, No. 20. Geological, zoological, and climatic history of the Great Basin; well written and illustrated; a primary source.
Boas, Franz
    1955   *Primitive Art,* Dover Publications, New York. Originally published in 1927; a classic work by a distinguished anthropologist.
Bolton, Herbert E. (editor)
    1950   "Pageant in the Wilderness," the Story of the Escalante Expedition to the Interior Basin, 1776, *Utah Historical Quarterly,* Utah State Historical Society, Vol. 18, Nos. 1, 2, 3, 4. Salt Lake City.
Brown, Vinson, and others.
    1958   *Wildlife of the Intermountain West,* Naturegraph, San Martin, California. 142 pages, paperbound; should be in your library.
Bryan, Alan Lyle
    1965   "Paleo-American Prehistory," Occasional Papers of the Idaho State University Museum, Number 16, Pocatello, Idaho. One of the most useful books for your library, a summary of evidence of Early Man in the Americas. A scholarly account; reads a little heavy.
Butler, B. Robert and Douglas Osborne
    1959   "Archaeological Evidence for the use of Atlatl Weights in the Northwest," *American Antiquity,* Vol. 25, No. 2, October.
Byerly, Perry
    1952   "Pacific Coast Earthquakes," Oregon State System of Higher Education, Eugene.
Carson Indian Agency
    1964   *Our Desert Friends,* State of Nevada, Public Instruction. For young people, about plants. Useful.
Cline, Gloria Griffen
    1963   *Exploring the Great Basin,* University of Oklahoma Press, Norman.
Coville, Frederick Vernon
    1904   *Wokas, a Primitive Food of the Klamath Indians,* Smithsonian Institution, Washington.
Cowles, John
    n.d.   "Cougar Mountain Cave," privately printed, Rainier, Oregon. Fifty pages, 40 plates, map. Illustrated story of the excavation of a Great Basin Cave by an amateur. Shows many projectile point styles, other artifacts.
Cressman, L. S.
    1936   "Archaeological Survey of the Guano Valley Region in Southeast-

ern Oregon," University of Oregon Studies in Anthropology, No. 1, Eugene.

1937   "Petroglyphs of Oregon," University of Oregon Studies in Anthropology, No. 2. Eugene.

1942   "Archaeological Researches in the Northern Great Basin," Carnegie Institution of Washington Publication 538, Washington. First major work on the subject.

1956   "Klamath Prehistory," Transactions of the American Philosophical Society, new series, Vol. 46, Part 4, Philadelphia. Excavations in Klamath villages; well illustrated, valuable reference.

1960   "Cultural Sequences at The Dalles, Oregon," Transactions of the American Philosophical Society, new series, Vol. 50, Part 10. Philadelphia. An Early Man site on the Columbia River.

1962   The Sandal and the Cave, Beaver Books, Portland. Popular account of the Indians of Oregon, including the Great Basin.

Cressman, L. S., Howell Williams, and Alex D. Krieger

1940   "Early Man in Oregon," University of Oregon Studies in Anthropology, No. 3. Eugene.

Daugherty, Richard D.

1956   "Archaeology of the Lind Coulee Site, Washington," Proceedings of the American Philosophical Society, Vol. 100, No. 3.

Davies, K. G., editor

1961   "Peter Skene Ogden's Snake Country Journal, 1826-27," The Hudson's Bay Society, London. Ogden was one of the first to see and record the Desert Culture in its final days.

Davis, Wilbur A.—See d'Azevedo and others.

1966

d'Azevedo, W., and others, editors

1966   The Current Status of Anthropological Research in the Great Basin, 1964, Desert Research Institute Technical Report, Series S-H, Reno. Papers presented at the 1964 Great Basin Archaeological Conference. Informative and interesting.

DeQuille, D.

1947   The Big Bonanza, Knopf. A reprint of the 1876 edition of the story of the Comstock Lode.

Ewers, John C., editor

1959   Adventures of Zenas Leonard, Fur Trader, University of Oklahoma.

Fenenga, Franklin

1953   "The Weights of Chipped Stone Points: A Clue to their Functions," Southwestern Journal of Anthropology, Vol. 9, No. 3, Albuquerque.

Fremont, Col. J. C.

1849   Exploring Expedition to the Rocky Mountains, Geo. H. Derby & Co., Buffalo. Several companies have published copies of this journal, which is now out of print but shows up occasionally in second-hand book stores. Good account of traveling in the Great Basin.

Geiger, Vincent and Wakeman Bryarly

1945   Trail to California, edited by David Morris Potter. Yale University.

Gould, Richard A.

1968   "Chipping Stones in the Outback," Natural History, Vol. LXXVII, No. 2, February.

Grant, Campbell

1966   The Rock Paintings of the Chumash, University of California Press, Berkeley. Beautifully written and illustrated in color. You will never know what wonderful artists the aborigines were until you see this book. Much about history, missions, artifacts.

1967   Rock Art of the American Indian, Thomas Y. Crowell Company, New York. Illustrates and informs about petroglyphs and pictographs throughout the United States.

Gruhn, Ruth
  1961   "The Archaeology of Wilson Butte Cave, South Central Idaho,"
         Occasional Papers of the Museum of Idaho State College, Pocatello.
Guernsey, Samuel J. and Alfred V. Kidder
  1921   "Basket-Maker Caves of Northeastern Arizona," Papers of the
         Peabody Museum of American Archaeology and Ethnology, Vol.
         VIII, No. 2, Cambridge.
Harrington, Mark Raymond
  1933   "Gypsum Cave, Nevada," Southwest Museum Papers No. 8, South-
         west Museum, Highland Park, Los Angeles. Beautifully written and
         illustrated. Out of print.
Heizer, Robert F. and John E. Mills
  1952   The Four Ages of Tsurai, University of California Press, Berkeley.
         A good story of the discovery and demise of one Indian village on
         the coast of California.
Heizer, Robert F. and Irmgard W. Johnson
  1952A "A Prehistoric Sling from Lovelock Cave," American Antiquity,
         Vol. XVIII, No. 2, October.
Heizer, Robert F. and Alex D. Krieger
  1956   "The Archaeology of Humboldt Cave," University of California
         Publications in American Archaeology and Ethnology, Vol. 47,
         No. 1, Berkeley.
Heizer, Robert F. and John A. Graham
  1962   Prehistoric Rock Art of Nevada and Eastern California, University
         of California Press, Berkeley.
Heizer, Robert F. and Martin A. Baumhoff
  1967   A Guide to Field Methods in Archaeology, The National Press,
         Palo Alto. A good reference work.
Hester, Jim
  1960   "Late Pleistocene Extinction and Radiocarbon Dating," American
         Antiquity, Vol. 26, No. 1, July.
Hill, Malcolm W.
  1948   "The Atlatl or Throwing Stick," Tennessee Archaeologist, Vol. 4,
         No. 4.
Howe, Carrol B.
  1968   Ancient Tribes of the Klamath Country, Binfords & Mort.
Jaeger, Edmund C.
  1957   "A Naturalist's Death Valley," Death Valley '49ers, Inc. Pamphlet.
  1957A The North American Deserts, Stanford University Press, Stanford.
         Descriptions and illustrations of the deserts and their flora and
         fauna.
Jennings, Jesse D. and Edward Norbeck
  1955   "Great Basin Prehistory; a Review," American Antiquity, Vol. 21,
         No. 1.
Jennings, Jesse D.
  1957   "Danger Cave," University of Utah Anthropological Papers, No. 27.
         The original concept of the Desert Culture resulted from the work
         done in Danger Cave. An excellent report, well written and illus-
         trated.
Jennings, Jesse D. and Edward Norbeck, editors
  1964   Prehistoric Man in the New World," University of Chicago Press,
         Chicago. A collection of papers by various authorities on Early
         Americans and other subjects. One of the books that should be in
         your library. Extensive bibliographies.
Kellar, James H.
  1955   "The Atlatl in North America," Indiana Historical Society Prehistory
         Research Series, Vol. III, Number 3, Indianapolis.
Kelly, Isabel T.
  1932   Ethnography of the Surprise Valley Paiute, University of California
         Publications in American Archaeology and Ethnology, Vol. 31,

No. 3. Excellent reference on the Northern Paiute, with many illustrations.
Krieger, Alex D.
1962 "The Earliest Culture in the Western United States," American Antiquity, Vol. 28, No. 2, October.
1964 "Early Man in the New World"—See Jennings and Norbeck, 1964.
Kroeber, A. L.
1953 "Handbook of the Indians of California," Bureau of American Ethnology, Bulletin 78, reprinted by California Book Company, Ltd., Berkeley.
Libby, Willard F.
1955 *Radiocarbon Dating*, The University of Chicago Press, Chicago.
Linton, Ralph
1924 "Use of Tobacco among North American Indians," Field Museum of Natural History, Anthropology Leaflet No. 15.
Loud, L. L., and M. R. Harrington
1929 "Lovelock Cave," University of California Publications in American Archaeology and Ethnology," No. 25, Berkeley.
Lowie, Robert H.
1963 *Indians of the Plains*, The Natural History Press, New York.
Mac Gowan, Kenneth and Joseph A. Hester, Jr.
1962 "Early Man in the New World," American Museum of Natural History, New York. Paperback. Excellent pre-history, well written, extensive bibliography. Should be in your library.
McGuire, Joseph D.
1899 "Pipes and Smoking Habits of the American Aborigines," Annual Report of the U. S. National Museum for the Year 1897, Washington.
Martin, Paul S.
1967 "Pleistocene Overkill," *Natural History*, Vol. LXXVI, No. 10.
Mayer-Oakes, William J.
1963 "Early Man in the Andes," *Scientific American*, Vol. 208, No. 5.
Moorehead, Warren K.
1910 *The Stone Age in North America*, Boston.
Morgan, Dale L.
1953 *Jedediah Smith and the Opening of the West*, University of Nebraska Press, Lincoln. Paperback. An excellent account of this indefatigable explorer.
Osborne, Douglas
1957 "Excavations in the McNary Reservoir Basin Near Umatilla, Oregon," River Basin Surveys Papers No. 8, Smithsonian Bureau of American Ethnology Bulletin 166, Washington. Much on the material culture of the Columbia River Indians.
Peets, Orville H.
1960 "Experiment in the Use of Atlatl Weights," *American Antiquity*, Vol. 26, No. 1, July.
Powell, J. W.
1961 *The Exploration of the Colorado River and its Canyons*, Dover Publications, New York. A reprint of Major Powell's account of his two trips down the Colorado in 1869-72. Much information on the Indians he met.
Price, John Andrew
1962 "Washoe Economy," Nevada State Museum Anthropological Papers No. 6, Carson City.
Ray, Verne F.
1963 *Primitive Pragmatists, the Modoc Indians of Northern California*, University of California Press. Ethnology of the Modoc Indians.
Rich, E. E., editor
1950 *Peter Skene Ogden's Snake Country Journals, 1824-25 and 1825-26*, The Hudson's Bay Record Society, London.

Rogers, Malcolm J.
    1966   *Ancient Hunters of the Far West*, Union Tribune Publishing Company, San Diego. Not a particularly useful book, although the articles in it by Wormington and others are helpful.
Seaman, N. G.
    1967   *Indian Relics of the Pacific Northwest*, Binfords & Mort, Publishers, Portland, Oregon.
Simpson, Capt. James H.
    1876   *Report of Explorations Across the Great Basin of the Territory of Utah*, U. S. Government Printing Office, Washington.
Spaulding, Kenneth A., editor
    1953   *On the Oregon Trail, Robert Stuart's Journey of Discovery*, University of Oklahoma Press, Norman.
Spier, Leslie
    1930   *Klamath Ethnography*, University of California Press, Berkeley.
Stansbury, Howard
    1852   *Exploration and Survey of the Valley of Great Salt Lake*, Lippincott, Philadelphia.
Steward, Julian H.
    1938   "Basin-Plateau Aboriginal Sociopolitical Groups," Bureau of American Ethnology, Bulletin 120. Washington.
Strong, Emory
    1960   *Stone Age on the Columbia River*, Binfords & Mort, Publishers.
Sutton, Ann and Myron
    1966   *The Life of the Desert*, McGraw-Hill Company, New York.
Tadlock, W. Lewis
    1966   "Certain Crescentic Stone objects as a Time Marker in the Western United States," *American Antiquity*, Vol. 31, No. 5, Part 1, July.
Thwaites, Reuben Gold, editor
    1904   *The Original Journals of the Lewis and Clark Expedition*, Dodd, Mead & Co., New York.
U. S. National Museum—Many of these reports of the Smithsonian Institution were used in the present text for references; the year of publication is included.
von Werlhof, Jay C.
    1965   "Rock Art of the Owens Valley, California," Report of the University of California Archaeological Survey, No. 65, University of California Archaeological Research Facility, Department of Anthropology, Berkeley.
West, George A.
    1934   "Tobacco, Pipes and Smoking Customs of the American Indians," Bulletin of the Public Museum of the City of Milwaukee, Vol. XVII. Two volumes, one of text and one of plates. An exhaustive study of the subject. Rare and expensive.
Wheeler, Lt. George M.
    1879   "Report of the U. S. Geographical Survey," Washington.
Willey, Gordon R.
    1966   *An Introduction to American Archaeology*, Prentice-Hall, Englewood Cliffs, New Jersey. Beautiful book, well illustrated.
Wilson, Thomas
    1899   "Arrowpoints, Spearheads and Knives of Prehistoric Times," Annual Report of the U. S. National Museum for the Year 1897.
Wormington, H. M.
    1957   *Ancient Man in North America*, Denver Museum of Natural History, Denver. A synopsis of all that has been discovered concerning Early Man in North America; illustrated, 271 pages, glossary, bibliography, index. This book should be in your library.
Yates, L. G.
    1889   "Charm Stones," Annual Report of the Smithsonian Institution for 1886, Washington.

Fig. 1. Desert scene near Inyokern, California.

Fig. 2. "They eat roots, lizards . . ."

Fig. 3 (left) Gathering seeds in the desert, in Southern Nevada. Carrying basket in the foreground. Fig. 4 (right) "They have good features and most of them have heavy beards." Both photos by John Hillers about 1873—Smithsonian Institution.

187

Fig. 5. "Buildings constructed of bullrushes, and resembling Muskrat houses." Photo by Vernon Bailey in Carson Sink, Nevada, about 1903—Smithsonian Institution

Fig. 6 (left) Stan Noonan examines a bedrock mortar on a terrace of Summer Lake. Fremont passed by this rock on Dec. 18, 1843. Fig. 7 (right) Wavecut terrace on Fort Rock.

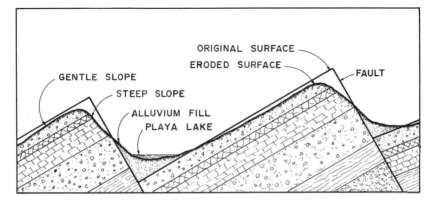

Fig. 8. Generalized cross section of a Great Basin landscape.

Fig. 9 (top) Earthquake fault, central Nevada, (bottom) "Slickensides" at Rattlesnake Point on Klamath Lake.

DISASTER IN 1872

ON THE DATE OF MARCH 26,
1872, AN EARTHQUAKE OF MAJOR
PROPORTIONS SHOOK OWENS
VALLEY AND NEARLY DESTROYED
THE TOWN OF LONE PINE.

TWENTY SEVEN PERSONS
WERE KILLED.

IN ADDITION TO SINGLE
BURIALS, 16 OF THE VICTIMS
WERE INTERRED IN A COMMON
GRAVE ENCLOSED BY THIS
FENCE.

Fig. 10 (left) Memorial plaque at Lone Pine. Fig. 11 (right) Earthquake crack in Humboldt Sink.

Fig. 12. The mountain of gravel in the center of the picture is a glacial moraine showing three different stages of the Ice Age. Near Convict Lake, California, in the Sierra Nevada Mountains.

Fig. 13. Channel eroded by outlet of Pleistocene Owens Lake. Little Lake and U.S. 395 in the background.

Fig. 14. Mono Lake, a remnant of extinct Lake Lahontan.

Fig. 15 (top) Wavecut terraces of Lake Lahontan, central Nevada, (bottom) pluvial Lake Chewaucan terraces near Paisley, Oregon.

Fig. 16. Possible pre-projectile point artifacts. (Top) Large bi-face tool from New Mexico, (center) choppers from central Nevada, (bottom) artifacts similar to fist axes. All to the same scale—Gerity collection.

Fig. 17 (left) Girls carrying water in watertight baskets. Photo by John Hillers about 1872—Smithsonian Institution. Fig. 18 (right) Ocala Cave.

Fig. 19. Lovelock Cave with Ruth standing in entrance.

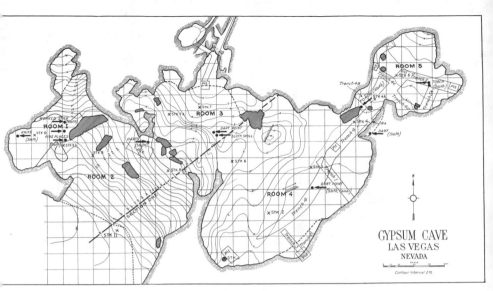

Chart No. 1

Fig. 20 (top) Fort Rock Cave, (bottom) view from entrance, Fort Rock in distant center.

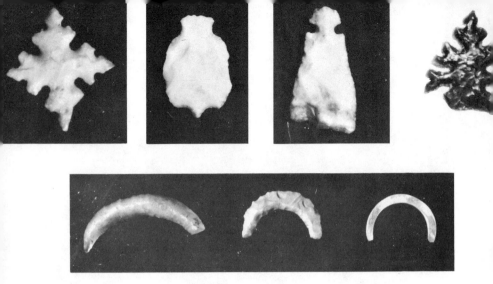

Fig. 21. Probably chipped ornaments. The curved pieces are believed to be nose ornaments because some of them are ground smooth—Miller, Luke and Arment collections.

Fig. 22 (left) The old arrow-maker and his daughter. Photo by John Hillers about 1872. Kaibab Plateau—Smithsonian Institution. Fig. 23 (top right) Obsidian point 6.5 inches long and 2.5 inches wide. The shaft would have to be over one inch wide to fit the stem; it is probably a knife meant for hafting. Found in Warner Valley, Oregon—Favell collection. Fig. 24 (bottom right) An obsidian core. Note the striking platforms on the top edges. The scale is one inch long. From the collection of Delmar Smith, Crater Rock Museum, Central Point, Oregon.

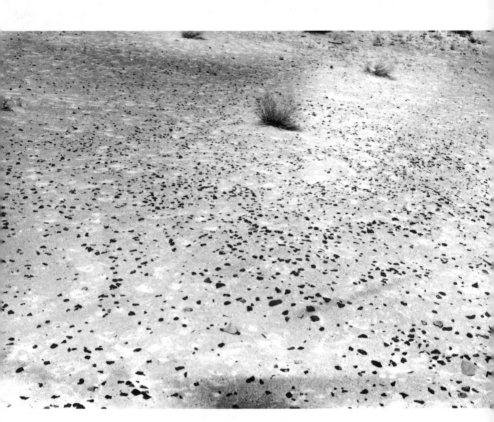

Fig. 25. Chipping detritus on an old camp ground.

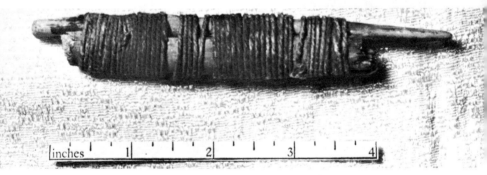

Fig. 26. Hafted chipping tool.

Fig. 27 (top) Projectile points found in the Great Basin—from many collections, (bottom) hafted atlatl foreshaft.

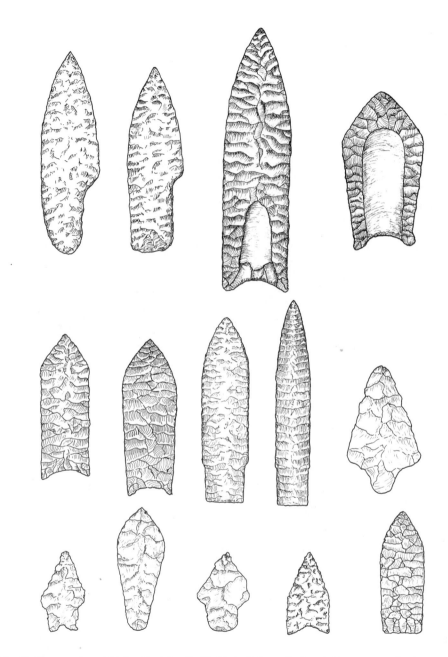

Fig. 28 (Top row from left) Sandia I, Sandia II, Clovis, Folsom; (2nd row) Plainview, Midland, Scottsbluff, Eden, Gypsum Cave; (bottom) Pinto Basin, Lake Mojave, Silver Lake, Meserve, Milnesand.

TYPE		SIZE	DISTRIBUTION			TOTAL
			DISTURBED SURFACE	UPPER BED	LOWER BED	
	1	Small Inter. Large	30 1 0	102 5 2	6 0 1	138 6 3
	2	Small Inter. Large	0 0 0	7 0 0	0 0 0	8 0 0
	3	Small Inter. Large	16 0 8	24 0 12	0 1 1	40 1 21
	4	Small Inter Large	7 1 12	9 5 22	0 1 6	16 7 40
	5	Small Inter. Large	12 1 0	11 0 0	0 0 0	23 1 0
	6	Small Inter. Large	7 0 9	28 0 24	2 1 3	37 1 36
	7	Small Inter. Large	3 5 19	3 20 101	0 3 13	6 28 133
	8	Small Inter. Large	0 0 3	0 0 18	0 0 2	0 0 23
	9	Small Inter. Large	0 0 0	0 0 9	0 0 12	0 0 12

Chart No. 2. Roaring Springs Cave Projectile Point Distribution (Dr. L. S. Cressman).

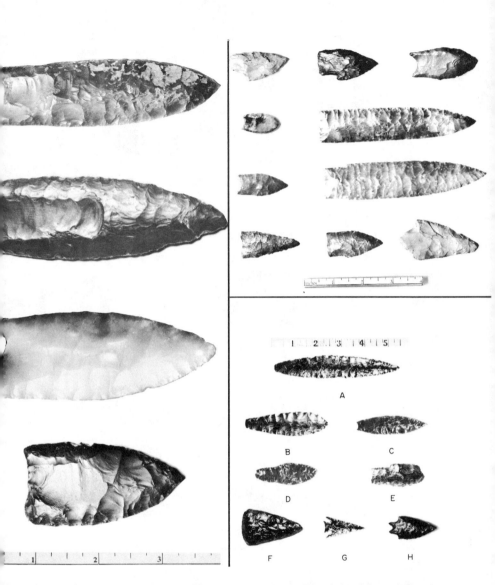

Fig. 29 (left) Clovis points from the West: (from top) near Malheur Lake, John and Georgia Crow; near Eugene, Oregon, Brent Kenyon; Washoe County, Nevada, Miss Ann Webb; near Blalock on the Columbia River, Ronald and Gary Zumwalt. All to same scale. Fig. 30 (top right) Early Man projectile point types: (top, from left) Sandia I, Sandia II, Clovis, Folsom, Eden, Plainview, Scottsbluff, Meserve, Milnesand, Gypsum Cave—Overman collection. Fig. 31 (bottom right) Desert arrow and dart points—Cowles collection. See text for description.

Fig. 32. Cougar Mountain Cave, John Cowles in entrance.

Fig. 33 (top row) Stemless point; basal notched and corner notched stemmed points. Fig. 34 (2nd row) Obsidian knife wrapped with buckskin for a handle, found in a Nevada cave—Nicolarsen collection. Fig. 35 (3rd row) Agate knife in wood handle, six inches long. Note that the handle has been used for a fire hearth. (Bottom) stemmed (right) and unstemmed knife blades—Luke and Shell collections.

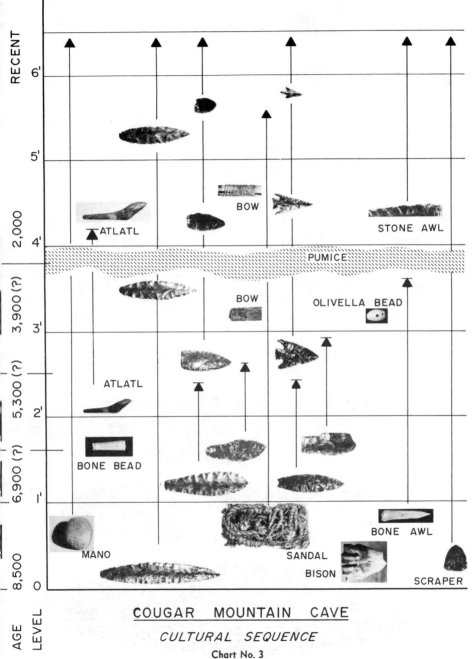

COUGAR MOUNTAIN CAVE

CULTURAL SEQUENCE

Chart No. 3

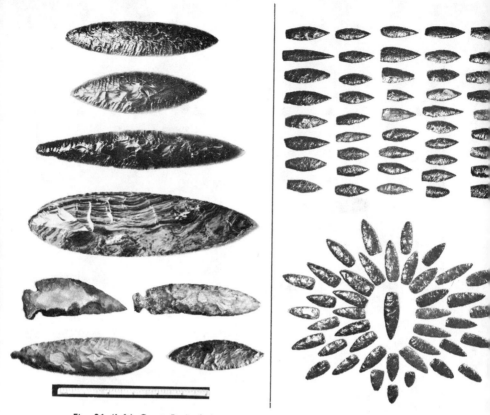

Fig. 36 (left) Great Basin knives. All to the same scale—Johnson and Favell collection.
Fig. 37 (right) Knives found in caches. Bottom photo by Norman Reimers.

Fig. 38. Cache of three knives, Northern Great Basin. The top knife is 11.5 inches long—
Loring collection.

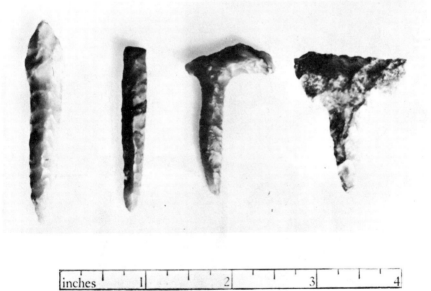

Fig. 39 (left) Scraper types. Fig. 40 (right) A large turtleback scraper—Nicolarsen collection.

Fig. 41. Stone drills.

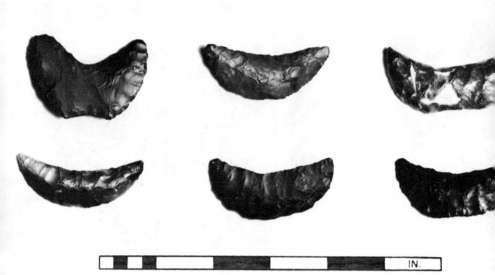

Fig. 42. Crescents—Nicolarsen collection.

Fig. 43. Perforated stones of unknown use—O'Shea, Lair and Luke
collections.

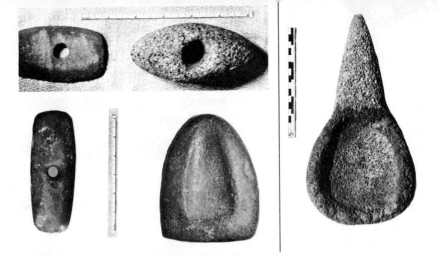

Fig. 44 (left) War club heads (?) and "piledriver"—Luke, O'Shea and Sanford collections. Fig. 45 (right) Handled container or lamp. Length 12 inches—Favell collection.

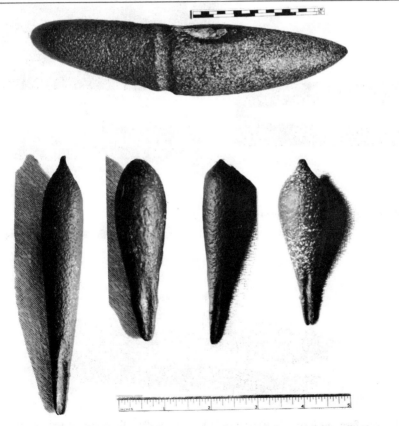

Fig. 46. "Icepick" (top) and charm stones—Samson, Luke and Lair collections.

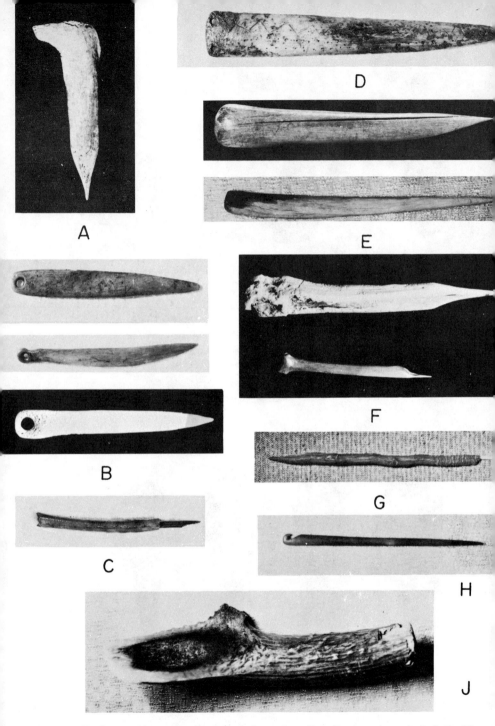

Fig. 47. Bone artifacts. A, scapula awl; B, eyed needles; C, composite awl; D, knife (?); E-H, awls; J, antler wedge—Gienger, Lair, Luke and Johnson collections.

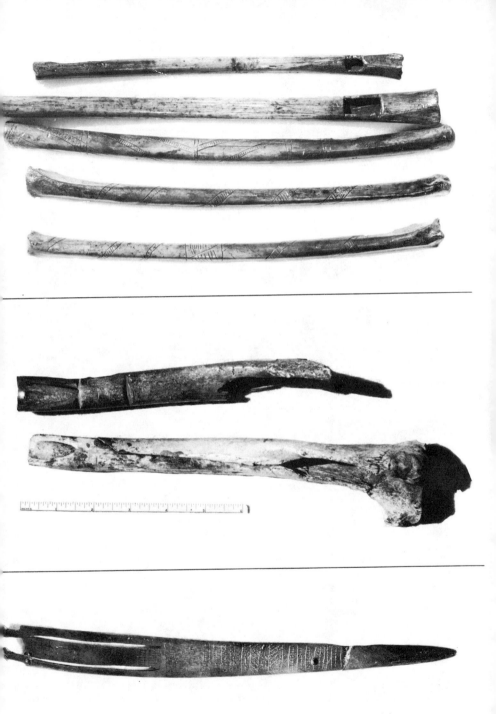

Fig. 48 (top) Decorated bone whistles, (center) bone gouges, (bottom) decorated bone ornament or tool—Gienger collection.

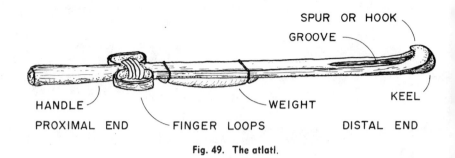

SPUR OR HOOK

GROOVE

HANDLE

WEIGHT

KEEL

PROXIMAL END

FINGER LOOPS

DISTAL END

Fig. 49. The atlatl.

Fig. 50 (top) Atlatl petroglyph, Valley of Fire, Nevada. Photo by Don Martin. (Bottom) Howard Hughes, petroglyph expert, with atlatl petroglyph, Little Lake, California.

Fig. 51 (left) Great Basin atlatls. (Top) The two Roaring Springs Cave atlatls and the Plush Cave atlatl—photo by L. S. Cressman, (center) the Nicolarsen atlatl with hafted Type III weight, (bottom) the Nevada Historical Society atlatl from Winnemucca Lake, photographed by the museum. Note the bone-flaking instrument in the handle. The distal end of the Nicolarsen atlatl is placed upside down in the photograph. Fig. 52 (right) Using the atlatl—Southwest Museum photo.

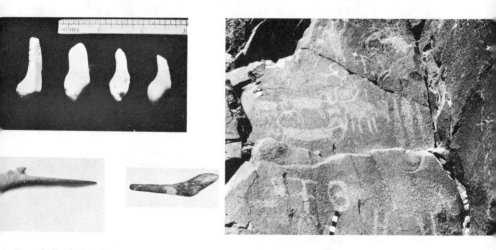

Fig. 53 (left) Atlatl spurs or hooks, stone (top) and wood. All to approximately the same scale—Lair, Cowles and Nicolarsen collections. Fig. 54 (right) Petroglyph showing hunters using atlatls. Note darts in mountain sheep, upper right center and lower right. Coso Range, California. Photo by Campbell Grant.

Fig. 55. Atlatl weights. (Top from left) Type I perforated stone and galena, banded Type III, from the Columbia River—McLeod and Selby collections. (Bottom) Type III weights—Ting, Lair and Sanford collections.

Fig. 56. The McLure atlatls. (Top) Obverse, side and reverse views of Specimen No. 1 showing weight and binding groove.

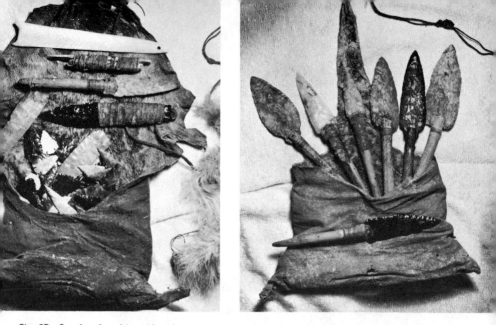

Fig. 57. Pouches found in a Nevada cave. Lower picture shows three knives and 100 projectile points from the pouch on the left. The right contains seven atlatl foreshafts—Nicolarsen collection.

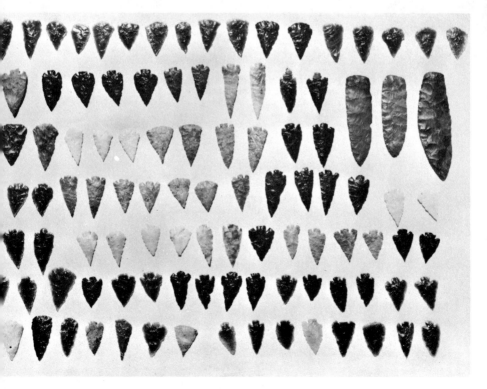

Fig. 58 (left) Planning the hunt. Note bows and quivers. Picture taken about 1872 by John Hillers in southern Nevada—Smithsonian Institution. Fig. 59 (right) Toy bow from a Nevada cave. Cressman (1942) found one in Roaring Springs Cave—Luke collection.

Fig. 60. Phragmites, the arrow shaft cane. Fig. 61. Wooden shaft imbedded in human ilium— Nicolarsen collection.

Fig. 62. Tools for making arrow and dart shafts. (Top) Abrasive stones for smoothing, (bottom left) straightener, used with heat, (bottom right) "spoke shave" for scraping—Johnson and Sanford collections.

Fig. 63. Petroglyph showing bow and arrow in use.

Fig. 64. Weaving a basket. On hut roof, seed beater; water bottle in foreground. Photo by John Hillers about 1872—Smithsonian Institution.

Fig. 65. Indian women gathering in the desert, burden baskets on their backs. The one on the right carries a winnowing tray. Their dress is modern but the baskets and hats have been the same for thousands of years. Photo by John K. Hillers, with the Powell expedition in 1871-1875—Smithsonian Institution.

Fig. 66. Seed grinding tools. (Top) Metate and mano, trough metate, (center) new and worn horned manos, handled mano, (lower) pointed and flat-bottomed mortars, roller pestle and mortar. No scale. The mortars are about 16 inches high—Favell, O'Shea, Gienger, Miller and Sweeney collections.

Fig. 67. Part of the Luke collection of metates and mortars.

Fig. 68. Bedrock mortars at the museum in Bridgeport, California.

Fig. 69. Metote west of Death Valley.

Fig. 70. Pinon pine trees.

Fig. 71 (left) Possible hook for harvesting pine nuts—Nicolarsen collection. Fig. 72 (right)
In the pine nut area. Note use of metate and mano, left center; also baby in cradle and
carrying baskets. About 1870, photo by John Hillers—Smithsonian Institution.

Fig. 73 (Top) Dugout canoes and wokas on Klamath Lake—Smithsonian Institution, (bottom) canoe paddle found four feet deep in peat at Klamath Lake—Pruitt collection.

Fig. 74 (left) Campbell Grant inspects a stone fence hunting blind near Inyokern, California. Fig. 75 (right) Hunting magic petroglyphs. Note atlatl behind the two largest mountain sheep; it has finger loops but no weight.

Fig. 76 (left) A jackrabbit—photo by Jim Anderson. Fig. 77 (right) Rabbit net fragment.

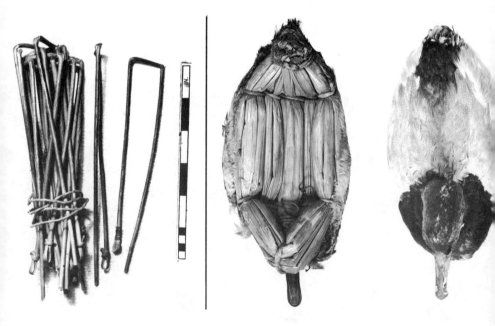

Fig. 78 (left) Parts for a trap or snare, found in a cave near Goose Lake. Cressman (1942) found similar pieces in Massacre Lake Cave—Warner and Wendler collection. Fig. 79 (right) Duck decoys, top and bottom views—Smithsonian Institution.

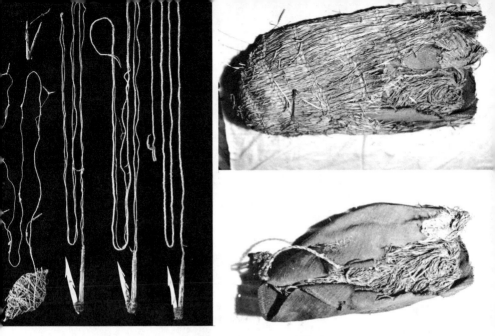

Fig. 80 (left) Fishing hooks and lines—Dr. Robert F. Heizer. Fig. 81 (right) Two nets found in a cache in a cave near Lakeview; (top) straw bag containing old basket (bottom) in which the nets are wrapped. Length of parcel, about two feet. The nets have not yet been unfolded—Warner-Wendler collection, in the Museum of Anthropology, University of Oregon.

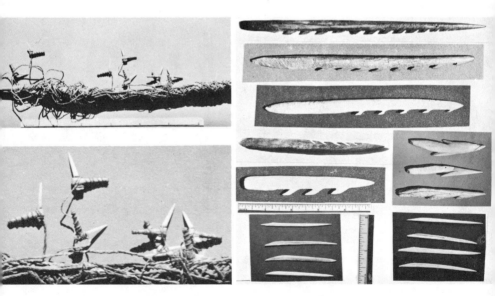

Fig. 82 (left) Fish line found in a Nevada cave, and enlarged detail of hooks—Luke collection. Fig. 83 (right) Bone harpoons (top) and points for composite fish hooks—Ting, Tieber and Sanford collections.

Fig. 84. Net weights. From top: perforated, notched, banded and bi-pointed—Royels, Ting and Sanford collections.

Fig. 85 (left) Canoe anchor—O'Shea collection. Fig. 86 (right) Flat cobble fish net weights—Favell collection.

Fig. 87. Habitations of the Desert Culture. Photo by John Hillers
about 1872—Smithsonian Institution.

Fig. 88 (right) House circle at Silver Lake, Oregon; two of eight in a row, (left) house circle
in the China Lake desert.

Fig. 89. Man in a rabbit skin robe—Southwest Museum.

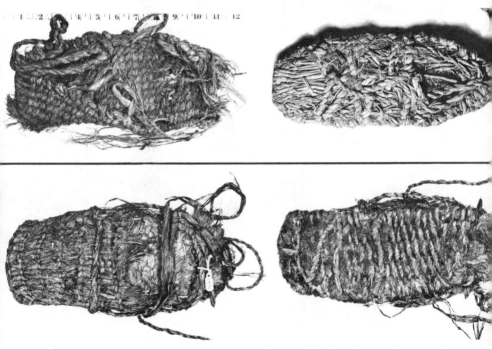

Fig. 90. Primitive footwear. (Left) Sagebrush bark sandal from Cougar Mountain Cave—
John Cowles photo; (right) tule sandal from the Nicolarsen collection.

Below are top and bottom views of a sagebrush bark sandal from Fort Rock Cave—
photo by L. S. Cressman.

Fig. 91 (Top) Ishi kindling fire with fire drill—Lowie Museum of Anthropology, University of California. Fig. 92 (bottom) Fire hearth and point for compound fire drill. Length about eight inches—Nicolarsen collection.

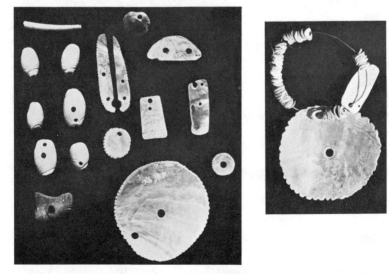

Fig. 93. Shell beads and ornaments: (upper left) dentalium; (next below) six olivella; (top center) glycymeris; (on string) beads made from saddle of the olivella. The perforated ornaments are abalone—Lair collection.

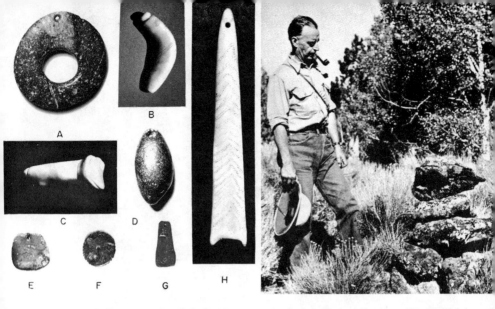

Fig. 94 (left) Pendants—Favell, Luke, Nicolarsen, Sanford and Lair collections. Fig. 95 (right) Dr. L. S. Cressman with spirit quest cairn, Klamath area—American Philosophical Society.

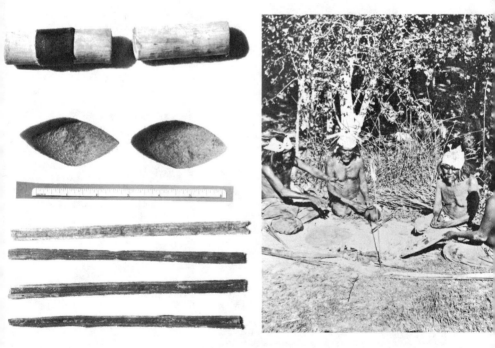

Fig. 96. Gambling pieces: (top) hand game "bones," (center) stone pieces once thought to be hand game pieces, (bottom) game counters—Gienger and Johnson collections. Fig. 97. Old men gambling. Photo by John Hillers about 1872 near present Las Vegas—Smithsonian Institution.

Fig. 98. Sixteen graduated stone balls (one was stolen) found in a cache, Northern Great Basin—Gienger collection.

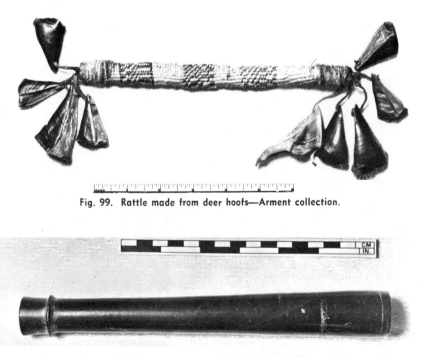

Fig. 99. Rattle made from deer hoofs—Arment collection.

Fig. 100. Stone tube pipe—Favell collection.

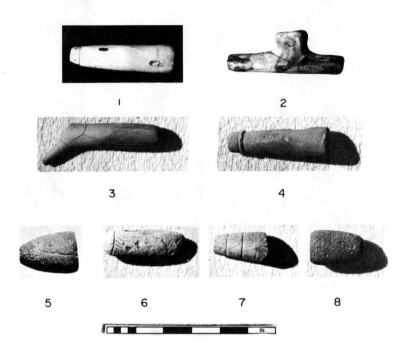

Fig. 101. Great Basin pipes—Munk, DePaoli and Sanford collections.

Fig. 102. Large tube pipe (?) ten inches long and three in diameter. Reub (R. A.) Long collection at the Museum of Anthropology, University of Oregon.

Fig. 103 (left) Unusual pipes from the Great Basin. Photo by Jimmie Thomas—Thomas and O'Shea collections. Fig. 104 (right) Section of broken pipe showing marks of stone drill—Sanford collection.

A

B

C

D

E

F

G

Fig. 105. Small stone carvings from the desert—Lair, Luke and DePaoli collections.

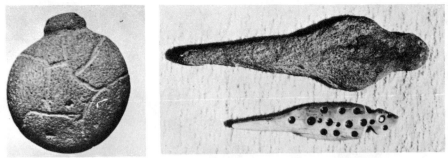

Fig. 106. Small effigies and carvings—Royels, Sanford, Shell and Rae collections.

Fig. 107 (left) Ruth examines a petroglyph at the Grimes Site near Fallon, Nevada. Bed of extinct Lake Lahontan in the background. Fig. 108 (right) John Cowles examines a petroglyph which may represent a camel, once plentiful in the Silver Lake area.

Fig. 109 (left) Fish petroglyph, Massacre Lake. Interested observer is Donald Martin who has taken more than 4,000 color slides from 400 western petroglyph sites. Fig. 110 (right) Emory with pit and groove or "rain rock," Grimes Site near Fallon, Nevada.

Fig. 111. Dr. Dale Ritter, in costume, with petroglyphs, Coso Range. Note size of figures. Hunter with bow, lower left, superimposed figures, left center. Dr. Ritter has an extensive collection of petroglyph photographs.

Fig. 112. Dot and circle design near Bly, Oregon. Note damage from rifle fire. Photo by Dr. Dale Ritter.

Fig. 113. Petroglyphs, Great Basin curvilinear. Top left photo by Glen Ainsworth.

235

Fig. 114 (left) Petroglyphs, Great Basin realistic.   Fig. 115 (right) Petroglyphs, Great Basin abs

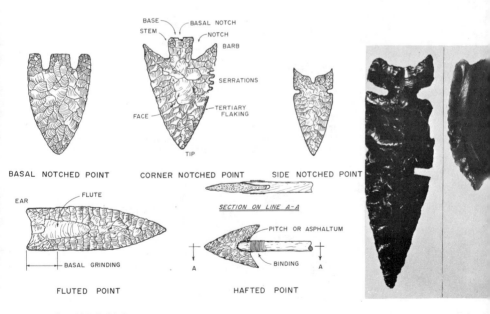

Fig. 116 (left) Projectile point types and terminology and method of hafting. Fig. 117 (right) Obsidian artifacts sectioned for hydration layer dating. Photo furnished by Peter Ting.

GEOLOGIC TIME CHART

AGE DIVISIONS			DOMINANT LIFE		TIME		
ERA	PERIOD	EPOCH	ANIMAL	PLANT	DURATION IN MILLIONS OF YEARS ERA	PERIOD / EPOCH	BEGINNING MILLIONS OF YEARS AGO *
CENOZOIC	QUATER-NARY	RECENT	MAN		63.011	1.011	0.011 / 0.011
		PLEISTOCENE					1 / 1
	TERTIARY	PLIOCENE	MAMMALS	FLOWERING TREES AND SHRUBS		62	12 / 13
		MIOCENE	BONY FISH				12 / 25
		OLIGOCENE	BIRDS				11 / 36
		EOCENE	SHELL FISH ARTHROPODS				22 / 58
		PALEOCENE **					5 / 63
MESOZOIC	CRETACEOUS		REPTILES	CONIFERS	167	72	135
	JURASSIC			CYCADS GINKGOS FERNS		46	181
	TRIASSIC					49	230
PALEOZOIC	PERMIAN		AMPHIBIANS INSECTS	SCALE TREES	370	50	280
	PENNSYLVANIAN (CARBONIFEROUS)			CORDAITES TREE FERNS		40	320
	MISSISSIPPIAN (CARBONIFEROUS)			CALAMITES		25	345
	DEVONIAN		SHARKS	PRIMITIVE SCALE TREES AND TREE FERNS		60	405
	SILURIAN **		LUNGFISH	PSILOPHYTES		20	425
	ORDOVICIAN **		CORALS BRACHIOPODS			75	500
	CAMBRIAN **		ECHINODERMS TRILOBITES	FUNGI ALGAE		100	600
PRE-CAMBRIAN	GRENVILLE OROGENY **		BEGINNING OF PRIMITIVE PLANT AND ANIMAL LIFE		4000		1000
	OLDEST KNOWN ROCKS IN NORTH AMERICA **						3200
	OLDEST KNOWN ROCKS (MURMANSK AREA) **						3400
	PROBABLE AGE OF THE EARTH						4600

*ADAPTED FROM KULP, 1961
**ROCKS OF THIS AGE NOT KNOWN TO EXIST IN OREGON

STATE OF OREGON
DEPARTMENT OF GEOLOGY
AND MINERAL INDUSTRIES
I.S EWEN
I7 JAN 61

Chart No. 4

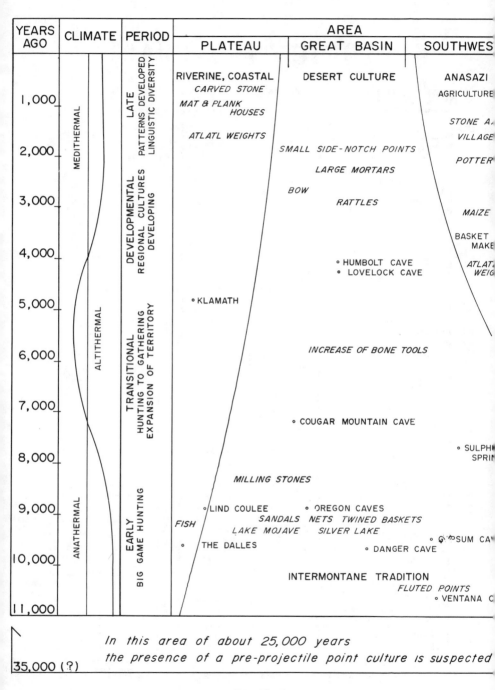

YEARS AGO	CLIMATE	PERIOD	AREA		
			PLATEAU	GREAT BASIN	SOUTHWES
1,000	MEDITHERMAL	LATE *PATTERNS DEVELOPED* *LINGUISTIC DIVERSITY*	RIVERINE, COASTAL *CARVED STONE* MAT & PLANK *HOUSES* *ATLATL WEIGHTS*	DESERT CULTURE	ANASAZI AGRICULTURE STONE A. VILLAGE
2,000		DEVELOPMENTAL *REGIONAL CULTURES DEVELOPING*		*SMALL SIDE-NOTCH POINTS* *LARGE MORTARS*	POTTER
3,000				*BOW* *RATTLES*	MAIZE
4,000	ALTITHERMAL			° HUMBOLT CAVE ° LOVELOCK CAVE	BASKET MAKE ATLAT WEIG
5,000		TRANSITIONAL *HUNTING TO GATHERING* *EXPANSION OF TERRITORY*	° KLAMATH		
6,000				*INCREASE OF BONE TOOLS*	
7,000				° COUGAR MOUNTAIN CAVE	
8,000	ANATHERMAL	EARLY *BIG GAME HUNTING*	*MILLING STONES*		° SULPH SPRIM
9,000			° LIND COULEE *FISH* *LAKE MOJAVE* ° *THE DALLES*	° OREGON CAVES *SANDALS NETS TWINED BASKETS* *SILVER LAKE* ° DANGER CAVE	° G SUM CA
10,000				INTERMONTANE TRADITION *FLUTED POINTS* ° VENTANA C	
11,000					

35,000 (?)	*In this area of about 25,000 years the presence of a pre-projectile point culture is suspected*

Chart No. 5

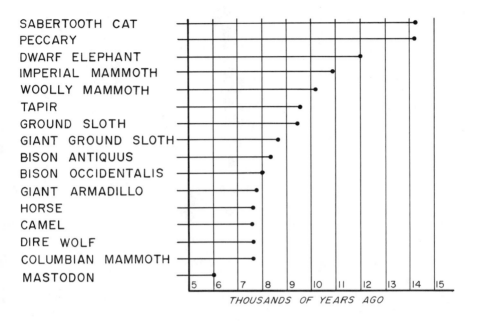

Chart No. 6. Timetable of the Great Extinction.

Some Native Plants Used by the Desert Culture

Fig. 118. Arrow Grass   Fig. 119. Blazing Star   Fig. 120. Buckwheat

Fig. 121. Century Plant

Fig. 122. Chia

Fig. 123. Creosote Bush

Fig. 124. Desert Sumac

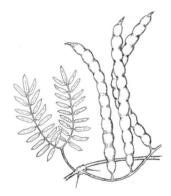

Fig. 125. Honeypod Mesquite

Fig. 126. Screwbean Mesquite

Flower

Fruit

Fig. 127. Mountain Mahogany

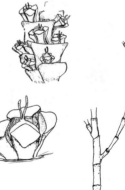

Fig. 128. Pickle Weed

240

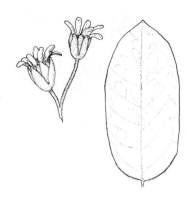

Fig. 129. Rice Grass   Fig. 130. Sego Lily   Fig. 131. Mule's Ears

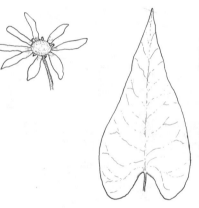

Fig. 132. Service Berry   Fig. 133. Balsamroot

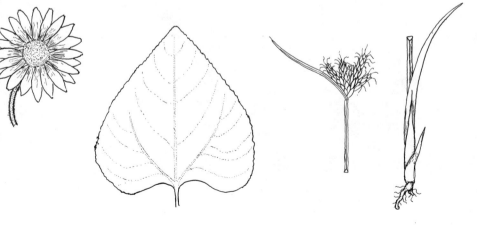

Fig. 134. Sunflower   Fig. 135. Tule Bulrush

241

Fig. 136. Tule Bulrush   Fig. 137. Joshua Tree   Fig. 138. Sego Lily

Fig. 139. Rice Grass   Fig. 140. Buckwheat   Fig. 141. Arrow Grass

Fig. 142. Balsamroot   Fig. 143. Blazing Star

242

Appendix

Dating Artifacts

It is only in the past few years that accurate dates have been assigned to archaeological material other than historical objects. There were estimates based on geological formations, depth of midden, state of decay, chemical change, and other phenomena, but the estimates had no hooks by which they could be attached to a definite peg on the timetable. Some of them assumed ridiculous proportions both above and below the norm, and there were a few red faces when the radioactive dating procedure was first used in 1948 by Dr. Willard Libby, an endeavor for which he was awarded the Nobel prize.

There are two types of dating in archaeology—relative and absolute. In relative dating an object is assigned an age with respect to another object, and this may be done by stratigraphy or seriation. If one object is below another in an undisturbed stratified site, it is obviously older; thus we know that Clovis points are older than the Folsom. The technique of seriation—a word meaning arranged in a series—is to assemble as much material as possible from different sites and determine the relative abundance; pottery sherds are very useful for this method. By analyzing the material in the series it is possible to find out which is older, as well as other information such as influence of other cultures. This method works because men are creatures susceptible to fashion, and any style loses its popularity after a time.

An important tool in relative dating is the fluorine analysis of bone. If the earth contains fluorine, and it usually does, the fluorine will be gradually absorbed by bone in a very slow process. Thus if human skeletal remains are found in or near a site containing bones of extinct animals such as the mammoth, and chemical tests show that the fluorine content is the same, then man and the mammoth lived about the same time. Since the rate of absorption of fluorine depends on variable factors, the absolute age cannot be known; what can only be known is that two things from the same area are or are not the same age. It was by this method that the famous Piltdown Man was proved to be a hoax.

A method of relative, and to a certain extent absolute, dating is by analysis of the hydration layer of obsidian artifacts. The surface of obsidian absorbs water and the composition is altered, forming a very thin layer on the surface. By exposing and measuring this layer, relative dating is possible. The rate of hydration is dependent on temperature and other conditions and can be applied, like fluorine dating, only to objects from the same area. However, if some obsidian artifacts from any particular area can be dated by absolute methods, tables can be set up like those of dendrochronology, and other obsidian artifacts from the same source can be dated by the thickness of the hydration layer. This method is still in the formative stages. Figure 117 shows two artifacts sectioned for analysis, furnished by Peter Ting of Reno. These were the first to be dated by the University of California Obsidian Hydration Laboratory; they proved to be 5,500 years old, and are from the 3,800-foot elevation on the shores of Pyramid Lake.

Of the methods of absolute dating, Carbon 14 is by far the most useful and widely used; dendrochronology is the most accurate. C14 is formed in the atmosphere by an interesting process. The earth is continually being bombarded from outer space with powerful rays called cosmic rays. When these rays enter the atmosphere they collide with atoms and release neutrons, an energetic particle that will change to a hydrogen atom in a few minutes. Some of them, before they decay, collide with and enter the nucleus of nitrogen atoms, ejecting other particles and changing the nitrogen atom, with an atomic weight of 14, to an isotope of carbon with an atomic weight of 14 instead of the normal 12. C14 is unstable and decays back to nitrogen at a constant rate that is unaffected by any outside influence.

C14 unites with oxygen to form carbon dioxide the same as ordinary carbon, and a significant portion of the atmosphere consists of carbon dioxide. This is the stuff, along with water and a few minerals for seasoning, upon which all life depends. The energy of the sun is used by plants to unite the carbon dioxide with water to form carbohydrates which are stored in their cells, along with proteins and other edible substances. The plants are consumed by animals which utilize the energy gained from the sun by the plants. Thus all living things, plant and animal, contain carbon in their cells and mixed with it is a very small but constant proportion of C14.

When the host—plant or animal—dies, no more carbon is being consumed to retain the balance, so the C14 in the cells disappears at a constant rate which has been shown to be about 15.6 disintegrations per minute per gram of carbon. This rate is such that one half of any given quantity of C14 will have disappeared in about 5,600 years. After the cells have been dead for 5,600 years, there would be only 7.8 disintegrations per minute per gram of carbon. When C14 decays it ejects a ray which can easily be detected with a Geiger counter. The scientist thus merely has to count the number of disintegrations per minute from a specimen to calculate the time since the cells died. For a process that sounds so simple, actually a very sophisticated and complicated apparatus is required. The cost of a test, formerly several hundred dollars, has been reduced over the years by improvements in the technique until now some of them cost less than $100.

Any organic material—one containing carbon—can be used for C14 dating but the best is charcoal and the next best is burned bone; they are the most liable to be pure and they have a high carbon content. Shell is also very good although subject to error, and wood or any kind of fiber can be burned to charcoal in the laboratory. While in theory, C14 is the ideal method of dating, it is beset with numerous pitfalls. There are so many things that can contaminate the specimen. Ground water can deposit organisms, rootlets can penetrate it, and fungus and bacteria are ever present; the specimen might even be intrusive and not belong where it is found at all. The tools used to gather the specimen must be free from oil and grease, and it must be wrapped in aluminum foil immediately to prevent radioactive material from the atmosphere from contaminating it. The specimen should be handled with clean steel tools and not touched with the hands. Any organic contamination will make the specimen seem younger than it is because it introduces more C14 into it.

The age obtained by a test is always expressed as so many years plus or minus so many more, as 1006 plus or minus 250 B.P. (before present) or B.C. The plus or minus figure is called a "sigma" and is a measure of the expected variation of the dates from specimens of the same source above and below the average of the tested sample. Because of sampling errors, laboratory conditions, length of time over which readings are taken by the counter, possible contamination, and other reasons, it cannot be expected that any two or more samples from the same source will give the same reading. A "sigma" is therefore always added to the prime date to show the probable discrepancy.

There does not seem to be much agreement between different authors about the quantity of material required for a suitable sample for C14 dating. The following appears to be about the minimum, but three or four times as much should be collected if at all possible: good clean charcoal, 1 ounce; wood, 4 ounces; grass or peat, 4 ounces; shell, 1 pound; guano, 1 pound; burned bone, 2 to 5 pounds; fabric, 4 ounces. It is important that any material be thoroughly dried so that no mold will form. Clean glass jars with tight lids are the best for storing samples, and complete data should be included. Many good samples have been lost because the labeling was inadequate.

— — —

Dendrochronology is a method of dating by the growth rings of trees. The width of the annual growth ring is determined by the climatic conditions. An exceptionally good year with plenty of moisture will produce a wide ring in all the trees in the region; a poor year will produce a narrow one. By tabulating rings from a great many samples that overlap it has been possible to construct a growth chart that goes back a little over 2,000 years. By taking a sample of wood from an archaeological site and comparing it to a chart for the same area, matching the growth rings, the sample can be fitted and the exact year in which it was cut determined. Dendrochronology is especially useful in the Southwest where trees were used for house beams.

— — —

It is well known that the magnetic north pole and true north are miles apart and that a compass will point not due north but to the magnetic north; whoever follows the needle will be led far astray. Furthermore, the magnetic north pole wanders slowly in a cycle that takes hundreds of years to complete.

When a mineral is heated, the atoms are agitated and if they become hot enough they are free to align themselves with the magnetic north; when they cool they remain in that position. If then the object has remained in the same place all the time—for instance a stone in a fire pit—the direction that the atoms are aligned can be determined by an instrument called a magnetometer. The position of the sample, of course, must be carefully marked to show its physical alignment with respect to the north pole before removal to the laboratory. Then, by determining the orientation of the atoms, the location of the north magnetic pole at the time the sample was heated can be found. By means of a chart showing the known positions of the magnetic pole over the years, the object can be dated, but it is necessary to know by some other means the approximate date, since in its swing the position of the pole passes the same point twice in each cycle, and has made many cycles. This method of dating is known as archeomagnetism.

— — —

A method of dating that gives with a fair degree of accuracy the last time an object was heated strongly, such as a potsherd, is thermoluminescence. The atoms in an object that is heated are slightly altered, when a bit of the same object is reheated to about 500 degrees Centigrade (932 degrees F.) the atoms emit light that can be measured by a very sophisticated instrument. The amount of light emitted is proportional to the number of years since the piece was last heated and the mean radioactivity of the object. The technique requires great precision and is subject to numerous difficulties, and the atomic reactions are complicated. The method appears very useful where no other satisfactory means of dating are available.

Preservation and Restoration of Artifacts

No universal rules for the preservation of perishable artifacts such as bone or wood can be given because of the many types of materials and degrees of deterioration, the recommendations here should be considered as a guide only. They are the ones we use and have found to be satisfactory. Preservation is a science, if you have a valuable artifact such as an atlatl or bone carving it is best to request help from your State Museum or University. Remember that once you have applied any preservative you are committed, none can be completely or satisfactorily removed again. Then too, many artifacts do not need preservatives, they will keep in good condition just as they are if given proper care.

There are certain things that you should *not* do. Never paint a wood, bone or stone artifact with varnish, shellac, finger nail polish or any other coating. It is unnecessary, gives them an artificial look, and ruins them for display or photography. Never let a bone or wood artifact dry rapidly in the open air. The outer surface will dry faster than the interior, shrink, and start to crack. We wrap the artifact in several layers of the ordinary kitchen variety of waxed paper and set it aside. We once found a prehistoric wooden bow in river mud, preserved by constant immersion in water. It was wrapped in several layers of waxed paper and put in a closet, it took months to dry but was nearly as hard as new when it did, and has been on display in a museum for ten years. Had the wood been badly decayed, of course, this method would not have worked. Never clean a metal artifact, especially copper or brass, in acid or any other solution. The finish or even the entire artifact may be ruined. Never scrub a stone artifact with cleaner or detergent, it will remove the patina that is part of the charm of the piece.

Preservation

A. Bone, Antler or Horn Artifacts:

1. Wet Specimens: Wrap in wet cloth or pack in wet sand until ready to preserve. If the material is hard and shows little or no deterioration, wrap loosely in several layers of wax paper, twist ends to avoid air circulation, and set aside to dry. Check every couple of days for a week or so to see if there is any tendency to crack; if so, treat as for fragile material. If the material is deteriorated or fragile, wash away any mud with a soft paint brush and drain on a paper towel, but do not let it dry. When drained, put it in a dish and cover with Solution No. 1 (see following section). Remove when bubbling ceases, drain and repeat the process until the specimen has absorbed all of the solution it will hold. Put it where it will dry slowly but do not wrap as the wrapping may stick. The solution will penetrate the specimen and cement the particles together.

2. Dry specimens: Pack in dry cloth or sand until ready to preserve. Brush away the sand and any other foreign material and treat with Solution No. 1 the same as for a wet specimen.

B. Wood Artifacts:

1. Use the same procedure as for bone and antler. Wet, decayed wood artifacts are very hard to preserve; when dry they shrink sometimes almost to nothing. Solution No. 3 is also good for decayed specimens.

C. Fiber Artifacts:

1. Baskets, twine, rope, and other artifacts made from fiber are difficult to preserve if wet and decayed. If artifact is well preserved, do not treat at all. If it needs treatment, clean with a soft brush and then soak in Solution No. 3, casein glue-water—thinned if necessary—for an hour. Remove and drain. Place on a smooth surface such as glass or micarta so it will not stick when dry, or better yet hang it up with a wire. Surround with a paper shield so it will not dry too fast. This solution, as well as No. 1, is good for preserving a fragile artifact in situ; it will be hard to clean after removal but it can be done with alcohol for Solution No. 1 and water for Solution No. 3.

D. Leather, Feathers, Fur, etc.:

1. Protect from insects. Keep dry. Leather can be softened with lanolin if needed.

E. Copper, Brass, Silver:

1. Never use any acids or other solutions, even if advised by a professional. A chemically cleaned artifact looks artificial and loses all its charm. Use only a very fine steel wool to scour away the corrosion—and sometimes a suede shoe brush on copper or brass. On rare occasions, where the corrosion is especially difficult, soak for an hour in water to which a little salt and vinegar have been added.

F. Glass Beads:

1. Wash in warm water and detergent; rinse and dry. Then wash in clear water containing a little household ammonia. Glass deteriorates when exposed to the weather and the polish cannot be restored.

G. Stone:

1. Some soft stones tend to separate at the laminations when dried. Treat as for bone or wood.

Preservative Solutions

Solution No. 1, shellac-alcohol: Mix one part white shellac (be sure it is the white variety) with nine parts alcohol or shellac thinner. Store in a tightly corked bottle until needed. Shake well before using.

Solution No. 2, celluloid-acetone: The simplest method is to thin ordinary household Duco or similar cement with about two parts of acetone. It can be made more economically by dissolving celluloid in acetone. *Warning*—the vapors of acetone are both poisonous and explosive. Use only in a well-ventilated room or outdoors.

Solution No. 3, casein glue-water: Thin ordinary household Elmer's glue, or similar glue with two or three parts of water and a little detergent. Store in a capped bottle.

There are other solutions, some of them quite recently concocted from plastic, but for all except the most sophisticated processes, any one of the above will be suitable. No. 1, shellac-alcohol, is principally recommended because it does not discolor or change the appearance of the artifact in any way. Then, too, it can be applied to wet artifacts because water has a high affinity for alcohol. It is the only solution the author keeps on hand. No. 2 is the stronger solution and should be used wherever strength is a factor, such as on an artifact that is liable to be frequently handled. No. 3 is excellent for preserving woven material, cordage, fiber, etc. It can be applied to artifacts in situ.

Restoration

It is ethical to repair and restore any artifact as long as it is not altered and no attempt is made to pass it off as undamaged. It is not ethical to rechip a broken projectile point or other chipped specimen, or to finish off the end if broken.

To cement broken stone artifacts together, first clean mating surfaces thoroughly with acetone or alcohol. Next, coat lightly with Duco cement, press tightly together, and hold for several seconds; then set so gravity tends to hold the parts together. It is nearly impossible to use tape, rubber bands, string, or other mechanical aids; but a box of clean, dry sand is very useful to hold the cemented specimen in position. Simply bury portions of it in the sand as required. There are other cements that are stronger than Duco, such as the Epoxy mixes and the cements used by amateur lapidaries, but they take much longer to dry.

To glue together wood specimens, use Elmer's or similar glue; it does not stain but it is not damp-proof.

For restoring stone artifacts with minor parts missing, water putty works well, and it is available at most hardware stores. It sets up very hard. Plaster of Paris or plastic wood are also good. Use water or oil colors to match the color of the artifact.

The author restores bone artifacts by powdering some similar bone from the same site, such as a splinter of animal bone. The powder is then mixed with Elmer's glue to make a workable paste for patching or filling. If care is used in selecting the repair material a good match can be obtained.

To remove the alkali patina on stone pieces from the desert, use fine steel wool.

Some Native Plants
Used By The
Desert Culture

By Ruth Strong

See pages 239 to 242 in the pictorial section

The Great Basin, with its wide range of temperature and elevation, offers an endless study of native plants. The visitor with a "What's that?" eye for unfamiliar botanical growth will need good technical manuals covering both desert and mountain species. He will want to pursue information scattered through explorers' journals, scientific studies, and government pamphlets.

It is less important that the layman name each plant correctly than that he observe with discrimination. He will enjoy his experience more as he recognizes that the plants change with the altitude, the moisture, and the soil. He will appreciate plant communities and will accept certain conditions of exposure and season. He will delight in the fragile relationship of vegetation and animals and will mourn the catastrophe of the Caucasian invasion.

The following list of twenty plants used by the ancient people is too brief to serve as a reference, but it may direct a beginner's attention to the satisfaction of systematic identification and the historic importance of plant life. Taxonomic confusion is one of the first obstacles the beginner will meet. The present writer has used Leroy Abram's *Illustrated Flora of the Pacific States* as a basis and has suggested the synonyms most often encountered as clues to further search.

ARROW GRASS

Phragmites phragmites
Phragmites communis

Family: grass. Other names: big grass, sugar cane, bamboo grass, wild broom corn, carrizo, common rush, common reed, giant reed. Paiute: *be ha be*. Moapa: *pah rump*. Elko Shosone— for smoking, *be hun du way a a*; for basketry, *hug a pi*; for arrow shafts, *weg we ko buh*. Perennial reed grass with long, creeping rhizomes growing in fresh-water marshes and stream sides. The stout jointed stems grow 8 to 12 feet tall and resemble bamboo. The plume flower panicle blooms from July to October.

This tall cane reed was used for atlatl darts and arrow shafts, prayer sticks, pipe stems, and loom rods. Harrington, in Gypsum Cave, found fragments of cane cut and trimmed, and suggested they were used as beads. The long leaves were woven into baskets, mats, screens, thatching, and cordage for nets and snares.

The tender roots were probably used for food, and the cane provided a valuable source of sugar. Edward Palmer, early plant hunter in the Southwest, relates that the Indians cut the reeds after an aphid had sucked the juices and secreted a honeydew on the stems and leaves. He described a sweet nourishing drink made with the honeydew crystals dissolved in water.

Dr. F. V. Colville says the Indians dried the stalks, ground them, and placed the flour near the fire where it bubbled like marshmallows and turned to taffy.

Other travellers tell of a practice the natives had of removing the crytallized droplets and forming the honeydew into balls of a sweet manna-like substance.

BLAZING STAR

Mentzelia laevicaulis

Family: loasa. Paiute name: *ku ha*. Perennial with stout white stems 1 to 3 feet tall. Toothed leaves lanceolate with barbed hairs. Flower, bright lemon-yellow with as many as 200 clustered stamens and 5 slender, oblong petals. Expanded flower may be 2 to 4 inches wide. Grows in dry washes and hillsides of arid Transition or upper Sonoran Zone. Blooms June to early September.

The Reese River people in north central Nevada burned off the brush and sowed the wild seed of the "gravy plant," blazing star. Steward says that all informants agreed there was neither ownership of land nor disputes arising from the harvest. He does add a story of a shaman who produced a heavy downpour of rain to discourage trespassers from the seed lands.

The blazing star names a various group of plants with stiff pinnate leaves covered with barbed hairs. Some species have large flowers, some small. Some species are perennial, some annual. Some flowers are pale yellow, some deep orange, but all bear seeds eagerly sought by the people of the Basin country.

We have often found plants on the dry hillside of the long highway grade north of Susanville, California. The tall white branched plants of *M. laevicaulis* bore both fresh blossoms and mature seed pods in early September. The small black seeds poured from the long-celled pods in a stream.

The Indians harvest the seeds in late summer and parch them with live coals skillfully shaken on a flat basket tray. The seeds might be stirred into hot water to make a thickened gravy or they might be ground in a stone mortar for *pinole*. *Pinole* is a ground meal made from small grass or flower seeds and is never cooked. This delicacy is served to honored guests in a small tightly woven basket. The guest takes a pinch of the meal with his fingers.

BUCKWHEAT

Eriogonum inflatum

Family: buckwheat. Other names: desert trumpet, pickle weed, Indian pipe. The perennial woody root stock gives rise to oval leaves that are all basal. The flower stalks are bare and 12 to 30 inches tall. The blue-green stems swell as they rise to a crown of branches flaunting tiny clusters of yellow flowerlets. The range is wide in the desert region of barren hillsides in the Great Basin, from California east to Colorado and New Mexico.

The buckwheat family is able to survive the most adverse conditions of the arid region. There are so many species that some are not readily recognized, but this strange plant (*E. inflatum*) is marked by the swelling of its hollow stalk. Late into the fall, dead and white, they stand tall on a dry hillside.

The young, tender stems in the spring have a pleasant sour taste. The seeds were gathered in the summer for *pinole* by most of the Basin people.

Another member of the buckwheat family, the sulphur flower (*E. umbellatum*), has several variants in color from yellow to red orange, which grow from sea level to the timber line in the western mountains. Some of the northern Paiute used the sulphur flower leaves brewed into a tea as treatment for colds and cough.

CENTURY PLANT

Agave utahensis

Family: amaryllis. Other names: maguey, mescal. Paiute name: *yant*. Perennial root and trunk underground, with great tuft of gray-green leaves with spiny teeth. Growing in colonies of the lower Sonoran Zone of the southwestern Basin, the plant after several years will send up a woody flower stalk 5 to 7 feet in height bearing yellow flowers in clusters.

In Gypsum Cave the most numerous traces of wild plants were quids, or chews, of "yant." The Indians roasted the young bud stalks in rock lined pits filled with hot coals, then chewed the sweet morsels until only a mass of fibers remained to be discarded.

Edward Palmer recorded in 1878 that the agave is in its prime for food just before the growth of the flowering stem. He adds that the heart of the swift growing bud cannot be eaten raw: it must be roasted. Palmer said that the highly nutritious "cakes of mescal" were traded by the Indians to the army posts.

When the stalk was cut off the sweep sap was collected and fermented for an intoxicating drink, but Palmer regrets that the process of making the fiery beverage, "not half so injurious as modern whiskey," was carried on in secret. He admired the stout rope made from the fibers of the leaves.

There are about a hundred species of the agave, chiefly found in Mexico, each producing its huge stalk of amaryllis flower after ten or more years of pre-blossom period. The superficial appearance of the agave, the sotols, the *nolinas*, and the yuccas will confound the casual desert visitor and he may try to call them all "century plants." The long leaves and large flower stalk will lead him to misuse of a common name. Once alerted to their difference he will find pleasure in their distinction, but he must carry his reference book in his pocket until he is sure of his knowledge.

CHIA

Salvia columbaria
Pycnosphace columbariae

Family: mint. Other name: desert sage. Paiute name: *posida chiapinole*. Annual after winter rains. Dark green leaves at the base are deeply cut and hairy. A square-stemmed stalk 6 to 16 inches tall bears 1 or 2 dense whorls of blue flowers from March to July. The plants are found on hillsides and gravelly soils of the Sonoran Zones of California, southern Nevada, Arizona, and New Mexico.

The chia seeds were gathered in great quantities, parched, and ground into *pinole*. Water might be added to make a mucilaginous gruel but usually the *pinole* was carried on a journey in a pouch to be eaten en route as the best protection against exhaustion. Early travellers recount that one small bag would nourish an Indian runner and would reduce his thirst while crossing the desert. Cortez found the natives using these seeds and Dr. Rothrock with the Wheeler survey in 1875 said that one soon acquires a fondness for the taste. Steward says that the people went to the Argus Mountains near Maturango Peak to gather chia.

CREOSOTE BUSH
Larrea glutinosa

Family: caltrop. Other names: *Larrea tridentata, Covillea tridentata*. Paiute names: *ya temp, ge roop*. Common evergreen shrub 3 to 9 feet tall, predominant in lower Sonoran Zone of the Mohave Desert to southern Utah. Closely related to the Chilean species *L. divaricata*. The grayish heavy-jointed branches are covered with dark green resinous leaves in simulated two-eared lobes. The yellow flowers in March and April are terminal with 5 long petals twisted like the blades of a propeller. The fruit is a small 5-part globe densely covered with silver hair.

The creosote is successful in a zone of scant rain with heat and drying winds. The heavy resin surface of the leaves prevents evaporation and after a rain produces a strong odor. Its bitter sap discourages browsing animals and its root spread an inhibitor to prevent other plants from trespassing in its living space. The branches harbor a scale insect which secretes a shellac product called "Sonora gum." The Papago and Panamint Indians mended their pots and glued their arrowpoints to shafts of ironwood and mahogany with this parasitic lac.

Creosote leaves brewed in a strong tea provided a tonic for ailments varying from colds to snake bite to kidney disorders.

DESERT SUMAC
Rhus trilobata

Family: sumac. Other names: squaw berry, squaw bush, skunk bush. Shoshone name: *a wimb, ut cup.* The desert form of this 2 to 7 foot bush grows on rocky hillsides from eastern Oregon to California, Utah, and Arizona. The pale yellow flowers appear before the tough, slender branches leaf out. This genus is named for the three-lobed leaflets which broaden at the outer ends.

The vigorous sumac is common in desert lands. Jaeger describes it as "a single hemispherical bush growing at the crest of sand hummocks or riding on strange sand columns. These columns are really pillars of granular gypsum, some 15 feet high, held in form in spite of constant winds by the numerous roots which fully branch and penetrate them. Each column crowning squawbush was once growing on top of a dune. The dune, still active, gradually moved on, leaving stranded the root-bound gypsum pedestal."

The slender withes of the shrub were used by the desert people as foundation for basketry. The peeled strands were used by the southern Basin tribes as a warp for their coiled baskets. Palmer in 1878 saw "the twigs soaked, bark scraped and split by mouth and hands. Baskets were built up by a succession of small rolls of grass, over which these twigs are firmly and closely bound. A bone awl is used to make holes under the rim of grass for the split twigs. The baskets are durable, hold water and hot stones for cooking." Specimens of similar basketry made from *Rhus trilobata* were recovered from Danger Cave.

The bright orange berries soaked in water made a refreshing tonic. Dried and powdered, they were stored for winter food. A cough medicine was steeped from the stems. Edith Murphey says that the best black dye was made from the twigs of sumac rolled with their leaves and boiled in a mixture of pinyon pitch and yellow ochre. She saw berries mashed and fermented to produce a dusty pink dye.

JOSHUA TREE
Yucca brevifolia; Y. arbovescens

Family: lily. Other name: Joshua. Young unbranched trees rise from large, tough roots deep in dry gravelly soil until they are 8 to 12 feet in height. The basal disk supports a cluster of bayonet leaves for several years until the first flowering, when the giant lily begins to branch. The mature tree may live 300 years and reach a height of 30 feet, with a spread of 20 feet.

The yuccas are of ancient origin. The Joshua tree waved its clumsy armloads of dagger leaves in the Tertiary period. In post-Pleistocene times it ranged over a much greater area of the Americas than it does today and was a favored food of the now extinct giant sloth, Nothrotherium. In Gypsum Cave, Nevada, the remains of the sloth were found in association with ancient man along with a contemporary desposit of yucca, creosote bush, spiny salt-bush, and the barrel cactus.

In 1844, when Captain Fremont crossed the Mojave Desert, he described the great tree yucca as "the most repulsive tree in the vegetable kingdom," but later when the pious Mormons were on their way to the promised land, they named it for the Biblical Joshua, because the branches seemed to point the way like a prophetic symbol.

The Joshua tree does not bloom every year, but if the rainfall is right the flowers appear on the ends of the branches in March and April. The pollen of the yucca is too heavy to be wind-borne, and each species has its own Pronuba moth (Tegeticula) to act in a partnership of mutual advantage. In this classic example of "living together," the night-flying moth collects the pollen, carries it to another blossom, and pushes it onto the stigma. Roger Tory Peterson says that the moth acts with deliberation "almost as if it understood the process." Having deposited the pollen, the moth crawls outside the fetid blossom to lay its egg inside the punctured ovary. Hostile as this formidable lily appears, the brilliant black and yellow Scott's oriole weaves its nest of yucca fiber and sits on the topmost dagger to sing its spring song.

The Panamint Indians of the Koso Range ate the top and center of the tender new bud and gathered the seeds in June for ground meal. The yucca leaves provide a fiber used in making sandals, mats, baskets, and cordage. The roots were used for soap in washing the hair, and the bright red feeder roots for a pattern in basket making.

HONEYPOD MESQUITE
Prosopis chilensis; P. glandulosa; P. juliflora

Family: mimosa. Paiute name: *ah pee*. Small tree or shrub, with wide-spread spiny branches, growing in thickets along desert washes of the lower Sonoran Zone. Drought resistance depends on 50 to 60 foot root system penetrating deep into the ground. Loses leaves with first frost but with the spring, bright green leaves and fragrant blossoms appear. Four to 8 inch pods mature in September and early October.

The most dependable food in the desert regions was the mesquite bean. Often when other seed crops failed, this drought-resistant bush provided a staple food rich in sugar. The protein is considerable in the bean itself, while the sugar is in the pulpy sponge of the pod. Cahuilla women ground the beans in a deep, pointed mortar set in the sand, made cakes from the flour, and dried them in the sun. Mojave women baked large pot-shaped cakes so hard they had to be broken with a stone. Atole, too, was sometimes made from the flour.

The Pima Indians fermented the sugar-rich meal into a favorite intoxicating drink. A gum exudes from the bark; it was gathered and used both as a candy and a dye. Bark from the roots was used as a poultice for stubborn wounds. Mesquite wood was made into projectile foreshafts and throwing sticks for hunting rabbits. The strong, straight limbs, hardened and sharpened in the fire, were used by the women for harvesting bulbs and roots.

SCREWBEAN MESQUITE
Prosopis pubescens

Family: mimosa. Other names: tornillo, screwpod. Paiute name: *quee ur*. This is a small shrub or tree not as common as the honey mesquite. It grows in bottomlands and canyon washes of the same area. Gray, barked twigs bear grayish leaflets in pairs and a spike of yellow flowers like a tuft of stamens. The beanpod is a peculiarly coiled, tight little cylinder. It can be seen along the Mojave River where the Las Vegas Highway crosses the sump of Soda Lake.

The screw bean was not as widespread as the honeypod, but after "cooking," the bean was much sweeter. Edward Balls describes the "cooking" process using no fire. The pods were placed in a large pit with layers of arrow weed (*Pluchea sericea*) and allowed to ferment for several days. Then the beans were taken out and dried. Palmer notes that every seed included an insect, a species of *Bruchus*, which became an ingredient of the meal. He added that when ground and mixed with water the sweet mixture was very palatable. Cakes made from the ground meal and baked hard in the slow-burning mesquite wood charcoal were often cached on a journey to provide against a hungry return. The wood of the mesquite is still the best fuel for a desert campfire.

MOUNTAIN MAHOGANY
Cercocarpus ledifolius

Family: rose. Paiute name: *too be*. Small tree 2 to 12 feet high with red-brown furrowed bark covered with downy hair. Leaves lanceolate, textured thick, tending to roll from the edges. Flowers greenish with no petal. Fruit red brown with long, twisting, furry, silver tail.

These small trees or shrubs grow to the very edge of the rimrock, even down the face of the most forbidding breaks in the ancient lava flows. There are perhaps 10 species of mahogany restricted to the Rocky Mountain and Pacific Coast region of the United States, extending southward through the Cordilleras of Mexico. Drought-resistant and evergreen, they accept the company of pinon and juniper, but often make lonely stands on arid outcroppings.

The sturdy trunk and stout branches provide hard, tough, and brittle wood that burns hot and clean. The Indians of Pyramid Lake scraped the inner bark to make a tea for "bad lungs" and colds. They used the bark tea for an eyewash and the young sprouts for a laxative and purge.

The wood was sharpened with an obsidian knife and hardened in hot ashes for arrow shafts, fish spears, and root-digging sticks. Edith Murphey records that a purple paint from a decoction of the bark was used as a protection against thunder and lightning. A further precaution was a piece of bark tied in the hair.

PICKLE WEED
Allenrolfia occidentalis

Family: goose foot. Other names: burroweed, iodine bush. A monotypic genus of western North America. Perennial erect half shrub with fleshy, jointed scale-like leaves. The flowers bloom June through August and are tucked into the scales of the terminal tip. The plant produces a great many seeds in late summer. Grows in alkaline soil of the Sonoran Zone of Central California, south through the desert and east to Utah, Texas, and Mexico. Much like it is *Salicornia ambigua,* also called pickleweed.

Most of the fill in Danger Cave is interpreted as residue after winnowing many tons of the tiny brown seeds of the pickleweed. Since the harvest must have been made in late summer and early autumn, the clue is strong evidence of an annual recurrent occupancy. Jennings says that the plants were probably gathered before the seeds were fully ripe and were allowed to dry in the cave, or near it. They were beaten out and winnowed as soon as the seeds were ready to drop. The young, succulent shoots may have been used for spring greens.

RICE GRASS
Oryzopsis hymenoides

Family: grass. Other names: Indian rice, sand grass. Paiute name: *wye, so pee va.* A bunchgrass of high nutrient value which will grow in arid sand regions in desert canyons and mountain sides up to an 8,000-foot elevation. Found on desert plains of the upper Sonoran Zone of eastern Washington, Oregon, and California, east to the Great Plains.

The seed of the rice grass is black and round and grows in abundance in its area, but the harvest time is limited. The seeds quickly drop when mature. This valuable food was gathered by the women; they caught bunches in one hand and cut the plant with a sharp bone sickle. Sickles and grass cutters were found In Lovelock Cave. Edith Murphey tells of seeing modern Indians pile the dry plants on canvas, then touch a match to the delicate stems, leaving the seeds on the canvas.

SEGO LILY
Calochortus nuttalli

Family: lily. Other names: mariposa, butterfly tulip, star tulip, cat's ears. Paiute name: *ko gi.* Leaves narrow, grass-like. Flowers cup shaped of 3 broad petals, white, pink, lilac, purple or yellow with dark purple spot or base crescent. Fruit a 3-celled pod with numerous black seeds. The dry, open pod often stands on its stout stem until the winter snows fall. Blooms May through June on dry hillsides and open plains at all elevations in the Basin country.

The Shoshone name "*Se gaw*" is used throughout most of the Great Basin for this graceful, tulip-like lily, but it is known in California by the early Spanish "mariposa," or butterfly lily. The stem, in different species 2 to 18 inches tall, marks a bulbous root buried deep in the dry ground. The bulb is the size of a walnut and eaten raw it is sweet and nutritious. The people of the desert dug them when the first buds appeared and roasted them in ashes or boiled them in baskets with hot cooking stones. In good years they stored the dried bulbs and made a wholesome bread from the meal.

In the Mojave desert the colorful mariposa *Calochortus kennedyi* may be only a few inches high, but its cluster of vermillion to orange flowers bear petals 1 to 2 inches long. It blooms after the rains from April to June.

In southeastern Oregon on the hillsides above Silver Lake *C. macrocarpus* covers the stony slopes of the Connley Hills near ancient rock shelters. In June, this splendid star tulip is held aloft on stems 18 inches high at 4,000-foot elevation.

Typically, the lily of the Great Basin—found from the California desert to southwestern Colorado, from creosote to the big sagebrush—is *C. flexuosis*. The stems are not erect, but lean on the ground or weakly twine on nearby shrubs; sometimes they are 16 inches long. The flowers are white, delicately tinged with lavender, and elegantly marked at the base of each petal with a purple spot and a yellow band.

SERVICE BERRY
Amelanchier alnifolia; Amelanchier utahensis

Family: apple-malaceae. Other names: shadbush, shadblow, sarvus berry. English name: Savoy or sorbus, associated with medlar tree. Shoshone name: *tu yem bee*. Shrubby tree 3 to 15 inches high in thickets of upper Sonoran and arid Transition Zones of the Great Basin to the Mojave Desert. Branches from the base, with bark smooth and gray. Pale green leaves usually strongly toothed above the middle; deciduous. Racemes of white flowers abundant. Fruit yellow to orange with sweet pulp and small seeds. Prolific seeder with ability to sprout repeatedly on stream banks or dry hillsides.

The early explorers were all glad to use the fruit of the service berry, either dried or fresh, mixed with meat or baked in cakes. Among the Indians it was a staple wherever available. Edward Palmer says the Indians boiled the berries in broth of fat meat and served them in feasts. The slender, straight branches were sought for arrow shafts, and Jennings found them used for atlatl mainshafts in Danger Cave.

BALSAMROOT
Balsamorhiza sagittata

Family: compositae. Other names: bigroot sunflower, arrow-leaf balsam, balsamroot. Shoshone name: *ah kerh*. Washoe name: *sugi laate*. Deep-seated perennial with a large, woody, resinous taproot. Basal leaves arrow shaped on stems 1 to 2 feet long. Flower head solitary, bright yellow; often measures 4 inches across. The 12 species of balsamroot are confined to the arid Transition Zones of western North America.

The balsamroot with a great tuft of arrow-shaped basal leaves on naked stems covers the rocky hills of the Great Basin from April to July. The Indians ate the early sprouts of silvery gray, hairy leaves for greens; they peeled and boiled the growing root to make a brew used in sweat treatment for the misery of rheumatism. In early summer they gathered the seeds from the heavy golden heads, winnowed, parched, and stored them for winter provision. Ground with mano and metate and cooked into an oily mush, the balsamroot was a valuable fare.

MULE'S EARS
Wyethia mollis.

Family: compositae. Paiute name: *wod zi kuh.* Stout perennial, dense clumps of woolly young leaves, becoming green with age. Ray flowers yellow, 2 to 5 on a stem. Open ridges and dry woods in arid Transition and Canadian Zones. Blooms May to early July.

The radiant Mule's ears sometimes flings 5 heads to a stalk, often surpassed in height by long, glossy elliptic leaves. It thrives on dry or moist hillsides in open sun, or makes a festive understory for the dignity of ponderosa pine.

The Indians used the roots to make a sweet, gummy, porridge, after fermenting the roots for one or two days on heated stones in an underground pit. The Nevada Indians ground raw roots and made a mixture with water to induce vomiting, while the Klamath used the mashed roots as a poultice for swelling and insect bites.

These robust plants were named for Nathaniel Wyeth, a Maine man and early explorer and trader in the Oregon country, who dared to build an American trading post under the very eyes of the all-powerful Hudson's Bay Company. On his first return across the continent in 1833, he remembered his friend in Philadelphia, Thomas Nuttall, and managed to take him several new plant specimens, among them this handsome member of the sunflower family.

SUNFLOWER
Helianthus annuus

Family: compositae. Annual, branched stems to a height of 1½ feet, reddish-purple disk flowers and yellow ray flowers make a large head 3 to 5 inches across. Cultivated, they attain gigantic size and weight. The stems are rough and hairy. Blooms July, August, and early September.

The flowering heads of the true sunflower *(Helianthus),* with their bright yellow-orange rays around a dark disk, are most easily confused with the Mule's ears *(Wyethia)* and the Balsamroot

(*Balsamorhiza*). Craighead suggests identification with a hand lens to show that the true sunflower seed appears four-angled and has two flat awns or bristles that point upward when young. The Indians recognized the *Helianthus* (helio—sun; anthus—flower) and used its roots for snake bite and rheumatism. They ate the rich oily seeds raw or parched them for bread. They extracted black, purple, and yellow dye from parts of the plant, and shredded the rough stalk to make fiber twine for their nets.

TULE BULRUSH
Scirpus americanus

Family: sedge. Other names: desert bulrush, cattail, flag. Shoshone name: *sa ip*. Perennial with long root stocks, leaves narrow and shorter than the sharply triangular, pithy stem. Spikelets from 1 to 7 in a cluster toward end of stem. Grows 2 to 6 feet tall in brackish or marshy places in the Sonoran through the Transition zones of the Great Basin. Other species, S. *nevadensis* and S. *validus* (S. *lacustris*) with stems round in cross section are also found in the alkaline, wet grounds of the old lake beds.

The caves of the Humboldt area produced great numbers of quids in the camp litter. The quids result from mastication of rhyzomes and tender leaves of *Scirpus americanus*. The quids are found as no more than pads of matted fibers, expelled from the mouth after the juices and soft connective tissues have been extracted by chewing.

Dr. Walter P. Cottam, of the University of Utah, reported that he experienced neither hunger nor thirst during one day of strenuous field work while he chewed the sweet starchy roots.

Edward Palmer, before 1870, saw desert Indians chew the roots as a preventative of thirst before starting a long journey. He also mentions the extensive use of the tule core as food, eaten raw or powdered into flour for bread.

All over the Basin the tule was heavily used for mats, cordage, and baskets. The shapely Klamath baskets were woven of split tule warp strands rolled in two-ply cord. The weft was shredded cattail, while the design was made from the dark-brown tule roots.

Books suggested for further study of plants used by the Indians of the Great Basin:

Abrams, Leroy and Roxanna Ferris
 1960 *Illustrated Flora of the Pacific States,* 4 vols. Stanford University Press, Palo Alto.

Arnberger, Leslie P.
 1962 "Flowers of the Southwest Mountains," Southwestern Monuments Association, Globe, Arizona. Pamphlet.

Balls, Edward K.
 1965 "Early Uses of California Plants," California Natural History guides, No. 10. University of California Press, Berkeley.

Craighead, John J. and others
 1963 *A Field Guide to Rocky Mountain Wildflowers,* Houghton Mifflin, Boston. One of the best to cover the plants and flowers of the Intermountain West.

Ferris, Roxana S.
 1962 *Death Valley Wildflowers,* Death Valley Natural History Association, Death Valley, California. 141-page paperback; very good.

Jepson, W. L.
 1925 *A Manual of the Flowering Plants of California.* University of California Press, Berkeley.

Medsger, O. P.
 1925 *Edible Wild Plants,* MacMillan, New York.

Munz, Philip A.
 1962 *California Desert Wildflowers,* University of California Press, Berkeley.
 1963 *California Mountain Wildflowers,* University of California Press, Berkeley.
 1965 *California Spring Wildflowers,* University of California Press, Berkeley.

Murphey, Edith Van Allen
 1959 *Indian Uses of Native Plants.* Desert Printers, Palm Desert, California.

Palmer, Edward
 1871 "Food Products of the North American Indians." Report of the Commissioner of Agriculture, pp. 404-28. Reprinted in *The Washington Archaeologist,* Vol. X, No. 1, February 1966. Seattle.

Reed, Flo
 1962 "Uses of Native Plants by the Indians." Department of Education, State of Nevada.

Saunders, C. F.
 1920 *Useful Wild Plants of the United States and Canada.* McBride and Company, New York.

Sweet, Muriel
 1962 *Common Edible and Useful Plants of the West.* Naturegraph Company, Healdsburg, California.

Train, Percy, J. R. Hendricks and W. A. Archer
 1941 "Medicinal Uses of Plants by the Indian Tribes of Nevada," *Contributions Toward a Flora of Nevada, No. 33, Bureau of Plant Industry.* U. S. Department of Agriculture, Washington.

Yanovsky, Elias
 1936 "Food Plants of the American Indian," U. S. Department of Agriculture, Miscellaneous Publications No. 237. Washington.

Glossary

A.D.: "Anno Domini" or "Year of our Lord." As a prefix it means the number of years after the birth of Christ.

Aeolian: Made or deposited by the wind.

Altithermal: A period when the climate was much warmer than it is now, from about 7,000 to 4,000 years ago.

Anathermal: Any period when the weather is about as it is now, but more specifically the period before the altithermal.

Archaic: Generally applied to the Eastern United States before agriculture or the invention of pottery.

Articulated: When a skeleton or parts thereof are held together by ligaments or are found in the same position as in life.

Artifact: Any object made by man, especially simple, primitive objects.

Aspect: a group of components that share the same traits.

Atlatl: A spear thrower (see text).

Basal grinding: Edges of the stem or hafted portion of a projectile point ground smooth to prevent cutting the binding used in hafting.

Basal thinning: The flaking of the stem or base of a projectile point to assist in hafting.

B.C.: "Before Christ." As a suffix it denotes years before the birth of Christ.

Biface: Having two sides, as a flaked blade.

Bi-pointed: Having a point on each end.

Blade: Chipped specimen with width less than one half of length.

Blank: An artifact blocked out to approximate shape and ready to finish.

Bolson: A flat desert basin surrounded by mountains.

B.P.: "Before Present." In C14 dating this usually refers to 1950.

Burin: A tool flaked to a point for inscribing or grooving bone or antler, generally in preparation for splitting for material to make tools.

Complex: A group of related traits forming a cultural unit.

Core: The piece of stone remaining after a series of flakes has been struck from it.

Cortex: The weathered surface of stone; an external layer.

Culture: Learned and inherited habits, techniques, ideas, and values of human beings.

Dendrochronology: Dating by tree rings.

Desert varnish: A black, shiny coating on some desert rocks (see text).

Flake: Chipped specimen with width more than one half of length; a piece struck from a core or blank.

Fluted: In archaeology, a projectile point with a flake removed at the base.

Focus: A group of components having similar but not necessarily identical traits.

Graben: A block of earth that has dropped down between two faults.

Graver: A flaked tool with a sharp spur or point; see text for difference between a burin and a graver.

Horizon: A level or stratum in a site; a level of development in a culture.

Horst: A block of the earth that has risen between two faults.

In situ: In the place it was originally deposited.

Intrusive: An object injected into a stratum after the original deposit was laid down.

Lanceolate: Lance shaped; narrow, long, and tapering.

Lithic: Pertaining to stone.

Loess: Fine, fertile, windblown deposit; pronounced "lo 'is."

Mano: A handstone for grinding meal, from the Spanish word for handstone "mano de piedre."

Medithermal: The period after the altithermal.

Metate: A flat stone upon which grain was ground with the mano.

Microlith: Small, sharp flakes or chips, generally set in rows in a haft for a saw-edged cutting tool.

Midden: The deposit of refuse that accumulates in a village site.

Moraine: Material eroded and eventually deposited by a glacier.

Morphology: The study of form and structure—generally without regard to function—of plants, animals, language, etc.

Patina: The deposit on an artifact caused by weathering or chemical action.

Petroglyph: A design (glyph) carved on stone (petro)—generally appearing on cliffs or immovable rocks.

Phase: A change or period in the culture during a focus.

Pictograph: A painting on a rock, generally on a cliff or immovable rock.

Plano-convex: With one side flat, the other convex.

Playa: An arid basin that is covered with shallow water at times.

Pluvial: A wet period in an ordinarily arid region.

Scraper: A tool, generally flaked, with an edge formed to scrape hides, wood, etc.

Seriation: Arranged or occurring in a series.

Serrated: Notched; having a series of saw-tooth projections.

Shard or Sherd: A fragment; if of pottery it is called a potsherd.

Site: A location showing signs of human occupancy.

Spatial: Existing in space.

Temporal: Of limited time, temporary.

Terrace: An old shore line of a river, lake, or sea.

Tradition: Cultural continuity of a specific trait.

Typology: Arranging by types for study.

Unifacially: On one face.

Varves: Thin laminations in a sedimentary deposit caused by seasonal flooding, often from melting ice.

Zone: An area having a limited range of physical and climatic features, imparting a suitable habitat for specific flora and fauna. Zones are greatly dependent on latitude and altitude.

Index

272